Visual Public Relations

This book brings together new and radical approaches to public relations which focus on the increasingly vital role that visual, sensory and physical elements factors play in shaping communication. Engaging with recent developments in critical and cultural theories, it outlines how non-textual and non-representational forces play a central role in the efficacy and reception of public relations.

By challenging the dominant accounts of public relations which center on the purely representational uses of text and imagery, this innovative collection critiques the suitability of accepted definitions of the field and highlights future directions for conceptualizing strategic communication within a multi-sensory environment. Bringing together global researchers in public relations, visual culture and communication, design and cultural theory, it provides a welcome inter-disciplinary approach which pushes the boundaries of public relations scholarship in a global cultural context.

This exciting volume will be of great interest to public relations scholars and advanced students of strategic communication, as well as communication researchers from cultural, media and critical studies exploring PR as a socio-cultural phenomenon.

Simon Collister is a doctoral researcher in Royal Holloway, University of London's New Political Communication Unit in the UK. He has published journal articles and contributed to edited collections on algorithmic public relations, innovative digital research methods and technology's impact on communication and news media. He is co-editor of Debates for a Digital Age: The Good, the Bad and the Ugly of our Online World (2015).

Sarah Roberts-Bowman, Ph.D. is a senior lecturer at Northumbria University, UK and formerly ran the MA Public Relations at the London College of Communication, University of the Arts, London, UK. Prior to entering academia, Sarah had 20 years' experience in PR practice holding senior roles in the public, private and not-for-profit sectors and has worked regionally, nationally and at a pan-European level.

Routledge New Directions in Public Relations and Communication Research
Edited by Kevin Moloney

Current academic thinking about public relations (PR) and related communication is a lively, expanding marketplace of ideas and many scholars believe that it's time for its radical approach to be deepened. *Routledge New Directions in PR &Communication Research* is the forum of choice for this new thinking. Its key strength is its remit, publishing critical and challenging responses to continuities and fractures in contemporary PR thinking and practice, tracking its spread into new geographies and political economies. It questions its contested role in market-orientated, capitalist, liberal democracies around the world, and examines its invasion of all media spaces, old, new, and as yet unenvisaged. We actively invite new contributions and offer academics a welcoming place for the publication of their analyses of a universal, persuasive mind-set that lives comfortably in old and new media around the world.

Books in this series will be of interest to academics and researchers involved in these expanding fields of study, as well as students undertaking advanced studies in this area.

Visual Public Relations

Strategic Communication Beyond Text

Simon Collister and Sarah Roberts-Bowman

Taylor & Francis Group

LONDON AND NEW YORK

First published 2018 by Routledge
2 Park Square, Milton Park, Abingdon, Oxon OX14 4RN

52 Vanderbilt Avenue, New York, NY 10017

First issued in paperback 2020

Routledge is an imprint of the Taylor & Francis Group, an informa business

British Library Cataloguing-in-Publication Data
A catalogue record for this book is available from the British Library

Library of Congress Cataloging-in-Publication Data
A catalog record for this book has been requested

ISBN 13: 978-0-367-66689-7 (pbk)
ISBN 13: 978-1-138-06466-9 (hbk)

Typeset in Times New Roman
by Apex CoVantage, LLC

Contents

Figures

Contributors

Editor biographies

Simon Collister is a doctoral researcher in Royal Holloway, University of London's New Political Communication Unit in the UK. His Ph.D. examines how media power functions in the semio-material dimensions of digitally-networked communication environments. He has published journal articles and contributed to edited collections on algorithmic public relations, innovative digital research methods and technology's impact on communication and news media. He is co-editor of *Debates for a Digital Age: The Good, the Bad and the Ugly of our Online World* (2015). His research interests include strategic communication, technology, materiality and theories of media power.

Sarah Roberts-Bowman, Ph.D., is a senior lecturer at Northumbria University, UK and formerly ran the MA Public Relations at the London College of Communication, University of the Arts, London. Prior to entering academia, Sarah had 20 years' experience in PR practice holding senior roles in the public, private and not-for-profit sectors and has worked regionally, nationally and at a pan-European level. Current research interests include visual and experiential practice, public affairs and competencies and the role of arts as an organisational facilitator.

Contributor biographies

Andrea Catellani, Ph.D., is Professor of Communication and Public Relations at the Communication School and member of the LASCO laboratory, Université catholique de Louvain, Belgium. He has published different books and articles on communication and textual analysis. His research interests include CSR (Corporate Social Responsibility) communication, environmental communication, ethics of communication, religious communication, semiotics and visual studies.

Jon Cope is Senior Lecturer in Public Relations at Westminster University, UK and a practicing PR consultant in the health and lifestyle sectors. His research interests span fashion communication, branding and graphic design history. He obtained his MA in Critical Global Politics from Exeter University in 2010.

Anna-Sara Fagerholm is Lecturer in Graphic Design and Programme Director of Graphic Design at Mid-Sweden University, Sweden. Her research is interested in how visual communication, design and visual strategies can make a difference in society.

Karina Göransson is Lecturer in Graphic Design and Director of Studies at the Department of Design at Mid-Sweden University, Sweden. Her research interests include visual communication and visual strategies, and in her studies she applies her experience of psychology from higher education.

Ian Horton, Ph.D. is Reader in Graphic Communication at London College of Communication, University of the Arts, London. He has published work on: oral history and text-based public art; colonialist stereotypes in European and British comic books; the relationship between art history and comics studies. His present research is focused in three related areas: experimental typography, Dutch graphic design and comic books. He is currently working on a book about the Dutch graphic design group Hard Werken to be published by *Valiz* in Spring 2018. He has presented conference papers on self-published comic books and creative freedom; experimental typography and curatorial practices; information design and graphic narratives and has recently been appointed as Associate Editor of the *Journal of Graphic Novels and Comics*.

Nick Lovegrove is Principal Lecturer and Programme Leader of the Graphic Design and Illustration course at the University of Hertfordshire, UK. His MA in Graphic Design, studied at London College of Communication used visual research methods to investigate public relations.

Kirsten Kohrs is currently Senior Lecturer at the University of Greenwich following an extensive and stellar career creating commercial communication. Her research interests focus around visual language.

Noureddine Miladi, Ph.D. is Associate Professor of Media and Communication at Qatar University and head of the Department of Mass Communication. He is co-author of *Media and Crises: The Art of Manipulation, Misinformation and Propaganda*, 2015 (ed. in Arabic) and *Mapping the Al Jazeera Phenomenon 20 Years On* (ed. 2016). He has also published widely in international refereed journals and books. He is editor of the *Journal of Arab and Muslim Media Research*, an international academic refereed journal in Arab media and culture. His research interests include social media and social change, media and democracy, youth, media and identity, media ethics and Al-Jazeera and public opinion.

Jessalynn Strauss, Ph.D. is an assistant professor of strategic communications at Elon University, USA. Her research examines the casino industry in Las Vegas, NV, exploring history, communication, and corporate social responsibility. Recent publications have included an examination of public relations by Las Vegas casinos and an examination of early corporate social responsibility in Las Vegas's mob-run casinos. In 2015, she published *Challenging Corporate*

Social Responsibility: Lessons for Public Relations from the Casino Industry (Routledge), which uses the gaming industry as a case study to consider the risks and rewards of corporate social responsibility.

Mark Wells is Senior Lecturer in Fashion Communications with Business Studies at the University of Brighton, UK and a practising interaction designer. His research interests explore the intersectionality of the digital and analogue spaces.

Acknowledgements

Books are often inspired by chance meetings, ad hoc conversations and events. The belief that public relations and strategic communications scholarship and practice needed to be explored 'beyond text' prompted us to host a conference in London in 2014. We were surprised and delighted by the response it received and so it was that this book was conceived as a result.

Our thanks go to all those fellow travellers who have contributed to the various chapters and we hope you will be as stimulated and challenged as we have been by the variety of subjects covered. Our aim is that this book will start a much-needed debate about the role of visual and spatial forms of communication in public relations scholarship and practice.

Books require numerous 'critical friends' and our thanks go to Kevin Moloney and his colleagues at Routledge for supporting us in our efforts from conception to publication.

Finally, an enormous thank you must go to our respective families without whose support and freely given space and time to pull our ideas together, this book would not have been possible.

Thanks go to Tim, Alfie, and Robbie Bowman and Sarah, Harry, Noah and Theo Collister.

Sarah Roberts-Bowman
Simon Collister
December 2017

1 Visual and spatial public relations

Strategic communication beyond text

Simon Collister and Sarah Roberts-Bowman

The inspiration for this book arises from a conference we organised in 2015 which set out to explore alternative perspectives on public relations – specifically focusing critical attention on the spatial, visual and performative dimensions of the field. The debates and conversations resulting from this event gave a clear indication that a further, deeper exploration of these dimensions of strategic communication would provide a valuable and timely contribution to the academic literature in two distinct ways.

Firstly, we believe that non-textual domains of media and communication have been left largely unexamined within the field of public relations and strategic communication. Starting an exploration of the visual and spatial aspects of the fields will play a significant role in closing – or at least, beginning to close – a conceptual gap in the literature. Secondly, such a project will initiate and encourage interdisciplinary thinking and approaches to public relations and strategic communication. As this chapter (and the collection itself) progresses the need to seek out and bridge conceptual divides with other, related fields, such as cultural and critical theories, design and anthropology will hopefully become clear.

In short, we are confident that by connecting broader perspectives on the visual and spatial dimensions of culture and media with public relations and strategic communication, a much-needed opportunity for furthering theories about, and research into, these fields can be developed.

This is particularly important in an increasingly complex and networked world in which traditionally distinct and disparate conceptual areas are becoming increasingly entwined. As will be argued in this chapter, thanks to rise of the internet, low-cost, multimedia-rich and location-based communication platforms the reality for strategic communication is that focusing on distinct channels or methods of communication (and communication management) is becoming increasingly problematic.

Based on this reality we argue that taking into account the wider visual and spatial domains of strategic communication will be crucial in allowing scholars to trace the parameters of and start to understand what contemporary media and communication scholarship could look like. Moreover, in so doing, the future directions for research and investigation can be identified and prioritised for further study,

Situating public relations and strategic communications in a socio-cultural context

In order to expand public relations and strategic communications' theoretical and applied horizons it is necessary to situate the disciplines in a conceptual context which allows the scholars contributing to this collection to effectively bridge and connect public relations studies with wider bodies of knowledge from the fields of, in particular, cultural and critical theory, design, sociology and anthropology. This is of no small importance given the relatively recent incursion of public relations scholarship into more critical and cultural accounts of the field and, crucially, the body of knowledge that underpins it.

Such an approach places this text firmly within the wider – ongoing – project initiated by Ihlen and Van Ruler (2009) and pushed forward by Edwards and Hodges (2011) which seeks to situate public relations scholarship in a wider societal and cultural domain and move the study of public relations beyond the functional preoccupation of management approaches as articulated in the early days of public relations scholarship by authors such as Grunig and Hunt (1984). It is important to note, however, that this does not mean that public relations falls into a functional-societal binary mode, but instead offers a more complementary perspective. Such a sociological account of public relations should be understood as

> not so much as an alternative [view of public relations] but as a macroview, one that is additional to the meso (management-orientated) and micro (people-oriented) views. PR as an academic discipline needs an understanding of how the PR function works and how it is *influenced by and influences social structures*
>
> (Ihlen, Ruler, & Fredriksson, 2009: 11) [our emphasis]

Such approaches to public relations importantly recognise the role of social structures in shaping the practice and reception of strategic communication and have been effectively applied to investigate and account for a range of important societal issues concerning power, legitimacy and the construction of meaning in everyday life (Cottle, 2003; Davis, 2000, 2002; Demetrious, 2013; Edwards, 2012; Grunig, 2000; Heath, 2010; Heide, 2009; Holtzhausen & Voto, 2002; Ihlen et al., 2009; McKie & Munshi, 2007)

Despite the importance of this growing body of work, it tends to root itself theoretically in socially constructed epistemologies whereby the phenomenological nature of communication, its symbolic and linguistic meaning, is foregrounded (Edwards & Hodges, 2011: 3). As Collister (2015) asserts, in order to maintain parity with contemporary theoretical accounts of culture, communication and society, public relations scholarship must seek out and address a fuller range of structures that are at work shaping society.

'Drawing on a neo-materialist ontology, Collister argues that when analysing the factors and forces structuring society it is much more powerful to start from a position of a 'generalized symmetry' (Callon, 1986: 200) between the materiality of the physical realm and the phenomenologically representative one; where 'the said as much as *the unsaid'* (Foucault, 1977: 195) becomes a central concern for the analysis of communication.[1]

Taking this perspective as its tentative start point, the book argues for a revised, interdisciplinary approach to the field of public relations and strategic communication that addresses how the visual and spatial domains of communication can be understood as extending the theoretical and practical range of the field into broader and cross-disciplinary non-textual realms. In so doing, the book aims to bring a set of refreshing multi-disciplinary perspectives to public relations and strategic communication scholarship and, additionally, provide fertile applied insight on which communication practitioners can reflectively engage and use to inform future practice.

Why visual and spatial?

Given that the scale and range of scholarly areas which could be addressed when thinking about the 'unsaid' in strategic communications is potentially extensive, it has been necessary to focused this book's attention on the two specific domains of image and space. These two areas have been selected due to the specific historical, conceptual and inter-disciplinary contexts in which this book originated, and which it now seeks to explore further.

First and foremost, the internet, and the digital media technology arising in parallel, has driven an exponential growth in visual (and multimedia) communication through the creation and sharing of images 'of all kinds, from photographs to video, comics, art and animation' (Mirzoeff, 2015: 6). The sheer proliferation in the use of images to mediate everyday life is, as Mirzoeff observes: 'astonishing' (*ibid*).

Larson (2015) notes that in 2017, 74 per cent of internet traffic is video (Larson, 2015) while in the same year there are on average 300 million photographs uploaded to the social network Facebook everyday (Anonymous, 2017) . . . While the ephemeral photo and video-based messaging platform, Snapchat, reports more than three billion 'snaps', i.e. images or videos, are created every day (Constine, 2017).

In addition to increased video efficacy, studies have demonstrated that Twitter posts containing images increase the likelihood if being shared with (i.e. 're-tweeted'), interacted with and saved by other users (Cooper, 2016). Similarly, Facebook posts that make use of imagery are likely to generate a 100 per cent increase in interaction among the social network's users (Pinantoan, 2015) and online articles that selectively include images demonstrated on average a 100% increase in the of shares it receives compared to text-only articles (*ibid*).

This evidence for the quantitative transformation in visual communication, although arising from recent and largely web-based studies, is reinforced through older studies that point to the increased *efficacy* of visual communication based on the assessment of stronger, psychological effects. For instance, Naijar asserts a 300 per cent improvement in information recall for visual communication over oral communication (Najjar, 1998), while recognition of information from visual communication on average doubles compared with text (Endestad, Helstrup, & Magnussen, 2003; Stenberg, 2006).

These potentially powerful effects of visual communication, taken together with the growth and adoption of visual culture as a distinct field of study has allowed scholars from different disciplines to engage theoretically and analytically with images as vehicles for communication and meaning-making. In turn, this fosters a conceptual environment that opens up new opportunities for research and practice within the field of public relations and strategic communication.

The increase in adoption of digital technology is also a driving factor in the book's interest in the role that space and place can play in shaping communication. The rise of GPS-enabled smartphones has created a situation whereby users produce, share and consume vast volumes of images, video and audio (as well as text) in real-time. Such media contains metadata, a type of data – often hidden or unseen by users – that expresses information pertaining to the physical environment, such as a user's location, the date, time as well as the type of device being used.

This means that increasingly individual and collective communication in physical space can be tracked and represented remotely (Boczkowski, 2010; Newman, 2011; Revers, 2015). In turn, this produces a scenario whereby conventional notions of distinct (digital) communication and the physical environment in which it occurs become intimately related to produce a locative media (Frith, 2015; Revers, 2015).

With such a locative media increasingly playing a central role in creating and shaping the physical and social conditions in which communication is produced and consumed the book's concerns with the visual and spatial can be brought together as a part of the conceptual field of affect theory. Here, affect refers to the 'encounters' and 'senses' (Gregg & Seigworth, 2009: 2) produced through inter-personal interactions between individuals, collective groups and the everyday material infrastructure of society.

From this perspective the book is keen to explore the notion of encounters with images and space as functioning as a form of 'pre-communicative context' whereby the visual, spatial and discourse environment surrounding or within which messages are produced and received play a vital role in influencing their reception, decoding or effect. Such a notion brings a number of cultural and philosophical fields into contact with the public relations discipline and opens up fertile research opportunities in both theory and applied practice. Moreover, while Cialdini (2016) has made initial steps towards this conceptual space in his recent work, pre-communication or 'pre-suasion' (Cialdini, 2016) as a line of scholarly enquiry remains largely overlooked in analyses of strategic communication.

Ultimately, these preceding developments, and the research opportunities they afford, bring to the fore the importance of addressing public relations and strategic communication studies from a number of different theoretical and practical stand-points. The next section of this chapter will set out the structure of the book and provide an overview of individual authors' contribution to this conceptual exploration.

Structure of the book

The first part of the book explores the visual dimensions of public relations show-ing the growing importance of visuality to strategic communication practice and discourse. chapter two addresses the issue of visual meaning-making and pub-lic relations. Locating her discussion within the pictorial turn in modern soci-ety (Mitchell, 1994) Kirsten Kohrs puts forward a framework to understand how visual communication works from a strategic communication perspective. Setting out a comprehensive account of the visual dimensions of communication, taking in semiotics, anthropology, non-verbal cues, such as body language, and visual rhetoric, Kohrs addresses the key questions of what do images do and how do images work in order to build out a framework for understanding and analysing the strategic use of images in communication.

In chapter three, Ian Horton provides a (mostly unwritten) history of the role of comic books and illustration with public relations. The role of such media forms provide a much valued perspective on the ways in which novel and visual narrative forms were adopted by public education campaigns in the US and UK. While Hor-ton argues for historically-relevant reading of the use of the comic form, he also highlights the importance on understanding the ways in which the communicative outcomes of the form have influenced the medium's development – a notion which may well have contemporary parallels in digital multimedia communication.

Finally, Jon Cope and Mark Wells in chapter four look at data visualization, one of the most fertile grounds for adopting new approaches to statistical narratives. They take both an historical and theoretical perspective drawing on the work of Otto Neurath, one of the earliest and leading figures in visual communication and his work known as 'isotypes' (that is, showing social, technological, biological and historical connections in pictorial form).

The second part of the book looks at the spatial dimensions of strategic com-munication. chapter five analyses the UK's National Union of Students and their management of the media narrative surrounding a public demonstration. Simon Collister argues that although the organisation's planned public relations activity in advance of the demonstration is successful in influencing the event's narrative in favour of its political agenda, the narrative is subsequently disrupted through the interactions of place and space with the demonstration participants. Focusing on the materiality of such spatial communication and the role of locative media in catalyzing a shift in the media narrative, Collister questions whether the analy-sis highlights the limits of conventional strategic communication management or outlines opportunities for further development of the discipline.

Building on this concept of space as having the potential to influence commu-nication, in chapter six Noureddine Miladi provides a deeper examination of the communicative function of public spaces. Drawing on a history of 'agora' – or central meeting places – in cities, Miladi uses philosopher's Henri Lefebvre's work on the production of social spaces to examine the symbolic, i.e. commu-nicative, effects of place in shaping society. Using contemporary and historical examples from across the globe's major cities, Miladi demonstrates the strategic communicative role that the materiality and physicality of public spaces and places – from parks, to statues, to squares, to designed public (and public-private) environments – have played in shaping social narratives.

Chapter seven, takes the argument of places and spaces as fulfilling specific communicative roles further by looking at the experiential nature of a strategically-designed museum. Jessalynn Strauss provides an analysis of Las Vegas' Mob Museum and its use of the physical environment to design an immersive experience for its visitors that both boosted the commercial success of the museum, but – crucially – also created a societal impact by helping redefine the identity of the city and its history. Strauss' analysis focuses on the role that public relations played in recognizing the significance of the museum's physicality and adopting this material opportunity to shape the resulting contribution to the city's perception.

Finally, the third part of this book presents new approaches to media and communication research to encourage scholars to step outside the all-too-often confines of traditional qualitative and quantitative methodologies. By identifying and experimenting with techniques from other scholarly fields, fresh insights into the theory and practice of strategic communication and public relations can be obtained.

In chapter eight, Nick Lovegrove outlines the development of a visual research methodology for enabling critical analyses of public relations – and in particular corporate communication. Adopting the stand-point of 'designer as reporter', Lovegrove approaches design as way of doing applied critical analysis of corporate brands to explore how graphic design's strategies of persuasion could be used to expose and critique public relations techniques.

Significantly, Lovegrove argues for this type of applied research as being an exercise in creating new artefacts, which should create new objects of knowledge. He demonstrates how this research approach can be adopted in two ways: firstly, Lovegrove outlines a new 'visual language' for analysing strategic communication in the media; then he demonstrates how this and other techniques can be used to investigate a corporate crisis case study.

In chapter nine, Andrea Catellani proposes an approach for analysing still and moving images online in order to understand the role of visual communication in discourse-building. Focusing its attention on environmentalist discourse from the NGO Greenpeace, Catellani sets out to explore whether there is evidence of 'post-humanitarian' tendencies Chouliaraki (2010) present in their organisational communication. This is achieved by adopting a semiotic methodology to identify a typology of images and video and then using this framework to assess the way the visual interacts with the textual dimensions of Greenpeace's public relations activity. In doing so, Catellani's work helps scholars analyse and understand the ways in which environmentalist discourses can be constructed through 'multi-modal' communication.

The notion of multimodality is explored further in chapter ten by Anna-Sara Fagerhom and Karina Göransson who share their perspectives on how experimental laboratory work can be used to achieve a truly multimodal research approach to strategic communication. Their contribution sets out how a range of innovative methods – drawn from the broader fields of advertising, graphic design and culture – can be used to investigate and test public relations activity across a fuller variety of affective 'encounters'. They demonstrate how understanding physiological signals combined with other techniques such as observation and interviews researchers can understand strategic communication's effect (and affect) on the unconscious. This provides fertile avenues for future research and experimentation to assess how communication activates all our senses and can help initiate deeper reflection on the ethics, strategies and methodologies for a fully pre-communicative context.

Finally, the concluding chapter of the collection draws together our thoughts and reflections on the direction of travel taken by the contributors. It returns to some of the theoretical concepts underpinning the text's genesis and – crucially – seeks to trace the common themes, challenges and opportunities presented in the preceding chapters as well as looking at the wider implications of such trends. By doing so, a future direction for research and scholarship, as well as applied practice, can be mapped out.

Aspirations for the book

The contributions to this book will hopefully provide researchers and practitioners with a fresh set of original and, at times, challenging, perspectives on public relations and strategic communications scholarship. It is important, however, to understand that the stand-points and approaches outlined above are not intended as an exhaustive evaluation of visual and spatial communications. Rather, this edited collection hopes to inspire different ways of thinking about the respective disciplines and encourage and foster greater interdisciplinarity within the fields of public relation and strategic communication.

Expanding on this notion, it is important to recognize that the term 'interdisciplinary' is over-used and used synonymously multi-disciplinary. According to Holley (2009) multidisciplinary is scholarship from more than one discipline that is often juxtaposed with little synthesis and connection. We suggest that this perhaps reflects the state of much public relations research, knowledge and practice. It is argued that public relations and strategic communication should embrace true interdisciplinarity that allows for greater integrative synthesis and stimulates innovation in both research and practice.

As Callard and Fitzgerald (2015) state in a new book on interdisciplinarity, it is a term that everybody invokes but few understand. True interdisciplinary approaches should challenge the underlying assumptions, bodies of knowledge and frameworks of the very disciplines under exploration – something we hope that this edited collection can help achieve.

Note

1 See Collister (2015) for a more in-depth account of neo-materialist impact on strategic communication.

References

Anonymous. (2017). The Top 20 Valuable Facebook Statistics: Updated August 2017. *Zephoria Digital Marketing Website*. Retrieved 27th August, 2017, from https://zephoria. com/top-15-valuable-facebook-statistics/

Boczkowski, Pablo. (2010). *News at Work: Imitation in an Age of Information Abundance*. Chicago: University of Chicago Press.

Callard, F. and Fitzgerald, D. (2015). *Rethinking Interdisciplinarity across the Social Sciences and Neurosciences*, London: Palgrave Macmillan.

Callon, M. (1986). Some Elements of a Sociology of Translation: Domestication of the Scallops and the Fisherman of St Brieuc Bay. In J. Law (Ed.), *Power, Action and Belief: A New Sopciology of Knowledge* (pp. 196–233). London: Routledge & Keegan Paul.

Chouliaraki, Lilie. (2010). Post-Humanitarianism: Humanitarian Communication beyond a Politics of Pity. *International Journal of Cultural Studies, 13*(2), 107–126.

Cialdini, Robert. (2016). *Pre-Suasion: A Revolutionary Way to Influence and Persuade*. London: Simon & Schuster.

Collister, Simon. (2015). Algorithmic Public Relations: Materiality, Technology and Power in a Post-Hegemonic World. In J. L'Etang, D. McKie, N. Snow & J. Xifra (Eds.), *Routledge Handbook of Critical Public Relations*. London: Routledge.

Constine, Josh. (2017). Snapchat Hits a Disappointing 166M Daily Users, Growing Only Slightly Faster. *Tech Crunch Website*. Retrieved 27th August 2017, from https://tech crunch.com/2017/05/10/snapchat-user-count/?ncid=rss

Cooper, Beth Belle. (2016). How Twitter's Expanded Images Increase Clicks, Retweets and Favorites [New Data]. *Buffer Social Blog*. Retrieved 2017, from https://blog.bufferapp. com/the-power-of-twitters-new-expanded-images-and-how-to-make-the-most-of-it

Cottle, Simon (Ed.). (2003). *News, Public Relations and Power*. London: Sage.

Davis, Aeron. (2000). Public Relations, Business News and the Reproduction of Corporate Elite Power. *Journalism, 1*(3), 282–304.

Davis, Aeron. (2002). *Public Relations Democracy: Politics, Public Relations and the Mass Media in Britain*. Manchester: Manchester University Press.

Demetrious, Kristin. (2013). *Public Relations, Activism and Social Change*. New York and Abingdon, Oxon.: Routledge.

Edwards, Lee. (2012). Exploring the Role of Public Relations as a Cultural Intermediary Occupation. *Cultural Sociology, 6*(4), 438–454.

Edwards, Lee, & Hodges, Caroline E. M. (Eds.). (2011). *Public Relations, Society & Culture: Theoretical and Empirical Explorations*. Abingdon: Routledge.

Endestad, Tor, Helstrup, Tore, & Magnussen, Svein J. (2003). Memory for Pictures and Words Following Literal and Metaphorical Decisions. *Imagination, Cognition and Personality, 23*(2,3), 209–216.

Foucault, Michel. (1977). *Discipline and Punish*. Harmondsworth: Penguin.

Frith, Jordan. (2015). *Smartphones as Locative Media*. Cambridge: Polity Press.

Gregg, Melissa, & Seigworth, Gregory J. (Eds.). (2009). *The Affect Theory Reader*. Durham, NC: Duke University Press.

Grunig, James E. (2000). Collectivism, Collaboration, and Societal Corporatism as Core Professional Values in Public Relations. *Journal of Public Relations Research, 12*(1), 23–48.

Grunig, James E. and Hunt, T. (1984). *Managing Public Relations*. New York: Holt, Rinehart and Winston.

Heath, Robert L. (Ed.). (2010). *The Sage Handbook of Public Relations*. Thousands Oaks, CA: Sage.

Heide, Mats. (2009). On Berger: A Social Constructionist Perspective on Public Relations and Crisis Communication. In Ø. Ihlen, B. V. Ruler & M. Fredriksson (Eds.), *Public Relations and Social Theory: Key Figures and Concepts*. New York and London: Routledge.

Ihlen, Øyvind, and van Ruler, Betteke. (2009) Introduction: Applying Social Theory to Public Relations. In In Ø. Ihlen, B. V. Ruler & M. Fredriksson (Eds.), *Public Relations and Social Theory: Key Figures and Concepts*. New York and London: Routledge.

Holley, Karri A. (2009). Understanding Interdisciplinary Challenges and Opportunities in Higher Education. *ASHE Higher Education Report, 35*(2), 1–131.

Holtzhausen, Derina R., & Voto, Rosina. (2002). Resistance from the Margins: The Postmodern Public Relations Practitioner as Organizational Activist. *Journal of Public Relations Research, 14*(1), 57–84.

Ihlen, Øyvind, Ruler, Betteke van, & Fredriksson, Magnus (Eds.). (2009). *Public Relations and Social Theory: Key Figures and Concepts*. New York and London: Routledge.

Larson, Kim. (2015). Building a YouTube Content Strategy: Lessons from Google BrandLab. *Think with Google Website*. Retrieved 27th August, 2017, from www.thinkwith google.com/marketing-resources/building-youtube-content-strategy-lessons-from-google-brandlab/

McKie, David, & Munshi, Debashish. (2007). *Reconfiguring Public Relations: Ecology, Equity and Enterprise*. Abingdon, Oxon.: Routledge.

Mirzoeff, Nicholas. (2015). *How to See the World*. London: Pelican.

Mitchell, W. J. T. (1994). *Picture Theory: Essays on Verbal and Visual Representation*. Chicago: The University of Chicago Press.

Najjar, Lawrence J. (1998). Principles of Educational Multimedia User Interface Design. *Human Factors, 40*(2), 311–323.

Newman, Nic. (2011). *Mainstream Media and the Distribution of News in the Age of Social Discovery*. Oxford, UK: Reuters Institute for the Study of Journalism, University of Oxford.

Pinantoan, Andrianes. (2015). How to Massively Boost Your Blog Traffic with These 5 Awesome Image Stats. *Buzzsumo Blog*. Retrieved 2017, from http://buzzsumo.com/blog/how-to-massively-boost-your-blog-traffic-with-these-5-awesome-image-stats

Revers, Matthias. (2015). The Augmented Newsbeat: Spatial Structuring in a Twitterized News Ecosystem. *Media, Culture & Society, 37*(1), 3–18.

Stenberg, Georg. (2006). Conceptual and Pereptual Factors in the Picture Superiority Effect. *European Journal of Cognitive Psychology, 18*(6), 813–847.

Part 1

Visual dimensions of public relations

2 Public relations as visual meaning-making

Kirsten Kohrs

Introduction

The visual culture and media theorist JWT Mitchell (1994), who coined the term the 'pictorial turn' to describe the (re-)orientation of modern society towards the visual, highlights that many questions regarding how visual communication works remain unresolved:

> The simplest way to put this is to say that, in what is often characterized as an age of "spectacle" (Guy Debord), "surveillance" (Foucault), and all-pervasive image-making, we still do not know exactly what pictures are, what their relation to language is, how they operate on observers and on the world, how their history is to be understood, and what is to be done with or about them
>
> (Mitchell, 1994: 13)

30 years on, all-pervasive image-making has reached record levels fuelled by omnipresent global access to technology and use of social media. An estimated more than 1 trillion photos are taken annually (Mylio, 2016). Google Photos, a photo storing and sharing site launched in 2015, boasts 200 million users who uploaded 13.7 petabytes (quadrillion bytes) of visual data including 24 billion selfies within a year (Sabharwal, 2016). Nearly 90 per cent of US adults use the internet, 77 per cent own a smartphone and 51 per cent a tablet (Smith, 2017). Nearly 80 per cent of US adults use social media sites (Smith, 2017), with 68 per cent using Facebook, 28 per cent Instagram and 24 per cent using Pinterest (PewResearch-Center, 2017). Almost 20 per cent of American households are 'hyperconnected,' that is, they contain ten or more smartphones, computers, tablets or streaming devices (Olmstead, 2017).

Clearly, the pictorial turn cannot be reduced to a 'straightforward replacement of language by pictures, books by television' (Boehm & Mitchell, 2009: 114) or the internet. However, images are not only ubiquitous, they are also central to 'questions of language, social and emotional life, realism and truth-claims, technology' (Mitchell, 2015: 154). Understanding how visual meaning-making works is, therefore, fundamental to understanding and engaging with stakeholders in Public Relations.

This chapter will explore the implications of the 'pictorial turn' for Public Relations and strategic communication, propose a systematic framework for understanding how visual communication works, and conclude by considering future directions for conceptual engagement with visual meaning-making.

Implications of the pictorial turn for public relations

Definitions of Public Relations are numerous and contested as the discipline is still evolving (L'Etang, 2013; Moloney, 2006; Smith, 2014; Theaker, 2016). Rather than engage in definitional debates, I will focus on core concepts of public relations, namely understanding stakeholders and communication.

It is possible to identify two influential paradigms in public relations communication. On the one hand, Grunig proposes the ideal of two-way symmetrical communication between organisations and stakeholders (e.g. Grunig, Grunig, & Dozier, 2002); on the other hand, in a more conflict-based understanding a multitude of voices battle for audiences in order to persuade and influence (Holbrook, 2014: 144 ff; Ihlen, Ruler, & Fredriksson, 2009) based on Bordieu's notion that 'actors struggle and compete to position themselves' (Ihlen, 2009). In the latter, meaning is negotiated through language. Language is, thus, both the locus of conflict and a weapon (Bourdieu, 1991; Ihlen, 2009; Moloney, 2006).

Indeed, an overwhelming flood of entertainment, infotainment, news, and fake news inundates today's publics via traditional mass media as well as social media vying for attention. World events are no longer framed in their salience and meaning by TV commentators or major newspapers. The virtual world is the new public sphere. Through activities such as uploading images, downloading stories, blogging and so on knowledge of the world is constructed.

These activities 'shape our participation as citizens without the pre-filter of anchored network news to package a national consensus' (Buck-Morss, 2009: 161). Language, verbal and visual, is at the forefront of the public sphere and thus Public Relations. It is the means by which the knowledge of the world is constructed and a powerful tool to influence or persuade audiences and mobilise support for a cause (commercial, political, social etc.). Understanding how visual language works in an age of all-pervasive image-making enables Public Relations to effectively manage perceptions and strategic relationships between organisations and stakeholders.

Perception is germane to shaping stakeholder opinion and attitudes. As a reflection of the *zeitgeist*, Oxford Dictionaries chose 'post-truth' as the word of the year 2016. It is defined as 'relating to or denoting circumstances in which objective facts are less influential in shaping public opinion than appeals to emotion and personal belief' (OxfordDictionaries, 2016). Images contribute to forming post-truth narratives. In his now infamous 2003 attempt to shape a narrative of the soundness of his actions in keeping America safe, President George W. Bush positioned himself under a banner 'Mission Accomplished' on a war ship, addressing military returning from battle to declare "In the battle of Iraq, the United States and our allies have prevailed" (Rifkin, 2015). However, it was not until 2010 that President Obama declared the combat mission in Iraq over, and, of course, the country is still highly politically unstable to date. Recently, in April 2017, after a North Korean show of power with a military parade and a missile test, images apparently showing American war ships heading towards North Korea were, in fact, revealed to be moving away (BBC, 2017).

Given the ubiquity and significance of visual commnication, the advancement of the visual image as the object of serious scholarly study has been charted (Dikovitskaya, 2005; Woodrow, 2010). Moving towards a theoretical framework to answer Mitchell's question how pictures work, that is for deconstructing and constructing effective visual communication, Public Relations can build on a plethora of existing scholarship.

Semiotics (Bouissac, 1998; Chandler, 2007; Cobley, 2010; Danesi, 2000) is probably the most widely used and best understood approach for visual meaning-making. Public Relations can build on landmark studies such as the groundbreaking early work in semiotics by Ferdinand de Saussure (1972/1983) on linguistic signs and Barthes's (1957/2009, 1964/1999) concept of 'myth' as a higher-level sign, Stuart Hall's influential concept of encoding and decoding of messages (1980) as well as, for instance, studies of advertising which often expose its ideological dimension (Goldman, 1992/2000; Messaris, 1997; Williamson, 1978/2002).

Outstanding existing cross-disciplinary scholarship on reading images includes the anthropologist Erving Goffman's (1979) seminal analysis of gender and power display in advertising. (For a meta-analysis of scholarship on power dimensions in advertising see Hall, Coats, & LeBeau (2005), for a recent corpus-based review of the language of gender in advertising see Kohrs and Gill (in press)). Superb contemporary scholarship in non-verbal communication focussing on body language includes Burgoon, Guerrero, & Floyd (2016); Giri (2009); and Knapp, Hall, and Horgan (2014) as well as Ekman on facial expression (2003). Deep and broad interdisciplinary expertise is also available in the form of the language of art (Fichner-Rathus, 2015, 2017; Lewis & Lewis, 2014; Ocvirk, Stinson, Wigg, Bone, & Cayton, 2013) and film studies (Bordwell & Thompson, 2013) as well as photography (Hirsch, 2015; Marien, 2010; Präkel, 2010; Wells, 2015). Visual rhetorical devices such as metaphor have been shown to exist (Forceville, 1998): further investigation of this topic can build on expertise such as Lanham's (1991) and Sloane's (2001) decisive work. Similarly, excellent extant scholarship on genre (Corbett, 2006; Duff, 2014; Frow, 2015) is a superb foundation for the investigation of genre in visual communication.

A plethora of outstanding existing scholarship is thus on hand to aid in advancing a systematic and comprehensive analysis of meaning-making in visual communication. To understand how visual communication works, the next section will first look at what pictures do, investigating differences between verbal and visual communication, followed by a proposal for a theoretical framework identifying how pictures work, that is a framework of dimensions of visual meaning-making and their components parts.

What do pictures do?

Images and their intrinsic properties of meaning-making have a different logic than words. For instance, a declarative verbal sentence such as 'A woman is wearing a red dress,' restricts its interpretation of meaning in that the dress is not blue, for instance, and in that the woman is not wearing trousers. However, the mental image of the dress and the woman that is formed individually will vary depending on socio-cultural context. A pictorial image of a woman wearing a red dress, on the other hand, generates no such ambiguities, though it may be open to a variety of interpretations.

In many ways, pictorial images can be less precise than words. Brummett argues that 'images are *relatively* more flexible at allowing differing, even conflicting attributions of meaning to the same text' (2015: 199) [original emphasis]. For instance, the Vietnam War Memorial in Washington D.C., a black wall listing the names of the 58,000 Americans who died in the Vietnam war, is a visual text which creates emotional common ground, a collective memory, as shared sense of community, without addressing the still extant controversy over the legitimacy of the war that utterances might provoke. Real agreement on the topic is elusive and but the image resolves conflict and contradictions rhetorically. It 'gives the public nothing to counter, nothing to object to; it simply exists as a visual, material statement' (Brummett, 2015: 199).

Exploiting a similar socio-psychological dynamic, cartoons (e.g. Warner Brothers, Walt Disney) were hugely popular in early US television as their animal characters allowed a distinct range of ethnic groups to enjoy and share an experience, without raising the controversial issue of race in a highly diverse country. Equally, today, advertising frequently shows figures from diverse ethnic groups (e.g. Caucasian, Asian, black) constructing an idealised post-racial world in order to be able reach the broadest possible target audience. The relative ambiguity of pictorial images 'allows appeals to solidarity, seems to create collective memories, and resolves social conflict with rhetorical effects' (Brummett, 2015: 200–201)

This evidence suggests, that rather than generating verbal debate, visual images, thus, appear to primarily elicit emotional responses. In terms of understanding stakeholders, this is a crucial dimension of images as 'affect appears to play a major role in how people represent and structure their social experiences'. (Forgas & Smith, 2003: 147). Research in social psychology and the behavioural sciences has long since established that human behaviour is irrational; decision-making, for example, is most often influenced by emotions rather than facts (Ariely, 2008; Kahneman, 2011). Images are thus a powerful means of engaging with stakeholders.

Meaning is negotiated through visual discourse. Terrorism, for instance, makes for an unlikely but fascinating case study for Public Relation initiatives with the objective of mobilising support (Holbrook, 2014). Audiences negotiate the meaning of terrorism based on a 'war of words and images carried by the mass media [. . .] conducted mainly by symbolic gestures of violence, ones that attempt to conquer the enemy through psychological intimidation rather than physical coercion' (Mitchell, 2005/2011: 298–299) such as the spectacle of the 9/11 terror attack on the on the iconic World Trade Center in New York.

Images, furthermore, take on a life of their own, 'beyond their historical, documentary function, detaching them from the strict rule of narrative, and releasing them into a world of verbal and visual associations' (Mitchell, 2005/2011: 305). Images of spectacle, such as the destruction of the World Trade Center, terrorist atrocities or toddlers in Arab countries learning to use heavy weapons, become memes, a term originally coined by Richard Dawkins (see also Blackmore, 1998; 1976/2006), to describe a cultural unit of transmission or imitation, a cultural replicator. A meme is a 'cultural element or behavioural trait whose transmission and consequent persistence in a population, although occurring by non-genetic means (esp. imitation), is considered analogous to the inheritance of a gene' (OxfordEnglishDictionary).

Images are thus relatively ambivalent in their meaning, primarily elicit emotions, are means of negotiating meaning as well as cultural replicators. But how do they work? Building on cross-disciplinary scholarship the next section will propose a systematic taxonomy of visual meaning-making, delineating its key dimensions as well as the individual building blocks which make up the dimensions.

How do pictures work?

Most scholars agree, that communication is a '*process of creating meanings between senders and receivers through the exchange of signs and symbols*. Messages originate as sender cognitions that are *encoded* (transformed into signals) *through commonly understood codes* and *decoded* by receivers (the signals must be recognized, interpreted, and evaluated)' (Burgoon *et al.*, 2016: 12) . However, as yet, we still do not understand exactly what the signs and symbols, that is, the basic units, of visual communication are or how they work individually and together. There is, furthermore, no established practice or consensus as to scope, methods, objectives or definitions in scholarly research into visual meaning-making (Kohrs, 2018).

The theoretical framework proposed here will build on long-established scholarly traditions and expertise of numerous disciplines such as the language of art and film studies, nonverbal behaviour, semiotics, rhetoric and genre theory. In each of these categories more systematic corpus-based research specific to visual communication needs to be carried out in terms of identifying the individual components of these dimensions and how they work individually and in conjunction. The following case studies can, however, provide an illustration of the potential power of a comprehensive and systematic understanding of visual meaning-making for public relations.

1. *The language of art*

In literature, the function of directing the attention of the reader/viewer to the most salient part is called foregrounding. Linguistic devices are used to 'enhance the meaning potential of the text, while also providing the reader with the possibility of aesthetic experience. [. . .] unusual forms of language – break[s] up the reader's routine behavior: commonplace views and perspectives are replaced by new and surprising insights and sensations' (van Peer & Hakemulder, 2006: 546).

The first dimension of visual meaning-making is the language of art. Its principles of organisation guide the arrangement of its building blocks, the five elements of art, namely line, colour, texture, shape, and value, to achieve a sense of visual order, create impact and direct the viewer's attention to what is most salient.

In the visual arts, avant-garde artists like Alexander Rodchenko (1891–1956), for instance, invented a radical new visual language to disrupt the viewers' commonplace perspective in the belief that art could have a functional purpose in building a utopian society. His choices among the basic elements of the language of art, colour, line, shape, texture and value, are striking. He seldom uses more than two colours in addition to black and white employs bold shapes. Rodchenko's famous 1924 advertising poster for the State Publishing House[1] is a good example of this remarkable new visual language. It is forceful, direct and eye-catching. Its dramatic font and a straightforward message seize the viewer's attention.

Rodchenko's visual language remains surprisingly modern. It is still current a hundred years later. The rock band Franz Ferdinand paid homage to Rodchenko by adapting and using his design for their 2005 album cover *You Could Have So Much Better*. Also, in a style that is very similar to Rodchenko's, Shepard Fairey created his iconic HOPE poster for Barrack Obama's 2008 presidential campaign.[2]

Most recently, this high-impact visual language can be found in countless (mostly anonymous) posters and disseminated over the internet during the 2016 US presidential election depicting Donald Trump, with a play on words: rather than 'HOPE' these posters carry the words 'NOPE' or 'GROPE' (Figure 2.1).

Figure 2.1 'Nope', US Presidential Election Campaign 2016: Donald Trump

Given the overall flexibility in meaning in pictures, words frequently occur in conjunction with an image to narrow down the number of possible interpretations. Removing some of the ambiguity of interpreting visual communication, words thus 'anchor' the meaning (Barthes, 1964). While Obama presents hope, Trump (Figure 2.1) is not acceptable as president of the United States (NOPE), also because of his inappropriate conduct towards women (GROPE).

In these images, further to the language of art, nonverbal behaviour, that is body language and proximity, is a second dimension of visual meaning-making which plays an important role in understanding the meaning of the images as the next section will elaborate.

2. *Nonverbal behaviour*

The term body language 'lumps together some conventional forms of non-verbal communication with other states or dispositions of a human body, voluntary or involuntary, identifiable as some kind of 'sign' to other people' (Matthews, 2014). Gesture, facial expressions and bodily movements communicate in addition to verbal language (Ponzio, 2006). Body language in images inevitably draws on and deploys socially shared codes and conventions from concrete social interaction, otherwise, it would not be possible to consensually interpret and assign meaning.

In Rodchenko's advertisement, the model's facial expression shows joy as she shouts the news about the availability of books on 'all the branches of knowledge.' In Shepard Fairy's 'HOPE' poster Obama's facial expression is contemplative and visionary while Trump appears highly emotional and aggressive, his brow is furrowed, his mouth contorted. Line of sight also contrasts in the visual representation of the two men: Obama gazes into the distance, the heroic pose of someone who is a visionary leader, while an angry Trump looks slightly down at the viewer. The image makers have, of course, made deliberate choices in representing their subject matter in a particular manner. The images, thus, convey attitudinal meaning, as they do not only communicate factual information but also feelings and attitudes of the producer toward the persons depicted (Wales, 2014).

Proxemics, first introduced by Edward T. Hall (1959, 1963), add further depth to understanding the dimension of nonverbal behaviour in visual meaning-making. It is the study of the personal space which individuals naturally maintain in social situations as an indicator of social relationships. Personal space is the culturally determined 'invisible, variable volume of space surrounding an individual that defines that individual's preferred distance from others' (Griffin, 2012: 105).

These spatial distances range from intimate to public space. The close framing of the portrait on the face in the posters suggests intimate distance to the portrayed, simply because only other human beings with whom we are very close are allowed access to such an intimate strata of an individual's personal space. The suggested close proximity to the aggressive Trump makes the virtual encounter (almost) as unpleasant as a real encounter would be and shapes perception of the depicted person.

Elements of the language of art, for instance colour, moreover underpin the reading of the images. The bright signal red colour across Trump's face further emphasizes aggression and emotional volatility in his facial expression while most of Obama's face is a cool, rational blue alongside some, but more subdued, red. Thus, the dimensions of visual meaning-making, language of art, body language and proximity, as well as words anchoring meaning, work in conjunction to establish the opposing characters of two American presidential candidates.

In Gordon Park's image *Ella Watson, Washington, D.C., Government Charwoman* (Figure 2.2), the entire upper body of the figure, Ella Watson, is depicted.

Figure 2.2 'Ella Watson, Washington, D.C., Government Charwoman' (1942) by Gordon Parks

As a viewer, we thus perceive her to be at a fairly close personal distance, though, not as close as Trump in Figure 2.1. The woman's upright posture, facing the viewer frontally, gives her dignity. Like Obama, the woman appears lost in thought, looking into the distance and not at the viewer. However, while Obama looks up to the right, Ella Watson looks left and slightly down. For a closer reading of this image, a further dimension of meaning-making, semiotics, is essential which will be elaborated in the next section.

3. Semiotics

As the analysis of the images above showed, knowledge of the context (for instance, the US elections of 2008 and 2016 for the political posters), has already added layers of meaning to the images. *Ella Watson* (Figure 2.2), is an image taken in 1942 by the photographer Gordon Parks while an apprentice at the Farm Security Administration which employed various photographers between 1935 and 1943, such as Dorothea Lange, famous for her *Migrant Mother*, documenting the hardship that particularly the rural population in the US suffered. Further to context, semiotics, the study of signs, unlocks additional dimensions of meaning.

Fundamental to semiotics is the differentiation between a literal message, denotation, and culturally cued associations, connotation, in visual meaning-making (Barthes, 1964/1999). Thus, Figure 2.2 denotes an African-American woman with a broom and a mop standing in front of an American flag. Proximity, the close framing of the image (upper body) and her frontal position, forces the viewer to engage with the woman. Her body language, the upright posture and pensive expression give her dignity, her gaze to the left and down suggest humility (cf. the aggressiveness of Trump's full frontal line of sight, looking down at the viewer and Obama's visionary leadership looking up into the distance).

The depiction of a broom and mop (denotation) connotes Watson's work, she is a cleaner. The image denotes an individual. The title of the photograph even reveals her name, Ella Watson. However, the American flag which dominates the picture suggests that the image depicts the human condition for African Americans in the United States about two decades before the Civil Rights laws were introduced.

This reading is underpinned by formal similarities (frontal facing figures, dominance of vertical lines, work implements held upright) which connote the iconic image, *American Gothic* (1930) by Grant Wood depicting a man and woman as a representation of rural American values.[3] For those who are aware of Wood's well known painting, Park's image juxtaposes traditional American values with the existential condition/human experience of African Americans.

The image furthermore creates affective meaning in that it effects emotional association in the viewer (Wales, 2014) through the dominant use of the American flag charged with patriotic meaning as well as through Ella Watson's display of quiet dignity in the face of the hardships of racisms. The political posters of Obama and Trump, of course, also exploit the patriotic connotations of the American flag in the form of the language of art, using the colours red, white and blue of the star-spangled banner.

The African American experience is also, however, almost inadvertently the focus of the next case study, a Pear's Soap advertisement (Figure 2.3), as it presents an entirely different point of view. Articulated, firstly, through the language of art the image communicates a cause-and-consequence conceptual relationship between the first and the second image through the use of a decorative frame which constitutes a connective marker (Sanders & Pander Maat, 2006: 593) between the two sequential scenes.

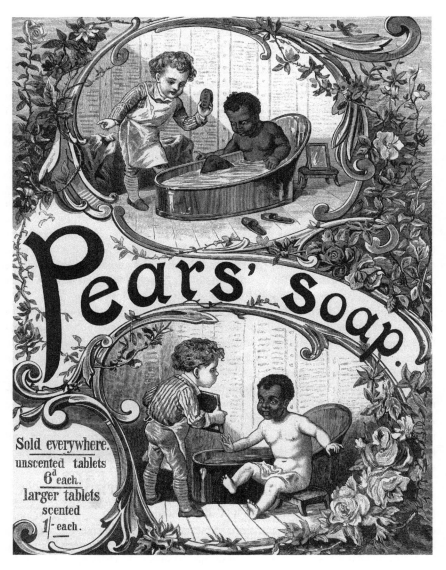

Figure 2.3 Advertisement for Pear's Soap (1885)

This is supported by continuity in terms of props, the viewer's perspective, characters, and so on between the two images. The producer's point of view and the meaning of the image is, secondly, articulated through the dimensions of nonverbal behaviour, in that the child is clearly delighted that his skin turned white after using Pear's soap. Thirdly, a visual trope, a further key dimension of meaning-making, is key to reading the image as will be elaborated in the next section.

4.   *Visual tropes*

Tropes or figures of speech are frequently employed in verbal language. A figure of speech is 'any form of expression in which the normal use of language is manipulated, stretched, or altered for rhetorical effect' (Matthews, 2007: 138). Tropes also exist in visual language.

In the Pear's Soap advertisement (Figure 2.3) dating back to the 19th century, the advertisers use unusual pictorial elements to illustrate that Pears' Soap is for 'improving and preserving the complexion.' The advertisement uses a visual marker, violating expectations of what is taken for granted and surprising the viewer. It 'foregrounds' (Wales, 2014) an element of the advertisement: the black skin of the child has turned white.

By highlighting a change in skin colour, that is making it prominent, the viewer's attention is focused on an unexpected and unusual conjunction of visual devices, forcing his or her attention and compelling new understanding and insight. In this case, the normal rules of continuity in a sequence of pictures are violated. The fact that skin colour is not fixed, but turns from black to white, suggests that a non-literal reading is required.

Pear's Soap advertisement is an example of a metaphor, in which a key feature (dirtiness) of a source object (laundry) is mapped on a target object (black skin). Black skin is washed white like dirty laundry, thus, 'black skin is dirty skin.' Furthermore, the foregrounded visual device is an example of another visual trope, namely a hyperbole, an amplification or exaggeration intended to intensify the emotional impact (Wales, 2014), or, in this case, create a humorous effect.

The figurative visual language, the visual metaphor (black skin is dirty skin), reveals the underlying belief system of the communicator. Less than 50 years after the abolition of slavery in Britain, it is likely that the Victorian audience shared the advertiser's belief system and thought the advertising amusing. However, a 21st century audience is likely to find the advertisement deeply offensive. This type of moral judgement is based entirely on the producer's and viewer's frame or knowledge of the world and imposed on the image (Tannen, 1984).

A further example of a visual trope is an antithesis. It is a visual rhetorical device, frequently used by the artist Martha Rosler, in which two contrasting ideas are brought together to engage the viewer emotionally. In her collages, Rosler opposes the ideas of a secure, affluent American lifestyle and the violence and death of the war in Vietnam. In *Patio View* from the series *House Beautiful: Bringing the War Home (1967–72)*[4] the viewer looks out from inside an ordinary, safe, affluent middle class home onto a war-torn street showing soldiers taking cover behind tanks and dead bodies.

The contrast is enhanced through the language of art; the black and white representation of the patio contrasts with the depiction of war in colour. The viewer feels some sense of the terror of war as it encroaches visually in our homes. Through the use of an antithesis, the viewer's emotional engagement with the violence of war is of a different quality to the typical way of watching war from a distance on television. The rhetorical figure of antithesis, in conjunction with the verbal anchoring through the title of the artwork, 'brings the war home' emotionally for the viewer.

The literary concept of foregrounding relates to the socio-psychological notion of a script, frame, or schema, all of which describe 'structures of expectation based on past experience' which 'help us process and comprehend stories [and] serve to filter and shape perception' (Tannen, 1984: 179). Visual tropes, thus, constitute an act of 'defamiliarisation,' that is an unfamiliar use of visual language in order to challenge habitual perceptions of the world 'for slowing down and intensifying the reader's perception' (Duff, 2014: 1).

The images analysed in the case studies above belong to a range of genres from advertising, political poster to art and documentary photography. The genre of an image provides further cues which guide the interpretation of the meaning of an image as the next section will illustrate in detail.

5.   *Genre*

In modern genre theory, genre is a 'recurring type or category of text as defined by structural, thematic and/or functional criteria' (*ibid*). The case studies represent different kind of genres, political posters, advertisements, documentary photography and art which can be distinguished by authorship, function, audience structures and reception. Genre provides a set of contextual clues on how to read a text. Seeking 'to control the uncertainty of communication' (Frow, 2015: 4), genres offer 'frameworks for constructing meaning and value' (Frow, 2015: 79).

In visual meaning-making, genre features usefully add a further layer of meaning invoking structures of knowledge beyond the aforementioned four dimensions of meaning-making, language of art, nonverbal behaviour, semiotics and visual tropes. Key components of the dimension of genre are 1) the functional component in which an actual or implied sender chooses a medium to achieve a communication objective, 2) the structural component or stylistic register, and 3) the subject matter of a piece of communication.

Firstly, a genre cues the speaking position or authorial intention of an actual or implied sender/producer. Potential interpretations of visual communication are, for instance, shaped by the knowledge that marketing departments, advertising agencies and photographers/illustrators create advertising to sell products or services, or, in the case of the political posters, artists like Rodchenko, Shephard Fairey (Obama HOPE) or unknowns (Trump NOPE/GROPE) not only seek to express their values and beliefs but also to influence and persuade. The choice of media, furthermore, underpins the interpretation. Photography, for instance, adds to the perception of realism/verisimilitude in documentary, posters use a high-impact visual language to draw attention appropriate to the viewing situation and so on.

Secondly, the structural component of genre is the stylistic register, that is, the choice between a highbrow and elaborate or a lowbrow style. The degree of complexity and sophistication, for instance, the choice of use of rhetorical devices such as visual tropes, guides the viewer's construction of meaning. In contemporary fashion advertising, for example, the boundary between the commercial realm and art is frequently fluid. The unique, creative style of a photographer makes for successful advertising as well as fashion spreads in iconic magazines like *Vogue* and *Vanity Fair* and works of art.

Thirdly, the theme or subject matter of a piece of communication as a genre component signals what has been invested with interest. Whether a bar of soap or the war in Vietnam is chosen as significant to be the subject matter of visual communication invokes knowledge structures in the viewer that guide meaning-making. Thus, genre activates 'certain possibilities of meaning and value rather than others' (Frow, 2015: 79).

Conclusion

This chapter has identified the implications of the pictorial turn for public relations in that images are a crucial means of negotiating meaning as well as cultural replicators, that circulate, proliferate, propagate, in short, spread like viruses and take on life of their own in a world of visual and verbal associations.

Understanding not only what pictures do but how they work is, thus, vital to engaging stakeholders and strategic communication in Public Relations. To avoid vague and impressionistic judgement, a systematic and comprehensive framework for understanding how pictures work was introduced which distinguished five dimensions of visual-meaning making, the language art, nonverbal behaviour, semiotics, visual tropes and genre, and isolated some of their respective building blocks through practical application to a number of case studies.

Examples of how visual meaning-making works can only be illustrative here, not only due to a lack of space in this chapter, but also since much more systematic corpus-based research needs to be undertaken to test the framework empirically, to build on it and to refine it. Even if, according to Mitchell (2010), we may never be done with asking what images mean and what their effect is, it is crucial to work towards a systematic, empirical, coherent, replicable and accessible framework confirming or contesting the relevance of the dimensions identified above as well as identifying and categorising the individual building blocks of each dimension with more specificity.

The importance of an accessible and usable theoretical model for (de-) constructing effective visual communication for the public space where countless actors struggle to position themselves cannot be overestimated, not only for public relations but for democratic discourse in general. Public relations specifically, however, would benefit from a better understanding of just how personal beliefs and public opinion can be shaped through visual communication in order to create stronger bonds with stakeholders and manage strategic communication more actively and effectively.

Notes

1 See: www.heritage-images.com/preview/2489339
2 See: http://npg.si.edu/blog/now-on-view-portrait-barack-obama-shepard-fairey
3 See: www.artic.edu/aic/collections/artwork/6565
4 www.artic.edu/aic/collections/artwork/195590?search_no=1&index=83

References

Ariely, D. (2008). *Predictably Irrational: The Hidden Forces That Shape Our Decisions*. New York: HarperCollins.

Barthes, R. (1957/2009). *Mythologies* (A. Lavers & S. Reynolds, Trans.). London: Vintage.

Barthes, R. (1964/1999). Rhetoric of the Image. In J. Evans & S. Hall (Eds.), *Visual Culture: The Reader* (pp. 33–40). London: Sage.

BBC (Producer). (2017, 29 May). North Korea tension: US 'armada' was not sailing to Korean peninsula. Retrieved from www.bbc.co.uk/news/world-asia-39638012

Blackmore, S. (1998). Imitation and the Definition of a Meme. *Journal of Memetics: Evolutionary Models of Information Transmission, 2.*

Boehm, G., & Mitchell, W. J. T. (2009). Pictorial versus Iconic Turn: Two Letters. *Culture, Theory & Critique, 50*(2–3), 103–121.

Bordwell, D., & Thompson, K. (2013). *Film Art: An Introduction* (10th ed.). New York: McGraw-Hill.

Bouissac, P. (1998). *Encyclopedia of Semiotics*. Oxford: Oxford University Press.

Bourdieu, P. (1991). *Language and Symbolic Power* (G. Raymond & M. Adamson, Trans.). Cambridge, UK: Polity Press.

Brummett, B. (2015). *Rhetoric in Popular Culture* (4th ed.). Los Angeles: Sage Publications, Inc.

Buck-Morss, S. (2009). Obama and the Image. *Culture, Theory & Critique, 50*(2–3), 145–164.

Burgoon, J. K., Guerrero, L. K., & Floyd, K. (2016). *Nonverbal Communication*. London: Routledge.

Chandler, D. (2007). *Semiotics: The Basics*. London: Routledge.

Cobley, P. (2010). *The Routledge Companion to Semiotics* (2nd ed.). London: Routledge.

Corbett, J. (2006). Genre and Genre Analysis. In K. Brown (Ed.), *Encyclopedia of Language & Linguistics* (2nd ed., pp. 26–32). Oxford: Elsevier.

Danesi, M. (2000). *Encyclopedic Dictionary of Semiotics, Media, and Communications*. Toronto: University of Toronto Press.

Dawkins, R. (1976/2006). *The Selfish Gene*. Oxford: Oxford University Press.

de Saussure, F. (1972/1983). *Course in General Linguistics* (R. Harris, Trans.). London: Duckworth.

Dikovitskaya, M. (2005). *Visual Culture: The Study of the Visual after the Cultural Turn*. Cambridge, MA: MIT Press.

Duff, D. (Ed.). (2014). *Modern Genre Theory*. Abingdon, Oxon: Routledge.

Ekman, P. (2003). *Emotions Revealed: Recognizing Faces and Feelings to Improve Communication and Emotional Life*. New York: Holt.

Fichner-Rathus, L. (2015). *Foundations of Art and Design* (2nd ed.). Stamford, CT: Cengage Learning.

Fichner-Rathus, L. (2017). *Understanding Art* (11th ed.). Boston: Cengage Learning.

Forceville, C. (1998). *Pictorial Metaphor in Advertising*. London: Routledge.

Forgas, J. P., & Smith, C. A. (2003). Affect and Emotion. In M. A. Hogg & J. Cooper (Eds.), *The Sage Handbook of Social Psychology* (p. 146). London: Sage Publications, Inc.

Frow, J. (2015). *Genre* (2nd ed.). Abingdon, Oxon: Routledge.

Giri, V. N. (2009). Nonverbal Communication Theories. In S. W. Littlejohn & K. A. Foss (Eds.), *Encyclopedia of Communication Theory* (pp. 690–694). Thousand Oaks, CA: Sage Publications, Inc.

Goffman, E. (1979). *Gender Advertisements*. London: The Macmillan Press Ltd.

Goldman, R. (1992/2000). *Reading Ads Socially*. London: Routledge.

Griffin, E. (2012). *A First Look at Communication Theory* (8 ed.). New York: McGraw Hill.

Grunig, L. A., Grunig, J. E., & Dozier, D. M. (2002). *Excellent public relations and effective organizations: A study of communication management in three countries*. Hillsdale, NJ: Erlbaum.

Hall, E. T. (1959). *The Silent Language*. Garden City, NY: Doubleday.

Hall, E. T. (1963). A System for the Notation of Proxemic Behavior. *American Anthropologist, 65*(5), 1003–1026.

Hall, J. A., Coats, E. J., & LeBeau, L. S. (2005). Nonverbal Behavior and the Vertical Dimension of Social Relations: A Meta-Analysis. *Psychological Bulletin, 6*(131), 898–924.

Hall, S. (1980). Encoding/Decoding. In S. Hall, D. Hobson, A. Lowe & P. Willis (Eds.), *Culture, Media, Language* (pp. 128–138). London: Hutchinson.

Hirsch, R. (2015). *Exploring Color Photography: From Film to Pixels* (6th ed.). New York: Focal Press.

Holbrook, D. (2014). Approaching Terrorist Public Relations Initiatives. *Public Relations Inquiry, 3*(2), 141–161.

Ihlen, Ø. (2009). On Bourdieu: Public Relations in Field Struggles. In Ø. Ihlen, B. v. Ruler & M. Fredriksson (Eds.), *Public Relations and Social Theory*. New York: Routledge.

Ihlen, Ø., Ruler, B. v., & Fredriksson, M. (Eds.). (2009). *Public Relations and Social Theory*. New York: Routledge.

Kahneman, D. (2011). *Thinking Fast and Thinking Slow*. New York: Farrar, Straus and Giroux.

Knapp, M. L., Hall, J. A., & Horgan, T. G. (2014). *Non-verbal Communication in Human Interaction* (8, International Edition ed.). Boston, MA: Wadsworth, Cengage Learning.

Kohrs, K. (2018). Learning from linguistics: rethinking multimodal enquiry. *International Journal of Social Research Methodology, 21*(1), 49–61.

Kohrs, K., & Gill, R. (in press). Confident Appearing: Revisiting 'Gender Advertisements' in Contemporary Culture. In J. Baxter & J. Angouri (Eds.), *The Routledge Handbook of Language, Gender and Sexuality*. Abingdon, Oxfordshire: Routledge.

Lanham, R. A. (1991). *A Handlist of Rhetorical Terms* (2nd ed.). Berkeley: University of California Press.

L'Etang, J. (2013). Public Relations: A Discipline in Transformation. *Sociology Compass, 7*(10), 799–817. doi: 10.1111/soc4.12072

Lewis, R., & Lewis, S. I. (2014). *The Power of Art* (3 ed.). Boston: Wadsworth, Cengage Learning.

Marien, M. W. (2010). *Photography: A Cultural History* (3rd ed.). London: Laurence King.

Matthews, P. H. (2007). *The Concise Oxford Dictionary of Linguistics* (2nd ed.). Oxford: Oxford University Press.

Matthews, P. H. (2014). *'Body Language': The Concise Oxford Dictionary of Linguistics* (3rd ed.). Oxford: Oxford University Press.

Messaris, P. (1997). *Visual Persuasion: The Role of Images in Advertising*. Thousand Oaks, CA: Sage Publications, Inc.

Mitchell, W. J. T. (1994). *Picture theory: Essays on verbal and visual representation.* Chicago: University of Chicago Press.

Mitchell, W. J. T. (2005/2011). *The Unspeakable and the Unimaginable: Word and Image in a Time of Terror: Cloning Terror: The War of Images, 9/11 to the Present.* Chicago: University of Chicago Press.

Mitchell, W. J. T. (2015). *Image Science: Iconology, Visual Culture, and Media Aesthetics.* Chicago: University of Chicago Prress.

Mitchell, W. J. T., & Hansen, M. B. N. (Eds.). (2010). *Critical Terms for Media Studies.* Chicago: University of Chicago Press.

Moloney, K. (2006). *Rethinking PR* (2nd ed.). Abingdon, Oxfordshire: Routledge.

Mylio (Producer). (2016, 16 April 2017). InfoTrends Worldwide Consumer Photos Captured and Stored, 2013–2017 Prepared for Mylio. Retrieved from http://mylio.com/true-stories/tech-today/how-many-digital-photos-will-be-taken-2017-repost

Ocvirk, O. G., Stinson, R. E., Wigg, P. R., Bone, R. O., & Cayton, D. L. (2013). *Art Fundamentals: Theory and Practice* (12th ed.). New York: McGraw Hill.

Olmstead, K. (2017, May 25). *A third of Americans live in a household with three or more smartphones.* Retrieved 26 May, 2017, from http://www.pewresearch.org/fact-tank/2017/05/25/a-third-of-americans-live-in-a-household-with-three-or-more-smartphones/

OxfordEnglishDictionary (Producer). (2017, 25 March 2017). "Meme, n.". *Oxford English Dictionary.* Retrieved from Home: Oxford English Dictionary.

OxfordEnglishDictionary (Ed.). *Oxford English Dictionary.* Oxford: Oxford University Press.

PewResearchCenter (Producer). (2017). Social Media Fact Sheet. Retrieved from www.pewinternet.org/fact-sheet/social-media/

Ponzio, A. (2006). Body Language. In K. Brown (Ed.), *Encyclopedia of Language & Linguistics* (2nd ed., pp. 78–85). Oxford: Elsevier.

Präkel, D. (2010). *The Visual Dictionary of Photography.* Lausanne: AVA Pubishing.

Rifkin, J. (Producer). (2015, 29 May 2017). 'Mission Accomplished' Was 12 Years Ago Today: What's Been the Cost Since Then? Retrieved from www.huffingtonpost.com/2015/05/01/iraq-war-mission-accomplished_n_7191382.html

Sabharwal, A. (Producer). (2016, 16 April 2017). Google Photos: One Year, 200 Million Users, and a Whole Lot of Selfies. Retrieved from https://blog.google/products/photos/google-photos-one-year-200-million/

Sanders, T., & Pander Maat, H. (2006). Cohesion and Coherence: Linguistic Approaches. In K. Brown (Ed.), *Encyclopedia of Language & Linguistics* (Second Edition), pp. 591–595. Oxford: Elsevier.

Sloane, T. O. (Ed.). (2001). *Encyclopedia of Rhetoric.* Oxford: Oxford University Press.

Smith, A. (Producer). (2017, 16 April). Record Shares of American Now Own Smartphones, Have Home Broadband. Retrieved from www.pewresearch.org/fact-tank/2017/01/12/evolution-of-technology/

Smith, R. (2014). *Public Relations: The Basics.* London: Routledge.

Tannen, D. (1984). What's in a Frame? Surface Evidence for Underlying Expectations. In R. O. Freedle (Ed.), *New Directions in Discourse Processing* (pp. 137–181). Norwood, NJ: Ablex.

Theaker, A. (2016). *The Public Relations Handbook* (5th ed.). London: Routledge.

van Peer, W., & Hakemulder, J. (2006). Foregrounding. In K. Brown (Ed.), *Encyclopedia of Language & Linguistics* (2nd ed., pp. 546–551). Oxford: Elsevier.

Wales, K. (2014). *A Dictionary of Stylistics* (3rd ed.). Abingdon, Oxon: Routledge.

Wells, L. (Ed.). (2015). *Photography: A Critical Introduction* (5th ed.). Abingdon, Oxon: Routledge.

Williamson, J. (1978/2002). *Decoding Advertisements: Ideology and Meaning in Advertisemnts.* London: Marion Boyars.

Woodrow, R. (2010). Reading Pictures: The Impossible Dream? *Analysis and Metaphysics, 9,* 62–75.

3 Comic books, science (fiction) and public relations

Ian Horton

Introduction

Comic books have a long but mostly unwritten history in the field of public relations yet they have had a significant impact on society throughout the twentieth and into the twenty-first century. Notable British examples from the 1980s included: AARGH! (Artists Against Rampant Government Homophobia) created to protest against Clause 28 of a government bill banning the 'promotion' of homosexuality, *Strip Aids* designed to raise awareness of Aids and Raymond Biggs' anti-nuclear weapon graphic novel *When the Wind Blows* (Sabin, 1993: 102–4). In the early 1980s the Department of Health created an anti-smoking campaign that pitted DC Comics Superman against the supervillian Nic O'Teen and more recently comic books have been extensively used in health campaigns across the world, a development that has received some critical attention through the emergence of the Graphic Medicine network and associated conferences for both academics and practitioners.[1]

Public relations comic books are just one sub-set of a wider field of practice that comic book artist and theorist Will Eisner has categorised as informational comic books and this study explores how public relations comic books differ from those that have a more commercial intent which might be considered as promotional or even belonging to the world of advertising. These terms will be defined specifically in relationship to ideas of public engagement using comic books from a range of different genres before focusing on examples from science (fiction) and concluding with a detailed examination of two recent examples in the public relations field: *Asteroid Belter: The Newcastle Science Comic* and *Dreams of a Low Carbon Future* both published in 2013.

The science-fiction genre has been a mainstay within British and American comic books since the 1930s, by focusing on examples of promotional and public relations comic books within this genre it is possible to explore how the tropes and conventions developed for entertainment purposes operate when used for different aims and objectives. The two main examples examined here are anthology comic books that build on a peculiarly British tradition in containing many short individual stories rather than one long narrative running throughout and were designed to engage schoolchildren of various ages in science based issues and topics. *Dreams*

Figure 3.1 Advertisement Superman Vs Nick O'Teen, Health Education Council, Department of Health, United Kingdom, 1980.

© Crown copyright.

Figure 3.2 Front Cover Asteroid Belter: The Newcastle Science Comic, 2013
(Art: Jack Fallows)

of a Low Carbon Future was produced by the engineers of the Doctoral Training Centre in Low Carbon Technologies at the University of Leeds with ESPRC
funding to examine and promoted solutions to climate change. *Asteroid Belter* was
produced as part of the British Science Festival held at Newcastle University in
2013 and was aimed at a younger audience to promote engagement with science as

Figure 3.3 Front Cover Dreams of a Low Carbon Future, 2013
(Illustration: Mark Wilkinson, Design: Benjamin Dickinson)

a topic more generally. The different modes of address employed in these examples will be explored in detail allowing for an examination of the complex relationships between illustration, information design and comic books when engaging with audiences. In addition to employing communication methods more commonly used in graphic design these different modes utilise features such as direct address of the audience to promote the 'truth' of the narratives being told, a device often associated with documentary comics and the space that exists between fictional and factual accounts of events (Mickwitz, 2016). This formal analysis concludes by considering of the notion of impact and public engagement and why comic books are such a valuable potential tool for the public relations profession.

Defining the field of public relations comic books

Although in the last twenty years Comics Studies has emerged as a distinct academic discipline there are still many aspects of the field that have received little critical attention and public relations comic books are one such neglected area.[2] In his article *The Funnies' Neglected Branch: Special Purpose Comics* Sol M. Davidson notes that

> 'The amazing thing is with all the millions of special purpose comics reaching and influencing their targeted audiences, that this comics genre is the least researched, appreciated, or collected branch of comic art.'
>
> (2005: 340)[3]

For Davidson, Special Purpose Comics is a broad category that includes 'Biography, Economics, Education, Entertainment, Government, History, Public Relations, Recreation, Religion, Sales, Science, Training, etc.' (2005: 340). His study includes many examples relating to these and other categories but there is little evaluation of the substantial differences that exist between them or of the similarities that cut across these fields. Public relations comic books form only a small part of Davidson's study and because they have generally received little attention there is a lack of precision in defining what exactly might count as belonging to this particular field. Davidson does however note that other terms have been used for these kinds of comic books.

'Other descriptive titles have been used to describe this neglected genre – giveaways, industrial comics, premiums, promics, promos. The *Comic Book Price Guide* uses the term promotional comics, and indeed, each comic was created to promote an idea, (*Eat Right to Win*), a product (*Chevrolet Fun Book*), or a purpose (*Making a Home for Wildlife*). Not entirely in jest, we propose the term impact comics for that describes their intent and, in large measure, their success . . . In every case, someone or some organization had a goal to accomplish, an objective to be attained – an election campaign to be won, a product to sell, a lesson to be taught, the environment to be saved – and some savvy, energetic risk-taker put his/her money into producing a graphic arts product that would help reach that goal.' (2005: 340).

The notion of impact is important for Davidson and suggests such comic books should be judged by their effectiveness in achieving their aims rather than by considering the visual and narrative structures employed. Measuring the effectiveness of any campaign tool is always difficult but an example from 1948 demonstrates the potential of public relations comic books. The American President

Harry S. Truman was running for re-election but was well behind in the polls to his Republican opponent Thomas E. Dewey. Realizing the severity of the situation the Democratic Party National Committee took the bold step of commissioning a sixteen-page biography titled *The Story of Harry S. Truman*. Three million copies of this rather sanitized and hagiographic biographical comic book were distributed to the core demographic of the Democratic Party and Truman went on to win the election by over one million votes (Smith and Duncan, 2009: 269–70). This causal link is difficult to prove but it is worth noting that in the decades that followed political parties in America used comic books for a number of different tasks such as educating and motivating voters, besides the most obvious application of attempting to win elections, which suggests that at the very least they believed public relations comic books could have a direct impact on the public (Davidson, 2005: 341–2, 356).

Davidson's term 'impact comics' has not been widely adopted but it does have some value when considering the aims of public relations comic books and can additionally be applied to other comic book genres. When examining the concept of genre in relation to mainstream comic book production Duncan and Smith confusing state that 'Usually distributed as giveaways, promotional comics help to advertise a product or a conviction or are a reward for having made a purchase' (2009: 216) In compounding advertising and promotional comic books they highlight the shared qualities of such publications but do not distinguish the substantial differences that exist between them in terms of purpose and intent. There is a considerable difference between creating a comic book to directly advertise or promote a product and one that wants to raise awareness of a conviction and it is the latter that is the focus of this study.

From the 1960s to the 1990s single-page advertising, promotional and public relations comic strips were often included in British boy's anthology comic books alongside the main adventure stories in the genres of action, sport and war. By examining examples of these comic strips in detail it is possible to differentiate between advertising, promotional and public relations comic books by highlighting their similarities and differences. An issue of the boy's adverture comic book *Valiant* from February 1971 contained three such strips, the first of these was an advert for a range of plastic model kits titled 'Airfix in Action' that employed comic book devices such as panels and speech balloons but did not strictly speaking tell a story but instead showcased the different model kits available.[4]

A second example from this issue contained a full page adventure story titled 'Kit Carter's Clarks Commandos' in which a group of teenage boys (the Clarks Commandos) find an injured bank robber and turn him over to the police, only in the final panel is there any reference to the Clarks' product line with an image of the shoes and the tag line 'Commandos are action shoes for tough assignments'. The final example from this issue of *Valiant* told the true life story of 'Brian Downey! Marine Commando!' who aged 17 quit his job as a miner in Newcastle and joined the Royal Marines. The final panel included the caption 'At 25 Brian's seen most of the world – from snow warfare exercises in Norway to jungle training in Johore Bahru, His next assignment? The Bahamas!'[5]

At one level this can be seen as a recruitment drive by the Royal Marines and the readers were encouraged to send away for the free Royal Marines booklet 'Britain's Commandos' but the juvenile readership of *Valiant* would have been too young to enlist and this comic strip is more readily conceived as a case of maintaining public relations with potential future recruits and raising awareness of the Royal Marines as a potential career choice. All three examples from *Valiant* employed the conventions of boy's comic book action and war stories to engage with readers but only the final one can be considered as an example of public relations as the others focus more on directly promoting or advertising products.

The origins of public relations comic books

There is a long history of American comic books being used for advertising purposes and it is this area we can detect the origins of the medium being used for public relations. As early as 1933 *Fortune* magazine devoted an article titled 'The Funny Papers' to the significant role comic strips played in newspaper sales highlighting the fact that most adults were regular readers of the 'Funnies' as these comic book newspaper supplements were called (1933: 44–9, 92, 95–6, 98, 101). The final section of this article focused on the emergence of advertising comic strips noting that in 1932 Comic Weekly sold over $1,000,000 of advertising space and highlighted some of their key characteristics

> 'The advertising strips have a close superficial resemblance to the genuine funnies although they are built around a sales talk instead of a gag. They are nearly always based on the Before and After theme. Their type is the old-fashioned (except that it seems not so old-fashioned) hair-restorer advertisement showing an absolutely bald surface before using the marvellous remedy and a luxuriant hair growth afterwards. Sample: Betty is pictured in tears because Jim does not call on her anymore. The other girls, sympathetic, contrive in some sweet, girlish way to insinuate that Betty has been "careless" and does not wash her underthings every day. This idea percolates and Betty is shown in the act of washing. In the last panel Jim is back again and cleanliness appears to be next to matrimony. This is a Lux advertisement.'
>
> (1933: 98)

These newspaper comic strips were created to advertise products through direct persuasion techniques an approach that was much derided in the *Fortune* article for undermining the values of the advertising and marketing professions. At the same time as these newspaper strips emerged in America a parallel development saw the creation of what were called at the time advertising premium comic books but which are better considered as examples of public relations comics. The originator of the premiums was Harry I. Wildenberg who worked as a sales manager at the Eastern Colour Printing Company. In the early 1930s he realised that it was possible to use spare printing capacity at the company to produce cheap comic books which could then be given away free to customers as a premium. Gulf Oil were the first to take up this idea and gave these comic books away at their gas stations and Wildenberg, with the help of another salesman M. C. Gaines, attracted a range of other companies for whom they produced premiums.

These other companies included Proctor and Gamble, Canada Dry, Kinney Shoes and Wheatena as well as a host of others that sold children's products, the comic books were generally produced in print runs of 100,000 to 250,000 but on occasion could reach runs of 1,000,000 copies. These premium comic books did not directly advertise the products but instead raised brand awareness and created band loyalty. These premiums had a major impact on the American comic book industry. In 1934 realising the popularity of these premiums Wildenberg and Gaines convinced the American New Company to distribute a 64-page comic book titled *Famous Funnies* at newsstands with a 10-cent cover price. Although not initially a success by Issue 12 *Famous Funnies* was making a substantial profit and other publishers soon followed their lead thus marking the beginnings of what became the American entertainment comic book industry (Goulart, 1991: 18–20).

Will Eisner was a key figure in the American comic book industry, as both a practitioner and theorist, who produced comic books for both entertainment and public relations purposes. Eisner was a highly successful comic book artist in his own right, producing the celebrated detective newspaper strip *The Spirit* in the 1940s and 1950s before leaving mainstream comic books to focus on the instructional and educational comic books he produced for The American Visual Corporation which he had founded in 1948 and whose clients included RCA Records, Baltimore Colts and the New York Telephone. He returned to the comic book industry in the 1970s going on to produce several semi-autobiographical graphic novels, such as *A Contract with God*.

In addition to his comic book work Eisner published several influential instructional books on the process of making comic books, these included *Comics and Sequential Art* in which he divided comic books into those created for entertainment purposes and those created to be instructional although he did stress that these two kinds of comic books can merge and crossover (1985: 153). He further differentiated instructional comic books into attitudinal and technical, where the technical comic books focused on conveying how a task can be executed precisely and efficiently. When discussing the potential for comic books to promote attitudinal change Eisner noted that

> 'Another instructional function of sequential art is conditioning an attitude towards a task . . . People learn by imitation and the reader in this instance can easily supply the intermediate or connecting action from his or her own experience. Here too there is no pressure of time as there would be in a live action motion picture or animated film. The amount of time allowed to the reader of a printed comic to examine, digest and imagine the process of acting out or assuming the role or attitude demonstrated is unlimited.'

(1985: 153–4)

To demonstrate this point *Comics and Sequential Art* included some examples of Eisner's own work produced for the State Employment Service by his company The American Visual Corporation. The main series he produced for them were nine full colour eight-page booklets collectively titled *The Job Scene* that looked at areas such as retail sales and health care with a view to explaining employment opportunities to students. They also produced comic books titled *The Power is Green* and *You're Hired* that looked respectively at gaining the necessary skills for employment and how to keep a job once employed (Davidson, 2005: 350–1).

Eisner's most significant and long-lasting client for The American Visuals Corporation was the U.S. Department of the Army for whom he created *PS Magazine the Preventative Maintenance Monthly* producing 229 issues between 1951 and 1972.[6] The comic book strips included in this magazine served two functions, at one level they were purely functional in instructing soldiers how to maintain and use their equipment, at another level these stories were meant to entertain and therefore intended to create attitudinal change amongst service men by engaging them with the tasks in hand.[7]

The main character employed in these comic strips was Joe Dope who had started out as a rather dumb soldier in some of Eisner's earlier war stories but was transformed into the 'hero' in the *PS Magazine* stories. In the story titled 'Joe Dope in 'How to Load a Truck'' from the first issue of the magazine we see Joe Dope berating another private for his lack of care in treating the army's equipment. The visual style was cartoonish and this, alongside the use of humour and colloquial language, it was hoped would allow the reader to engage more fully with the message being communicated. The strip also used infographics, diagrams and more realistic visual styles to give variety to the narrative and provide more accurate information on the task being explained (Fitzgerald, 2008).

The American armed services had already utilized comic books for public relations, all be it with a propaganda dimension during the Second World War (Chapman, Hoyles, Kerr and Sheriff, 2015: 101–24). In 1942 the Graphics Division of the Office of War Information commissioned research by the advertising agency Young and Rubican into how to produce effective posters to communicate the war effort. One of their recommendations was that comic strip elements should be included in the posters as this would allow for empathy and identification with recurrent characters. Although the Office of War Information did not produce their own comic books in this period they did closely monitor the content of commercial comic books and strips and sent out a monthly guide to newspaper, magazine and comic book publishers about what constituted suitably patriotic content (Chapman, Hoyles, Kerr and Sheriff, 2015: 101–24).

One publisher Magazine Enterprises uniquely produced two war comic books *United States Marine Corp* and *The American Air Forces* in close collaboration with the armed services using photographs they provided in narrative sequences and as source material for comic strip illustrations. Interestingly *United States Marine Corp* included two humorous recurring characters, Monte and Trip, in a similar vein to Eisner's Joe Dope and presumably with the same aim of creating identification and empathy.

Figure 3.4 'Joe Dope in How to Load a Truck' PS Magazine June 1951 Vol 1 No. 1 p. 14. (Story and Art Will Eisner)

Figure 3.5 'Joe Dope how to Load a Truck' PS Magazine June 1951 Vol 1 No. 1 p. 15. (Story and Art Will Eisner)

Magazine Enterprises, as the name suggests, was a commercial publisher and since the earliest days of the comic strip well known recurring characters had been used to advertise products (Davidson, 2005: 350–1). In the 1970s DC Comics by then a subsidiary company of Warmer Communications, decide to monetize their main superhero characters for advertising, promotional and public relations purposes. This activity was itself promoted in a brochure DC Comics produced in 1979 that showed the superheroes themselves making promotional comics and included tag lines such as 'Let us start working for YOU!' and 'The graphic way to present your marketing message'. The brochure listed over 30 companies and organisations that had successfully used comic books and many of these, such as General Electric, MacDonalds and Pizza Hut, would have used them mainly for marketing and advertising.

However, other organisations listed like, the Anti-Defamation League, the National Mental Health Association and the United States Public Health Commission would have no product as such to sell so would have been using them primarily for public relations. The brochure furthermore drew on support from the advertising and marketing industries with supportive quotes from publications such as *Advertising Requirements* and *Sales Management*. A quote from *Premium Practice and Business Promotion* included in the brochure stated 'Few premiums can rival the wide acceptance enjoyed by comics amongst our kids – or the variety available to the advertiser who uses them to promote his products'. This reveals the main of use of these comic books as free giveaways with promotional intent and indicates that the industry was taking the medium seriously as a public relations tool.

The fact that DC Comics not only licensed the superhero characters but also created the artwork ensured that the brand was not damaged by the resulting comic books. Although not a comic book the series of posters created by DC Comics for the British Health Education Council in the early 1980s show the creativity this afforded in action (see Figure 3.1). These anti-smoking posters pitted Superman against a specially created new character Nick O'Teen whose uniform consists of a dingy tar-soaked brown cape and suit with a smoking cigarette butt on his head. Nick O'Teen's crumpled figure is in stark contrast to the brightly-coloured Superman who lifts Nick O'Teen with one hand while crushing a packet of cigarettes in the other proclaiming 'Help me crush the evil Nick O'Teen! Hijacker of health, foe of the fit. Never say yes to a cigarette!'

From this brief history of public relations comic books it is clear that they were from the outset closely associated with: the newspaper advertising strips that proceeded them, free giveaway 'premiums' and the emergence of the American comic book as a mainstream medium in the 1930s. Of course, public relations comic books did share some of the aims of advertising, promotional and mainstream comic books in terms of engagement which is why later companies such as DC Comics were able to monetised their most popular characters for public relations purposes. However, Eisner's work and theories demonstrate that the biggest difference between these different kinds of comic books is that those created for public relations were focused on achieving attitudinal change in their audiences.

Comic books, science (fiction) and public engagement

In examining contemporary public relations comic books that promote the sciences using the science fiction genre it is important to establish some of the key conventions in this genre and consider how they have been represented previously in comic book form. Comic books and magazines played a key role in communicating scientific knowledge and technological innovation in Britain following the Second World War.[8] From the 1950s onwards British comic books such as; *Eagle, Robin* and *Swift*, and children's magazines; *Look and Learn* and *World of Wonder*, employed visual strategies that synthesised illustration, information design and the narrative form of comic books in providing a positive image of scientific achievements.[9]

The relationship between illustration, information design and comic book conventions in these examples can be complex but in its most basic form it can be seen in directional arrows that guide the viewer through the narrative construction of a confusing series of comic book panels. However, some of the most compelling uses of information design in these examples were when these devices were employed alongside illustration and comic strips in the communication of historical, scientific and technological knowledge. *Look and Learn* and *World of Wonder* covered these scientific and technological topics with an educationally focused agenda which was made evident in David Stone's 'Editorial' to the first issue of *Look and Learn*

> '*Look and Learn* is not a comic, or a dusty old encyclopaedia pretending to be an entertaining weekly paper. It is really like one of those fabulous caravans that used to set off to strange and unknown places and return laden with all sorts of wonderful things . . . Today, the world changes at a rate undreamt of even by our mothers and fathers . . . Of necessity, newspapers and television must adapt themselves to today's frantic pace, and many of us find ourselves bewildered by ever-changing headlines rushing by like racing cars at Silverstone. Many people, tiring of newspapers, turn to papers which thrive on what is called "escaping." . . . Between these two extremes there must be what the Ancient World called the Golden Mean, and what we would call a happy medium. A happy medium means a nice balance between fact and fiction, between information and entertainment, between, if you like, laughter and tears. It is our hope that *Look and Learn* will be the most happy medium of all. But you must be the judge of that.'
>
> (Holland, 2006: 6–7)

The *Eagle*, founded with clear didactic purposes in the early 1950*s*, had similarities to *Look and Learn* in including cutaway drawings of technological marvels, half-page sporting comic strips on keeping a straight bat and explanatory strips looking at scientific discoveries. One comic strip serialised in the *Eagle*, 'Professor Brittain Explains', examined the technological innovation of the period such as TIM the talking telephone clock, the mechanics behind London Underground ticket machines and the scientific principles behind radar technology. The pipe-smoking Professor Brittain would explain each week's topic to two school children and in addition to using comic strip features such as panels and speech balloons it employed infrographics, maps and technical drawings. In terms of address Professor Brittain directly talked to the children throughout in lengthy explanatory speech balloons and often in his closing remarks invited empathy with the reader by addressing them directly. The aim of ensuring reader engagement was continued at the end of the strip with the request 'Any Questions: Please write to Professor Brittain, c/o *Eagle*, if you have any questions or problems you would like him to deal with.'

Although these examples employ some narrative strategies they were essentially factual in terms of content. There is, however, a significant link to some of the science fiction and fantasy stories that were also published in these comic books and magazines. For example, Frank Hampson's 'Dan Dare: Pilot of the Future' was the flagship comic strip in the *Eagle* and Don Lawrence's 'The Trigan Empire' was an important comic book element in *Look and Learn*. These stories of the future and far away worlds framed the illustrated articles and comic strips promoting contemporary scientific and technological innovations, taking them away from the factual and firmly into the world of the imagination. Hampson's artwork on the *Dan Dare* strip has been described as representing ' . . . the most perfectly realised modernist future in the history of British science fiction.' and notable for ' . . . its aestheticization of technology with its sleek and streamlined spaceships and its many functional gadgets' (Chapman, 2011: 63). The strip has also been directly linked to the perception of science and technology in this post-war, a period where

'The future imagined in 'Dan Dare' embodies the idealism of the Festival of Britain where technology is both functional and employed for the benefit of mankind . . . It is also for the most part a utopian future'

(Chapman, 2011: 63).

Clearly other comic strips in the *Eagle* dealing with contemporary science and technology such as 'Professor Brittain Explains' would then have been read in relation to this vision of the future which was framed as full of utopian promise.[10] The concept of utopia has been a longstanding trope within the science fiction genre and it is possible to trace representations of such visions for the future in contemporary public relations comic books.

The examples of science fiction comic books and children's magazines from the 1950s and 1960s examined above enjoyed mainstream success employing relatively conventional comic book techniques and narrative structures. The 1970s saw new developments with innovative techniques and narrative structures being employed in a range of comic books and graphic novels aimed directly at an adult market. Jean Giraud who worked under the pseudonym of Moebius was an important figure in this development as a writer and artist as well as being co-founder of the French science fiction/fantasy magazine *Métal Hurlant*. His story *Upon a Star* from 1983 is typical of his later science-fiction comic book work in its themes if not its creation. The original seven-page version was commissioned by the chairman of Citroen to be given away as a gift to the company's branch managers, as a public relations tool in promoting brand loyalty. Moebius kept the central element of the plot, the 'mythical car', the Traction, manufactured by Citroen in the late 1930s, when adapting the original version into the forty-page story *Upon a Star* for Citroen that then inspired a series of sequels titled *The Aedena Cycle* (Moebius, 1988).

In this longer version of the story the two main characters, the mechanics Stel and Atan, are called to repair a refinery, which they find deserted, on an asteroid circling a planet. The asteroid is drawn towards the planet's surface, and crashes destroying their spaceship. After the crash a Citroen Traction is the only form of transport still working and they use this to drive to the only signs of life on the planet. These signs emanate from an immense pyramid surrounded by abandoned spaceships that resemble the minarets of an Islamic city, and a tented encampment containing representative members of all the species in the known universe, all drawn to the planet by the pyramid that grants them eternal life. They have been waiting for a pilot to take them to the 'legendary paradise planet of Aedena'. Stel who has an inner affinity with all mechanical devices is this pilot. He is the only person who can enter the pyramid and as he enters it transforms into an ark spaceship that takes the form of the two chevrons that make the Citroen car badge. The story finishes with Stel apparently guiding the spaceship to Aedena as it heads out into deep space. The Citroen Traction, described by Stel as 'a jewel that can take us to the end of this world!' plays the central role in this story, it is the vehicle that allows them to reach the settlement and is symbolically reinforced in the image of the spaceship that allows them to reach paradise (Moebius, 1988).

As well as being a public relations tool this story playfully uses the concepts of both utopia and dystopia. Utopia is represented by the paradise of Aedena which the technocrat Stel pilots them towards, its antonym the notion of dystopia is represented by the deserted then destroyed asteroid, the mainly uninhabited planet and the abandoned spaceships. The pyramid that transforms into a spaceship also feeds into dystopian notions of an unknowable technological force. When discussing the representation of technology by Jack Kirby in American superhero comic books Hadfield has noted that

'The phrase the *technological sublime* indeed suggests an attitude of worshipful awe. It seems to me that Kirby's work reveals a less celebratory, more ambivalent sense of the technological sublime, something more in keeping with how I read Burke's definition of the sublime . . . That definition is fearful – or rather *fear-based* . . . the use of high-tech motifs to represent vast forces that not only are ineffable and awful . . . but also might result in shock, estrangement, or madness.'

(2012: 145–6)

Similar dystopian ideas of shock and awe were present in the graphic novel *When the Wind Blows* created by Raymond Biggs in 1982. The cover image showed the main characters Jim and Hilda, a placid elderly British couple in front of the mushroom cloud of a nuclear missile explosion. The story starts with Jim returning to his home, set in an idealised English countryside, after reading the newspapers reporting the threat of nuclear war in his local library. As the narrative unfolds war is announced and the nuclear strike ensues, Jim follow the government advice on dealing with this eventuality as outlined in the public information booklet *Protect and Survive*, which was published in 1980 and also employed comic book conventions. What follows is a black comedy that contrasts Jim and Hilda's naive belief that they will survive, by hiding in their hastily constructed self-made shelter using advice from *Protect and Survive*, with the reality of the radiation sickness that kills them. On its release *When the Wind Blows* was referenced in a Parliamentary debate on the subject of Britain's military defences

> 'Defence now means defence against a nuclear attack. The gentleman who produced the document "When the Wind Blows" – I think that it was sent to all hon. Members – did a great service to the House and to the public, who may subsequently have the opportunity of reading the book. It spells out in graphic terms the ridiculous deception that is being played on the British people. I refer to the argument that there is a defence against nuclear weapons.[11]

Although produced commercially for entertainment purposes *When the Wind Blows* had a significant public relations impact in terms of attitudinal change. The fact that a copy was sent to all Members of Parliament was significant and shortly after this the Labour Party adopted a unilateral nuclear disarmament policy, a course of action that must in part have been a reaction to the story by party members and the public.

Dreams of a Low Carbon Future was produced by the Doctoral Training Centre in Low Carbon Technologies at the University of Leeds in 2013 and designed precisely to create an impact similar to that of *When the Wind Blows*.[12] Edited by James McKay and Benjamin Dickinson and funded by the ESPRC and the Royal Academy of Engineering the aim of the publication was, as the title suggests, to raise awareness about the dangers of global warming and to highlight the potential solutions being devised by engineers and scientists. The resulting anthology comic book had high production values, mimicking those of a graphic novel, and was created through collaborations between school children, engineers and scientists, comic book artists and illustrators, to imagine, examine and promote solutions to climate change.

The stories in *Dreams of a Low Carbon Future* draw on key conventions from the science fiction genre that can be divided into two main types, those that show potential dystopian futures and those that demonstrate utopian solutions to the problem of climate change. The cover illustration by Mark Wilkinson is an example of the latter with a utopian future city depicted in a manner typical of science fiction illustrations such Dan Dare from the *Eagle* (see Figure 3.3). However, this cover image is informed by new engineering concepts and is an example of bio-design with organic materials and design principles being used to create a

Figure 3.6 'Tour of KL2.0 2098' Dreams of a Low Carbon Future 2013
(Created by James Mckay, Nicole Cant and Lara Salih)

Figure 3.7 'Dystopia: Welcome to Judd City – 2045' Dreams of a Low Carbon Future 2013

(Created by Judd Blackmorre, Lara Salih, Thomas Fletcher, Jasmine Gaunt, Olivia Rogers, James Mackay, Hannah James)

sustainable megacity of the future. This positive view of the future is reflected in stories such as 'Tour of KL2.0 2098' which demonstrate a range of potential solutions to global warming and climate change such as new methods of carbon capture and innovations in energy production.

Other stories such as 'Dystopia: Welcome to Judd City – 2045' show the devastation that might be wrought by global warming and the kind of dystopian society that might emerge. In this narrative it is suggested that a ruling elite controls Judd City by exploiting slave workers, called 'subbers' or sub-humans, and by extracting the last remaining fossil fuels through fracking to support a consumerist society in denial of the impact of climate change.

Both of these stories are narrated by Professor Kwerblodie, an alien visitor to Earth. He is introduced in the opening story in *Dreams of a Low Carbon Future* and appears throughout as our guide who is there to provide an objective and external viewpoint to the issues facing the world in this period of crisis. In this first story, he demonstrates how energy operates in a manner similar to the Professor Brittain comic strips discussed earlier by directly addressing the readers and using scientific facts and supporting infographics. Many of the other stories in *Dreams of a Low Carbon Future* employed devices from the realm of information design such as diagrams, maps and directional arrows to explain the more complex scientific ideas accurately as it was essential that the information provided by the scientists and engineers was presented clearly to the reader.

Information design was used even more extensively in *Asteroid Belter: The Newcastle Science Comic*, edited by Lydia Wysocki and Paul Thompson and produced as part of the British Science Festival held at Newcastle University in 2013, perhaps because it was aimed at a younger audience than *Dreams of a Low Carbon Future*.[13] This intended younger audience was reflected in the simple cartoonish graphic style employed throughout *Asteroid Belter* and by being printed on newsprint so it looked and felt like a traditional British children's anthology comic book (see Figure 3.2). *Asteroid Belter* did not focus exclusively on issues of climate change and global warming, which might be predisposed to depictions of dystopian and utopian futures, instead it was a more general science comic book designed to look at a range of scientific subjects and introduce them to new audiences. It explored topics such as botany, geology and quantum physics, with several stories examining health issues often with a rather juvenile sense of humour as demonstrated in titles such as 'A Guinea Pigs' Guide to Cancer Drug Trials' and 'A Day in the Life of a Poo'. Even though representations of dystopia and utopia are mainly absent from *Asteroid Belter* there are references to other science fiction conventions such as space travel with characters taking a day trip to the moon or going to witness a supernova explosion. Time travel is another well-known science fiction convention employed and is a central theme in three stories in *Asteroid Belter*, 'Felix and Chuckney in Time Travel Rocks', 'Time travel is . . . Awesome' and 'How to Train your Robot', this final example uses the language of information design to incorporate a game for the reader to play and the resulting comic strip can be considered both instructional and entertaining.

Figure 3.8 'How to Train your Robot' Asteroid Belter: The Newcastle Science Comic 2013
(Comic: John Miers; Science: John Hedley)

One feature that *Asteroid Belter* and *Dreams of a Low Carbon Future* share is the convention of the mad scientist or learned professor that has its roots in mainstream science fiction and adventure comic books such Professor Brittain in the *Eagle*. Such characters appear in several comic strips in *Asteroid Belter*: in one example a real-life professor, Brian Randell of Newcastle University, explains his research into the history of computing, in another strip Professor Yakka explains how to make a rocket out of a plastic bottle, baking soda and vinegar. These examples are relatively straight-forward narratives but the most telling of these kinds of comic strips is titled 'Astoundishing Science' and explicitly deconstructs the notion of the mad scientist.

The mad scientist invents a cat crossed with a speaker, called Boomboxcatbot, that rebels against him and declares 'It's not science, it's just silly . . . Imaginative

Figure 3.9 'Astoundishing Science' Asteroid Belter: The Newcastle Science Comic 2013
(Story and art: Oscillating Brow; Colours and letters: Paul Thompson)

stories are great, but I'm fed up with these 'mad scientist' clichés! . . . . Science is amazing but it isn't about 'boffins' and weirdness'.

Conventions from the science fiction genre have been adopted and adapted from mainstream comic books to inform the narratives in *Asteroid Belter* and *Dreams of a Low Carbon Future*. Will Eisner suggested that instructional comic books should entertain as well as inform and it is possible to argue that in these example of science (fiction) public relations comic books this is achieve by working with established genre conventions using well-understood reader expectations. The focus in this study has been on the use of the science fiction genre in public relations comic books but there is some scope to examine how conventions adopted from other comic book genres; for example, documentary, sports or war, might operate within the realm of public relations.

Where these public relations comic books differ from the mainstream is in how they engage with their audiences. This is achieved in three different ways; the first of these is through the modes of address noted above where the reader is directly addressed by the characters in the stories, a feature that is relatively rare in the mainstream but is commonplace in many public relations comic books. A second feature used to ensure audience engagement is the use of instructional devices drawn from the visual language of information design such as maps, diagrams and directional arrows; these devices also appear occasionally in mainstream entertainment comic books but are much more prevalent in those created for public relations purposes.

A third feature that *Asteroid Belter* and *Dreams of a Low Carbon Future* utilize is the fact that they were produced collaboratively with the children who make up their target audience. This feature distinguishes contemporary public relations comic books from those in the past, where the reader was spoken to but did not have its own voice, and ensures that at least some of the target audience are directly engaged with the issues at stake. We have seen that Davidson defined public relation comic books as 'impact comics' because of the way that they have a direct purpose in wanting to promote an idea or a concept and this notion of impact fits well with Eisner's suggestion that these comic books promote attitudinal change. Taken together these ideas of audience engagement, impact and attitudinal change suggest that comic books can be a valuable tool within the public relations profession.

Notes

1 The Graphic Medicine website (www.graphicmedicine.org/) was founded by Dr Ian Williams in 2007. In the last decade the Graphic Medicine network has grown extensively and runs regular international conferences and has its own book series published by Penn State University Press.

2 For an overview of the emergence of Comics Studies as an academic discipline see Matthew J. Smith and Randy Duncan (Eds.) (2017) *The Secret Origins of Comics Studies*. Basingstoke: Routledge.

3 Davidson's article is the only substantial study of the topic and was in part written to note that he had donated his substantial personal collection of such comics to the University of Florida's George A. Smathers Libraries. Such comics are by their very nature ephemeral and it is only through building personal collections or donations by

other collectors like Davidson that the topic can be studies in any depth. A more recent study from 2011, Richard L. Graham's *Government Issue: Comics for the People 1940s-2000s,* examines some of this material in detail but as the title suggests it only addresses comic books published by the American government and therefore provides only a partial account of the field.

4 *Valiant,* 20th February 1971, IPC Magazine Ltd.
5 Downey served with the Royal Marines from 1960 to 1978. Details recorded in an oral history project for the Imperial War Museum. www.iwm.org.uk/collections/item/object/80032295.
6 The entire run of *PS Magazine the Preventative Maintenance Monthly* has been scanned and made available for researchers by Virginia Commonwealth University Library Digital Collections. http://dig.library.vcu.edu/cdm/landingpage/collection/psm
7 For a discussion of the psychology behind the educational potential for comic books see Paul Aleixo and Krystina Sumner (2017) 'Memory for Biopsychology Material Presented in Comic Book Format.' *Journal of Graphic Novels and Comics* 8 (1), pp. 79–88 and Paul Aleixo and Claire Norris (2013) 'Planarian Worms, Shock Generators and Apathetic Witnesses: Teaching Psychology and Graphic Novels.' *Psychology Teaching Review* 19 (1), pp. 36–43.
8 The ideas examined here are based on a paper titled 'Look and Learn from a World of Wonder' delivered at *Science, Imagination, and the Illustration of Knowledge* the *4th International Illustration Symposium* in Oxford in 2013.
9 *Look and Learn* was published between 1962 and 1982. Another boy's comic book *Ranger* (1965–66) which included the science fiction story 'The Rise and Fall of the Trigan Empire' (later simply titled 'The Trigan Empire') was merged with *Look and Learn* in 1966. Another children's magazine *World of Wonder* (1970–75) was merged with *Look and Learn* in 1975. The *Eagle* was published between 1950 and 1969 when it was incorporated with another boy's comic book *Lion.* 'Dan Dare: Pilot of the Future' was dropped as the lead story of the *Eagle* in the mid-1960s. The *Eagle* was revived in 1982 and carried on with Dan Dare as a central character until its final demise in 1994.
10 The relationship between British superheroes such as Dan Dare and the social discourses surrounding science fiction and technology are explored in detail in Chris Murray (2017) *The British Superhero.* Jackson, MS: University Press of Mississippi.
11 As reported in hansard.millbanksystems.com/commons/1982/feb/15/defence#column_62
12 For information on *Dreams of a Low Carbon Future* see https://cdt.engineering.leeds.ac.uk/dtc-low-carbon-technologies/research/DreamsofaLowCarbonFuture.shtml. In November 2016 McKay and Dickinson released *A Dream of a Low Carbon Future* a revised and refined version of the original comic book focused on the single idea of depicting a sustainable world for the future.
13 For information on *Asteroid Belter: The Newcastle Science Comic* see http://newcastle sciencecomic.blogspot.co.uk/.

References

Aleixo, Paul and Norris, Claire (2013). 'Planarian Worms, Shock Generators and Apathetic Witnesses: Teaching Psychology and Graphic Novels.' *Psychology Teaching Review* 19 (1): 36–43.

Alexio, Paul and Summer, Krystina (2017). 'Memory for Biopsychology Material Presented in Comic Book Format.' *Journal of Graphic Novels and Comics* 8 (1): 79–88.

Chapman, James (2011). *British Comics a Cultural History.* London: Reaktion Books.

Chapman, Jane, Hoyles, Anna, Kerr, Andrew and Sheriff, Adam (2015). *Comics and the Worlds Wars: A Cultural Record.* Basingstoke: Palgrave Macmillan.

Davidson, Sol M. (2005). '"The Funnies" Neglected Branch: Special Purpose Comics.' *International Journal of Comic Art* 7 (2), Fall/Winter: 340–57.

Eisner, Will (1985). *Comics and Sequential Art*. New York: W. W. Norton.

Fitzgerald, Paul E. (2008). *Will Eisner and PS Magazine*. New Castle, Pennsylvania: Hermes Press.

'The Funny Papers.' (1933). *Fortune*, April.

Goulart, Ron (1991). *Over 50 Years of American Comic Books*. Lincolnwood, IL: Publication International Ltd.

Graham, Richard L. (2011). *Government Issue: Comics for the People 1940s-2000s*. New York: Abrams Comicarts.

Hatfield, Charles (2012). *Hand of Fire: The Comics Art of Jack Kirby*. Jackson, MS: University Press of Mississippi.

Holland, Steve (2006). *Look and Learn a History of the Children's Magazine*. Available at www.lookandlearn.com/history/Look-and-Learn-History.pdf.

Mickwitz, Nina (2016). *Documentary Comics: Graphic Truth-Telling in a Skeptical Age*. Baisingstoke: Palgrave Macmillian.

Moebius (Jean Giruad) (1988). 'Upon a Star.' in Moebius (Jean Giruad), *Moebius 1: The Collected Fantasies of Jean Giraud*. (English Translation by Jean-Marc and Randy Lofficier). London: Titan Books. (Unpaginated).

Murray, Chris (2017). *The British Superhero*. Jackson, MS: University Press of Mississippi.

Sabin, Roger (1993). *Adult Comics: An Introduction*. London: Routledge.

Smith, Matthew J. and Duncan, Randy (2009). *The Power of Comics*. New York: Continuum International Publishing Group.

Smith, Matthew J. and Duncan, Randy (Eds.) (2017). *The Secret Origins of Comics Studies*. Baisingstoke: Routledge.

4   Picturing statistical narratives

A century of data visualisation in public relations practice

Jon Cope and Mark Wells

Introduction

Early in his 1936 explication of Isotype, Otto Neurath emphasises his central assertion in all-caps: 'WORDS MAKE DIVISION, PICTURES MAKE CONNECTION' (Neurath, 1936, 18). Today, his typographically amplified message continues to resonate strongly with public relations (PR) practitioners. Since their resurgence coinciding with the development of the visual web from around 2010, infographics and other forms of data visualisation continue to proliferate to the point at which their production has become almost routine in public relations practice.

In this chapter, we survey the subject of graphic design – focusing on infographics – in the healthcare PR sector. We highlight antecedents from the past century, with Isotype – the radical 'International Picture Language' initially developed between 1925 and 1934 in Vienna as a public education tool – as the fulcrum. We compare Isotype's concept of the 'transformer' – responsible for deciding 'what is worth transmitting to the public' (Neurath & Kinross, 2009, 78) – with today's healthcare PR practitioner, responsible largely for communicating persuasively on behalf of powerful corporations. In so doing, we examine the tensions between the informational/educational and rhetorical/persuasive functions of infographics, questioning the PR practitioner's role as public 'trustee' (Neurath & Kinross, 2009, 116) as well as that of the graphic designer who, it is argued, ought to 'serve the needs of society' (Twyman, 1975).

Our overall aim in this chapter is to understand the reasons for the ongoing popularity of infographics as a PR tool, questioning their use and usefulness in practice to understand whether a need will continue to exist for such visual representations of data in the future.

Boxout 1   What is Isotype? How it works

What is Isotype?

Arguably the most significant influence on contemporary infographics, 'Isotype' – the International System of TYpographic Picture Education – was initially developed in 1925 by the Austrian philosopher, political economist

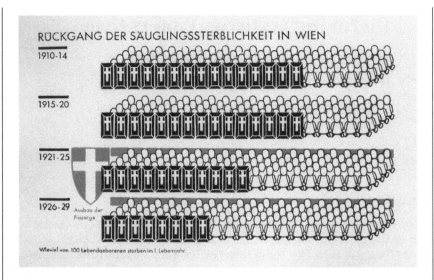

Figure 4.1 Chart illustrating 'Declining Infant Mortality Rates in Vienna', designed for the Museum of Society and Economy (c. 1930)

Used with permission: (*Otto and Marie Neurath Isotype Collection, University of Reading*)

and data visualisation pioneer Otto Neurath (1882–1945) together with collaborators including the graphic artist Gerd Arntz (1900–1988) and Marie Reidemeister (1898–1986). It was the first systematic attempt to produce a universal visual language capable of 'representing all aspects of the physical world' particularly to less educated groups, such as workers and schoolchildren (Burke, 2009, 211). Initially known as the Vienna Method of Pictorial Statistics, Isotype was first deployed at Vienna's Museum of Society & Economy from 1924, to represent social facts pictorially, making statistics visually pleasing and therefore memorable. Exhibits included charts and diagrams reflecting specific health and societal problems in Vienna at the time. (Burke, 2009). From the 1920s until the early 1970s, Neurath and his colleagues successfully expanded the Isotype concept for use in books for adults and children, national public health campaigns, public information films and publicity materials for companies including ICI.

How it works

Emerging from Modernist ideals of minimalism and functionalism, Isotype's clear-cut pictograms combine the simplicity of Constructivism with the typographic simplicity of Bauhaus and have had a significant influence on graphic illustration styles from the 1920s to the present day, particularly in the field of information design and data visualisation. The Isotype pictograms illustrate quantitative information by assigning a unit value to a representative symbol (e.g. one human figure to depict a population of 100,000) and repeating this figure as required. Although often presented

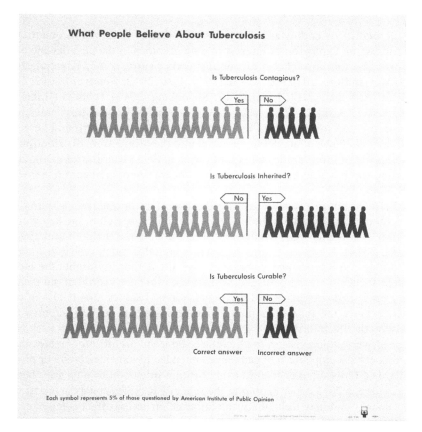

Figure 4.2 'What people believe about tuberculosis': illustration from the brochure Tuberculosis: basic facts in picture language, National Tuberculosis Association, New York (Neurath & Kleinschmidt, 1939)

Used with permission: (*Otto and Marie Neurath Isotype Collection, University of Reading, UK*)

as a 'system' or 'language', the strictures of Isotype are minimal: a sign should always represent the same figure, and signs should be displayed in horizontal lines in groups of five or ten. Thus, a greater number of things is always represented by a greater number of signs, not by changing the size of a single sign (whereby it is not clear whether it is the height, width, area or some other dimension that is to be considered). The system works best when visualising different quantities for comparison.

A description of the Isotype Picture Language in a publicity poster for Compton's Pictured Encyclopaedia (1939) for which Neurath and his team produced a series of 43 Isotype charts announced: 'they stimulate attention, interest, imagination, and understanding. They leave the student with a permanent "visual memory" of what he has learned. They train him to new and clearer ways of thinking for himself." (Burke, 2013, 323)

Review of the literature

The PR industry's enthusiasm for telling the stories that inhabit quantitative data follows an explosion of interest in data graphics in the past decade or so, supported by the publication of popular texts (Tufte, 1983; Klanten, 2008, 2010; McCandless, 2010, 2014; Yau, 2011; Few, 2012; Rendgen, 2012; Cairo 2013, 2016; Krum, 2014; Lima, 2017; Shaoqiang, 2018), toolkits (Iliinsky & Steele, 2011; Kirk, 2012), a wide range of specialist websites[1] and online tools[2] dedicated to presenting and producing data visualisation. There also exists an abundance of academic research into the production, distribution and consumption of infographics and other forms of data visualisation (Dur, 2014) including some within the science and healthcare sectors (Bucchi & Saracino, 2016; Shin, 2016).

A 2014 literature review covering the use of infographics in journalism, risk communication and psychology notes copious research in the key areas of attention, comprehension, recall, appeal and adherence (behavioural change) (Stones, 2014). However, while the review includes much research focusing on familiar graph types and comprehension, the author highlights the lack of research focusing on 'embellished infographics that are visible in the contemporary press and commissioned by organisations' (Stones, 2014, 1) – in other words, exactly the type of popular, pictorially enhanced infographics used widely by the PR industry.

Indeed, very little exists in the literature about the use of infographics by PR practitioners as components of campaigns intended to influence brand or product choice. The few examples that do exist mention infographics only peripherally. For example, a 2013 paper exploring the role of PR professionals in a post mass media society and how technology and information access affect democracy outlines the concept of 'Long Now' thinking, 'a focus on the future that necessitates collaboration, putting the community ahead of the individual or organization, and enacting democratic ideals' (Kent, 2013). The author recommends the use of 'high-quality infographics rather than eye-candy' in this approach to communications, delivered by senior managers and organizational leaders rather than by 'interns tweeting' (Kent, 2013, 343).

In the public health sphere, Guidry et al. (2017) briefly mention the use of infographics by PR practitioners working on behalf of global health organizations using social media as a vehicle for crisis communication in infectious disease outbreaks. The authors remark on the strength and volume of visual communications using Twitter by Medicines Sans Frontieres (MSF) around the 2014 Ebola crisis, compared to the efforts of the US Centers for Disease Control and the World Health Organisation. MSF – the authors claim – is 'more savvy and strategic in using visual-driven social media platforms to communicate about pandemic-related health risks' (Guidry et al., 2017, 8), perhaps partly as a result of using infographics.

Broadening the scope beyond infographics but using a historical approach to analysing contemporary graphic design practice in public health, Paul Stiff and colleagues' use of 19th-century documents to discuss information design principles (Stiff et al., 2010) has influenced more recent discussions of the contribution of typography and information design to health communication (Walker, 2017).

Infographics in the pharmaceutical industry

The lack of research into the use of infographics in PR campaigns generally, suggests that a more extensive analysis of this phenomenon would yield many interesting and useful observations for PR practitioners and scholars. However, in this chapter, we focus on the use of infographics to support PR campaigns in the healthcare sector, particularly within the pharmaceutical industry. PR activity for the healthcare sector (which refers largely to the pharmaceutical industry) contributes income to 15–17% of UK PR practitioners (PRCA, 2016, 25), with healthcare one of PR's biggest growth areas in both the UK and US (PRCA, 2016; PR Council, 2016). In addition to its financial contribution to the PR industry, there are several reasons for our interest in the use of infographics for pharmaceutical PR.

First, pharmaceutical PR depends heavily on the communication of complex data, providing evidence not only of product safety, efficacy and quality, but also illustrating the impact of any condition that a product is intended to treat, the likelihood of developing the condition and the need for new therapeutic options – often around unpalatable topics. As health PR consultant Catherine Nestor notes 'Communication specialists in healthcare constantly grapple with how to get people's attention on issues they may not want to hear about' (Roberts & Wright, 2017, 32).

Infographics offer PR practitioners in this sector a way to circumvent low levels of data literacy,[3] low health literacy[4] and deliberate information avoidance among the general public, while also potentially facilitating the clear, objective and compelling presentation of data to highly data literate health professionals who may not otherwise have the time, interest or inclination to pay attention to pharmaceutical company data. This was described to us succinctly by Andrea Smart, marketing director of Parker Design, a UK agency offering infographic design to clients in a variety of sectors, including pharmaceuticals as 'making the truth more apparent' (Smart, 2017).

However, there also exist obvious risks in presenting data in ways that are highly simplified – even simplistic – where there is a significant commercial imperative to persuade as well as simply inform, particularly as the public tends to place greater trust in numerical information than in other types of data (Stones & Gent, 2015a). As Deroy Peraza, Creative Director of New York design agency Hyperakt told us, "What's attractive to pharmaceutical companies is that these objects [infographics] seem trustworthy, but in reality every infographic has an editorial bent. There is selective data being presented – it's not a complete picture. It always has the agenda of whoever is commissioning it at its core." (Peraza, 2017).

Second, the promotion of pharmaceutical products is highly regulated, in part due to the 'information asymmetry' between 'experts' who manufacture and sell medicines, and their end consumers, who are unlikely to be equipped with the knowledge and understanding to make independent judgements on medicines' safety, quality or efficacy (World Health Organisation, 2013). This involves restrictions on the promotion of prescription medicines, most stringent in the case of patients/consumers (often referred to as laypersons). Indeed, while the promotion of prescription medicines directly to the general public ('direct to consumer' or 'DTC' promotion) is illegal in every country except the US, New Zealand and Brazil, it remains possible to use communications tools – including infographics – to influence health professionals, patient groups and the general public. In an interview for Gorkana (the UK-based media database and media analysis service), healthcare PR account director Ruth Wheatley outlines the need for expertise in regulation:

> "In an industry as heavily regulated as pharmaceuticals, it's also essential to understand the rules within which companies, and journalists, must operate. All healthcare PRs go through a significant number of hours of compliance training during their careers. We are experts in the clauses of the Association of the British Pharmaceutical Industry (ABPI) Code, the process the European Medicines Agency (EMA) goes through to evaluate new medicines, and what an US Food and Drug Administration (FDA) breakthrough designation actually means. We know how precise we have to be and how clinical trial results should be presented. We know how to reference every single point in a press release, but also how to tell the story despite the jargon."
>
> (Bylykbashi, 2016)

But clearly, knowledge of the regulatory environment also provides understanding of how to push boundaries. As Janet Kettels, vice president of communications and PR for pharmaceutical giant Allergan International explains: "The art of pharmaceutical public relations is what you do in the spaces that are available." (Lane, 2017, 31). Such attitudes have prompted several high-profile investigations. For example, a widely reported study from 2006 by the global federation of consumer groups, Consumers International, found that: "pharmaceutical companies in Europe are now using alternate pressure points, such as patient groups, students and pharmacists, coupled with revised, and arguably unethical, marketing tactics, particularly using the internet through chat groups and product information websites. In addition, companies employ a range of special techniques which all aim at the same effect: to appear to offer all the available information about 'modern' diseases (especially so-called lifestyle diseases, such as stress and poor eating habits) and create a need among consumers to demand drugs to deal with the problems." (Consumers International, 2006, 6).

Third, there can be little doubt that infographics are now *routinely* produced as outputs for PR campaigns on behalf of the pharmaceutical industry. Indeed, it is the very 'routineness' of infographic production in pharmaceutical PR that first drew our attention to the subject as an area for further investigation. We have personal, professional experience of this, having worked on infographics as part of PR campaigns for clients in the pharmaceutical industry, but the phenomenon is well known and acknowledged by the PR industry itself. Even the most cursory search of pharmaceutical companies' online media centres and social media accounts reveals hundreds of examples. In a recent magazine feature describing the planning cycle for a new pharmaceutical product launch, Kate Hawker, head of EMEA healthcare at Burson-Marsteller says: "With six months to go [until launch], work starts on materials: content, releases, *infographics*, video blogs and patient case studies for all the different audiences – generally in English." (Benady, 2017, 20) Infographics have thus become part of the *standard toolkit* for pharmaceutical product public relations. Where a phenomenon has become part of normal, routine procedure in any professional sphere, its presence must warrant further enquiry.

Infographic rhetoric and public relations

Put simply, an infographic comprises 'a mix of image and text working together to convey specific information' (Guidry, 2016, 661). Unlike standard, aesthetically minimal data visualisations produced by computer algorhythms, infographics are typically manually produced, digital illustrations that present 'a personalised treatment of information, are specific to a dataset (they cannot be reused with others), are aesthetically rich (with a strong visual content keyed to engaging readers and sustaining their interest) and are relatively poor in data (since each piece of information must be coded manually).' (Iliinsky & Steele, 2011, 5–6)

These descriptions make infographics seem entirely objective in their presentation of information. Indeed, graphic design scholar Per Mollerup describes the infographic as a specific type of graphic design 'that works with objectivity and clarity of expression' (Mollerup, 2013, 14) and asserts that information designers consciously strive to make information as factual, objective and unambiguous as possible. Furthermore, despite Otto Neurath's role as an agitator for social change, even Isotype has been described as 'a diagrammatic strategy that strives for maximal transparency and minimal iconicity, aiming to convey information as clearly as possible by avoiding all aesthetic or pictorial rhetoric.' (Hartle, 2017, 100).

But what about the role of rhetoric and persuasion? Neurath was certainly hopeful that statistics could serve as a tool for change (Neurath, 1927). Likewise, it is our contention – shared with others (e.g Roberts & Wright, 2017) – that data is almost never presented to particular audiences or the general public merely to inform of the presence of the data itself. Rather, it is presented with a purpose and – especially when presented by PR practitioners and embellished by the use of graphic design – its purpose must surely be intended to persuade viewers to a certain point of view.

In his critique of academic summaries of the functions of design, Malcolm Barnard is swift to dismiss any attempt to exclude a rhetorical function. Persuasion, he claims, is critical, arguing that all graphic production has a rhetorical function. 'What is the point of a graphic sign that has no effect on anyone?' he asks. (Barnard, 2005, 15). Persuasion was the opening 'theme' in a 2017 exhibition at the Wellcome Collection, focusing on the use of graphic design in health communication (Roberts & Wright, 2017). Indeed, why would PR practitioners devote so much time and energy to the production of infographics if they perceived no persuasive purpose in doing so? It could perhaps be argued that PR agencies might urge clients to fund production of anything at all to generate fee income for the PR agency. There is also recognition that the presence of infographics in support of PR campaigns offers advantages in terms of search engine optimisation.[5] However, today, there can be little doubt that infographics produced by the pharmaceutical industry exist not only to inform, but also to persuade. As Deroy Peraza notes, 'a client's agenda, their preferred way of seeing an issue is edited into the infographic by the selection of content you put in it.' (Peraza, 2017).

Boxout 2   What are infographics?

What are infographics?

Infographics are of three kinds: static, interactive and motion (Lankow et al., 2012). For this chapter, we focus on the static form described by Li and Moacdieh (2014) and others (e.g. Bateman, 2010; Stones & Gent, 2015a) as 'embellished infographics'. Such infographics may include data 'embellished' by other graphic devices 'from small decorations to large images and visual backgrounds' intended to enhance the aesthetic appearance of their data. (Bateman, 2010, 1) Many such examples incorporate pictograms or symbols of the sort popularised by the Isotype system and its disciples, such as Nigel Holmes in the 1980s.

In our experience, these are the types of infographic most used by PR practitioners in the pharmaceutical sector. Unlike animated, interactive or other forms of moving image infographic, they have low production costs and may pass more quickly through pharmaceutical companies' notoriously slow legal, medical and regulatory approvals procedures.

Static infographics are quick to produce, easy to distribute directly or via social media platforms and – if effectively conceived and designed – require only a relatively short period of attention to communicate their message. Explaining the pitfalls of interactive elements within online infographics, As Dominikus Baur writes: "85% of page visitors simply ignore them, missing out on information hidden behind interaction. On top of that, interactives are expensive to make – they have to work across devices, using trackpads and fingers. They're error-prone and can tarnish the publication's reception within their audience." (Baur, 2017)

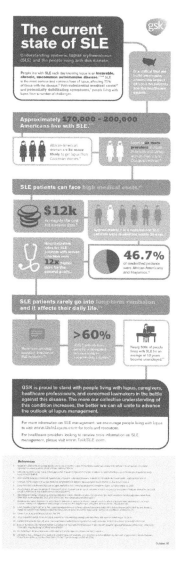

Figure 4.3 Produced in October 2016 by Edelman Public Relations in the US for the British pharmaceutical company, GlaxoSmithKline, this infographic (available at the time of writing at: http://us.gsk.com/media/930780/gsk_sle-infographic_11_2_16.jpg) is intended to illustrate 'the current state of systemic lupus erythematosus' in the US. It is a typical example of an embellished, static infographic in 'skyscraper' format (i.e. tall and thin). It uses a variety of data, embellished with colour, typography and icons designed to attract attention. The ratio of data to embellishment (or 'chart junk' as Tufte (1983) calls it) is relatively low and it includes a range of academic references, in order to comply with regulations around information produced by pharmaceutical companies and made available to the public.

(Copyright GSK: used with permission)

It is worth noting that according to some industry professionals (e.g. Peraza, 2017; Smart, 2017), current trends indicate a shift away from long-form (or 'skyscraper') infographics with multiple data points in favour of single data-point social media 'tiles'. We see clear evidence today, that rather than attempting to tell a 'whole story' with one infographic, PR practitioners are using infographics to communicate smaller sections of stories, intended to coalesce into a whole when viewers explore them further.

Infographics and the graphic turn in pharmaceutical public relations

The use of infographics for pharmaceutical PR coincides broadly with the rise of social media and the 'visual web' (Lewine, 2014). However, their rise in popularity is also linked to the phenomenon of 'content marketing'. This term, coined in the late 1990s, describes the practice (from the 19th century onwards) of brands attempting to strengthen consumer relationships by providing useful information, rather than simply promoting product purchases. Examples of content marketing include publications such as the 1888 Johnson & Johnson publication, *Modern Methods of Antiseptic Wound Treatment* (Johnson & Johnson, 1888) or the more widely known Michelin guides (1900 – present), vast content databases such as 'Think With Google', as well as much more ephemeral artefacts such as infographics, 'how to' guides, or 'expert' feature articles.

The precise point at which infographics became firmly embedded within the content marketer's 'toolkit' is obscure, but by 2013 several websites and online tools including Visual.ly and Plot.ly devoted wholly or largely to collating, searching, presenting and producing infographics had appeared (and in some cases, subsequently disappeared). Coinciding with this timing, infographics emerged as standard components of content toolkits for pharmaceutical PR campaigns from around 2010 to the point where they are routinely presented today (Lane, 2017).

Although the presentation of data to health professionals has always been fundamental to pharmaceutical companies' efforts to market their products, there is little evidence to suggest widespread use of infographics by pharmaceutical industry PR campaigns prior to the start of the 21st century. Indeed, while marketing of drugs by pharmaceutical companies to the medical profession has long been a way of influencing medical opinion and practice (Seale, 2003) activities of the type associated with contemporary PR or medical education[6] campaigns have only truly flourished from the 1950s onwards. Despite this, it is possible to trace the lineage of data visualisation for communications purposes in health and the pharmaceutical industry to an earlier era.

Many scholars (e.g Tufte, 1983; Friendly, 2007) highlight the links between contemporary infographics and the graphic vocabularies introduced in the eighteenth-century by J.H. Lambert (1728–1777) and William Playfair (1759–1823), early pioneers of the visual display of information to show relationships between variable quantities. Playfair is credited with inventing most of today's graphic charts – line and bar (Playfair, 1786) and pie and circle (Playfair, 1801). Playfair shared Otto Neurath's opinion that 'the eye is the best judge of relative proportions' (Burke, 2013, 11) Lambert and Playfair themselves followed in the footsteps of John Amos Comenius's revolutionary children's textbook *Orbis Pictus* (1658), one of the earliest printed approaches to 'the problem of how to spread enlightenment with the help of methods of visualization' (Neurath, 1931).

In the 1820s, Baron Charles Dupin (1784–1873) is credited with creating 'perhaps the first modern-style thematic statistical map' and 'the first application of graphics in the social realm' with the 1826 'Carte figurativ de l'instruction populaire de la France' (Dupin, 1826), representing the rate of enrolment of male students for each 'department' in France (Friendly, 2007). Some thirty years later, in 1855, Dr John Snow (1813–1858) produced his famous 'dot map' showing deaths caused by London's third cholera outbreak (1853–54) close to the Broad Street water pump in London's Soho district. The map was an early demonstration of the power of epidemiological data to explain disease transmission – in this instance,

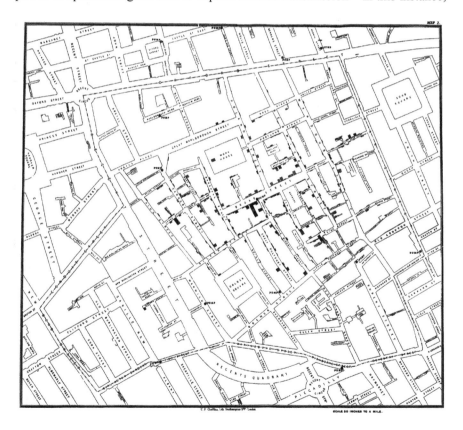

Figure 4.4 Dr John Snow's 1855 map shows the location of deaths from cholera during the Broad Street pump outbreak in London's Soho during 1854, showing London at a scale of 30 inches to 1 mile.

via the water supply rather than as was previously believed, through the 'miasma' of infected air. Snow himself died at 45 of complications resulting from a stroke before his research was accepted.

The rhetorical use of information graphics for health and societal improvement is also apparent in the famous 'rose', 'coxcomb' or 'polar area' diagrams (1858) created by Florence Nightingale (1820–1910) that showed mortality statistics of the British army in the Crimean War. Nightingale used the diagrams – which showed unequivocally that many more soldiers died of disease and the consequences of wounds, than directly as a result of combat – as part of her successful campaign to improve hygiene in the treatment of soldiers during battle.

In mid 19th century France, civil engineer Charles Joseph Minard's (1781–1870) famous chart depicting Napoleon's 1812 Russian campaign (Minard, 1861) incorporated innovative techniques developed for displaying flows of people

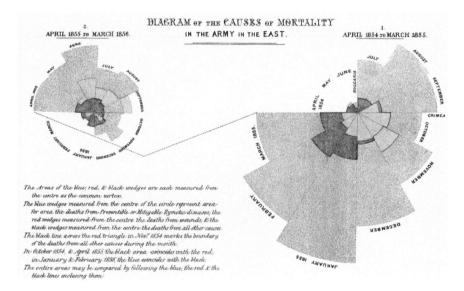

Figure 4.5 'Diagram of the causes of mortality in the army in the East' from Florence Nightingale's 1858 publication, Notes on Matters Affecting the Health, Efficiency, and Hospital Administration of the British Army. This graphic shows the number of deaths due to preventable diseases (dark grey), those caused by wounds (light grey), and those due to other causes (black). The wording reads: The areas of the blue, red, and black wedges are each measured from the centre as the common vertex. The blue wedges measured from the centre of the circle represent area for area the deaths from Preventable or Mitigable Zymotic diseases, the red wedges measured from the centre the deaths from wounds, & the black wedges measured from the centre the deaths from all other causes. The black line across the red triangle in Nov. 1854 marks the boundary of the deaths from all other causes during the month. In October 1854, & April 1855, the black area coincides with the red, in January & February 1856, the blue coincides with the black. The entire areas may be compared by following the blue, the red, & the black lines enclosing them.

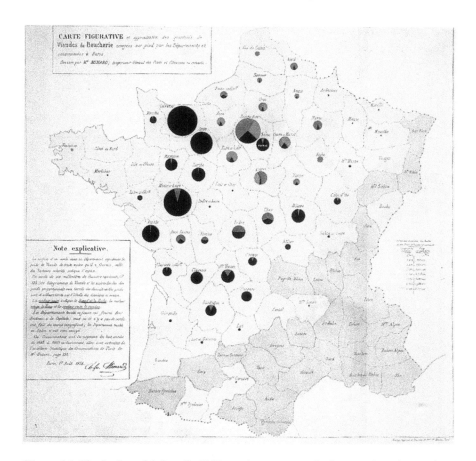

Figure 4.6 Charles Joseph Minard's 1858 map incorporates pie charts to show the numbers of cattle sent from different regions of France for consumption in Paris.

across the dams, canals and bridges that Minard was responsible for constructing. However, an earlier Minard map from 1858 using pie charts to represent the cattle sent from around France for consumption in Paris clearly lends more to contemporary infographic styles.

While Michael Friendly contrasts the mid- to late nineteenth century's 'golden age' of statistical graphics with the early twentieth century's 'modern dark ages' of visualisation (Friendly, 2007), there are several interesting instances of an increasingly sophisticated approach to design and illustration with a health-related, educational purpose emerging at in this period. Fritz Kahn (1888–1968), the German gynaecologist, science writer and 'infographics pioneer' (Von Debschitz & Von Debschitz, 2013), for example, worked with designer/illustrators such as Fritz Schüler to produce visual stories about the human body (Fig. 4.7) in his 1926 publication *Das Leben des Menschen* (Human Life).

Figure 4.7 Fritz Kahn uses infographic style in this 1926 illustration to depict the biology of smelling a roast dinner, showing the sensation of smell and the process of salivation that occurs in response.

Used with permission: Thilo Von Debschitz

However, it is Otto Neurath (1882–1945) in the period directly following the First World War who is widely acknowledged as the instigator of modern infographic styles. Born in Vienna in 1882, where he worked until 1934 as a philosopher, social activist, museum director and visual education pioneer, Neurath was also a skilled promoter of events and ideas. Indeed, although the formalised practice of PR was still in its infancy in the early 20th century, Neurath may have crossed paths with a young Edward Bernays, founder of modern propaganda (or, as he termed it: public relations) who was born in Vienna nine years after Neurath (but emigrated to America in childhood).

Largely responsible for publicizing the activities of the Vienna Circle (the influential group of scientists and philosophers based around the University of Vienna from 1924–1936 of which he was a founder member), Neurath used the language of mass advertising to promote the project of social and political Enlightenment (Vossoughian, 2011). He also vigorously promoted his International Picture Language (later, Isotype), throughout Europe and America, leading to commercial partnerships with publishers and other private, voluntary and statutory sector organisations worldwide.

But although Neurath was not a PR practitioner, his specialist team – comprising 'transformers', working with scientists, medical experts, and graphic artists responsible for translating the data into compelling visual narratives – was a prototype of a contemporary creative agency (Burke, 2016). It was this approach to information

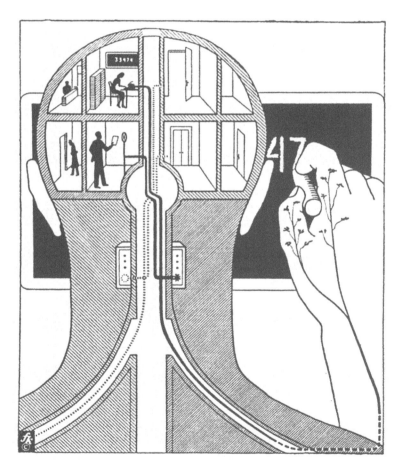

Figure 4.8 In this 1939 illustration, Fritz Kahn attempts to show the 'left-sidedness' of the brain in controlling speech, writing and object handling.
Used with permission: Thilo Von Debschitz

design that Sue Walker believes is particularly relevant to health communication. 'Transformer' was a term devised . . . to mean the person who worked with original and often scientific data and information to produce explanations (usually in the form of charts) that could be understood by ordinary people. This way of working often involved close collaboration between the Neuraths [Otto and Marie] and leading scientists or medical professionals, as was the case with their work for the National Tuberculosis Association (NTA) in the USA in the 1930s.' (Walker, 2017: 102–3)

The work for the NTA involved production of a series of educational public display materials that were reproduced and exhibited over 5,000 times and seemingly met with great success, although the stripped back Isotype aesthetic led to an overly homogenised version of the US population that has come under critical scrutiny in recent years (Mitman, 2011).

Neurath and his NTA collaborator, H.E. Kleinschmidt even published a short booklet in 1939 entitled *Health Education by Isotype*, advocating principles that remain relevant to health communication today. The publication received a positive and pun-heavy review at the time in the *American Journal of Public Health*: 'Every public health worker-administrator, engineer, nurse, as well as educator-will profit by exposing himself to this Isotype infection, for it tends to make one immune to that common ailment, rush of brains to the head.' (Patterson, 1939)

After fleeing the Nazi invasion of mainland Europe in 1940, Otto and Marie Neurath arrived in England just as 'enemy aliens' were being interned. Upon their release in 1941, they settled in Oxford. Together, they founded the Isotype Institute and until the end of WWII, worked on books and films of 'soft propaganda' on behalf of the UK Government Ministry of Information. Several projects involved health, including diagrams for a film about blood transfusion. Following Otto's death in 1945, Marie travelled to West Africa producing, among other materials, pictorial posters for the Nigerian Ministry of Health. (Neurath & Kinross, 2009, 61)

At around this time, the prescription medicines market grew rapidly, with branded drugs becoming increasingly important to pharmaceutical company profits. Naturally, competition intensified, leading to an increasing investment in cutting-edge techniques to promote medicines to health professionals and consumers at the borders of self-regulation and national legislation (Greene & Herzberg, 2010). In addition to rapid developments in the practice of public relations, Roberts & Wright note how the commercial need to differentiate companies 'went hand in hand with the rise of the designer as brand developer' (2017).

In 1953, the American Pharmaceutical Manufacturers Association (APMA) developed an industry PR primer (APMA, 1953) and urged all pharmaceutical firms to develop their own PR offices. Three years later, the US pharmaceutical industry's trade associations created the Health News Institute, a PR organisation ostensibly aiming to educate consumers about medicines using tactics such as symposia for health and medical journalists, fact sheets and 'speaker kits' (precursors to today's PR toolkits) including facts, statistics and 'quotable quotes' for company spokespeople (Phillips-Fein, & Zelizer, 2012).

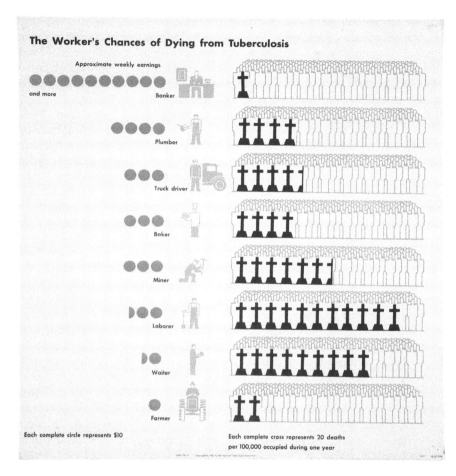

Figure 4.9 'The worker's chance of dying from tuberculosis': illustration from the brochure Tuberculosis: basic facts in picture language, National Tuberculosis Association, New York (Neurath & Kleinschmidt, 1939).

Used with permission: Otto and Marie Neurath Isotype Collection, University of Reading, UK.

By the 1960s in the US, PR (publicity) stunts for prescription medicines were not uncommon. In 1961, Roche launched its tranquilizer, Librium, by inviting journalists to watch the drug used to calm a wild lynx (*Life*, 1960). Early predecessors of today's infographics perhaps first emerged at this time in the form of 'backgrounders'. These 'seemingly legitimate news articles about new pharmaceutical developments' were published in popular magazines, written by journalists who appeared to be neutral, professional freelancers, but had actually been commissioned by pharmaceutical industry trade bodies.

The requirement for more innovative forms of promotion was also apparent in both the US and Europe, where graphic display of information, including advertising, brochure design, packaging, patient information and internal communication materials also underwent radical change, influenced by the stylistic cues of Modernism, Russian Constructivism, and the Bauhaus and Swiss graphic design movements. As an early advocate of these styles for the production of clear, instructive graphic design, Neurath's impact is also significant.

A contemporary of Neurath, the German graphic designer Will Burtin (1908–1972) was among the pioneers of graphic design for the pharmaceutical industry. In 1949, while working as art director for *Fortune* magazine (a role he left in later the same year), Burtin was appointed art director for the Upjohn pharmaceutical company, first redesigning the firm's corporate identity and then moving on to the company journal *Scope*, dedicated to pharmaceutical research.[7] A proponent of simple, minimal sans-serif typography, Burtin's approach to design echoed elements of Isotype as well as the prevailing International Typographic Style, Switzerland's influential post-war graphic design movement. However, nowhere within the pharmaceutical industry was this aesthetic turn better realized than at the Swiss pharmaceutical and chemical company, J.R. Geigy A.G.

Throughout the 1950s and 60s, Geigy broke new ground with its approach to design and public relations. The 'Geigy style' – developed by more than 50 designers working for the company between 1941 and 1970 – emerged from within the company's propaganda department (renamed 'publicity department' in 1966), itself founded in 1941 in response to Geigy's 'dynamic growth', and in preparation for the post-war period (Janser & Junod, 2009, 16). In the 1950s, consistently more than two-thirds of the propaganda department's efforts were devoted to the pharmaceuticals division (*ibid*, 15), evidently perceived to have the greatest marketing potential despite intense competition. The department, led for its 29-year existence by René Rudin, gave visitors 'the impression of a precisely thought-out, modern' operation, responsible for all aspects of advertising, packaging, direct mail, exhibition materials and filmmaking (*ibid*, 15). In 1948, Rudin was joined by art director Max Schmid, who developed the graphic approach that flourished until his departure in 1969 – when Geigy merged with CIBA to form CIBA-Geigy. During this period, infographics were often incorporated into information produced by Geigy (and other pharmaceutical companies) for internal audiences and other stakeholders including shareholders and health professionals. As Roberts & Wright et al note:

> The graphic language developed by Geigy was instrumental in connecting the pharmaceutical company with doctors. They in turn prescribed medication to maintain health, treat illness and relieve chronic pain. The design can be seen as pivotal in both improving patient quality of life, and saving some lives, too.
>
> (2017, 143)

In 1996, CIBA-Geigy merged with Sandoz to form Novartis – which today maintains Geigy's graphic traditions as one of the most prolific producers of infographics for health professionals, patients' associations and consumers.

While Geigy's contribution to pharmaceutical communication was significant, it was not until the 1980s that the practice of pharmaceutical (or 'healthcare') PR started to become recognised, refined and promoted as an agency speciality. It was at this time, that the pharmaceutical industry began to reconsider traditional promotion approaches that relied on communicating solely to health professionals, principally by replacing paid advertising with PR techniques (Pines, 1999). Julie Donohue (2006) described the examples of the analgesic Syntex, which, following its UK launch in 1978 quickly became a topic of discussion on talk shows, leading to rapid acceleration in its use. Such activities prompted pharmaceutical companies to consider direct communication with the public. Burson-Marsteller established its healthcare practice in 1979, claiming to be the first PR agency to do so (Genesis Burson-Marstellar, n.d.). It served mainly pharmaceutical companies, becoming listed as the top ranked US healthcare PR firm by the early 1990s (O'Dwyer, 1991: 32). Burson-Marsteller's first pharmaceutical product launch took place in 1983 when the agency introduced Schering-Plough's antiviral drug, Interferon.

As pharmaceutical PR flourished throughout the 80s, so did the graphical display of information, precipitated in part by the contributions of Edward Tufte to public interest in data visualisation with the publication of *The Visual Display of Quantitative Information* in 1983 (and subsequent publications in 1986, 1990 and 2006). According to Tufte, by 1983, between 900 billion and 2 trillion images of statistical graphics were being printed globally each year (Tufte, 1983). While these were not all infographics as we understand them today (and only a small fraction would be intended for general public consumption) it is clear that by the early 1980s, the turn towards data visualisation was firmly established.

Between the 1980s and the early 2000s, the use of information graphics for public consumption flourished, in particular as critical components of newspaper journalism, with publications such as *USA Today*, *The Washington Post* in the US and *The Sunday Times* and – latterly – *The Guardian* in the UK. Technology enabled printing to become cheaper and of a better quality, full colour imagery could be used more freely and the importance of design and layout increased. These developments allowed designers to create a visually engaging product using a greater range of visual aids, including information graphics. In turn, this drove developments in format. For example, The Guardian was redesigned in 1988 to permit more creative and visual flexibility, with subsequent developments in the early 2000's to utilise the ability to print large images. In 2014, the Guardian sought to enhance its digital output by merging its visual journalism, data journalism and audience development teams and a move to a 'bold, striking and beautiful' tabloid format planned for 2018 as part of a cost-cutting exercise. (Sweeney, 2017)

This revolution in printing technology coincided with easy access to desktop publishing (DTP), providing designers with the ability to control the whole publishing and design process. The resulting proliferation of graphics used to communicate stories to the public did not go unobserved by the PR industry, which adapted the ways in which it presented materials to journalists for publication, gradually prioritizing the graphical display of information. In recent years, scholars have suggested that infographics can multiply the number of page views for news stories by up to 30 times (Dick, 2017, 498).

However, it was not until the emergence of online social networks, designed to host user generated content, that infographics burst into public consciousness. Launched in 1997, SixDegrees is widely considered to be, what we now recognise as the first social networking site, offering features (user profiles, friend lists and educational affiliations) that are now commonplace among the key social media platforms. Whilst SixDegrees was a popular platform, user demands were too advanced for the technology of the time. Other sites such as Friendster (2002), MySpace (2003) followed, but all paled into obscurity following the launch to students in 2004 of Facebook. It was at this point that the development of technology, such as digital cameras and faster internet speeds, could match the demands of the user. This created a multimedia user generated platform for the masses that created an increased demand for the visualisation of complex datasets whilst simultaneously creating large amounts of data itself.

Launching in 2006, Twitter failed to allow users to upload images until August 2011, before launching Twitter Images in September 2012. The following year, Twitter adapted its timeline functionality to provide previews of Twitter photos (and videos from the short form video service, Vine), instead of forcing users to click on a link to view visual content hosted by an external service. At this stage, uploading a photo counted for 24 of the 140 characters permitted per post. So, while images (particularly those using graphics to depict complex data, or embedded text) permitted users to drastically increase the amount of information communicated with each Tweet, it was not until May 2016 (the same year it launched mobile photo uploading functionality) that Twitter announced that media such as photos and videos (and the person's Twitter handle), would not count against the 140 character limit.

These seismic developments in social media technology occurred alongside, and also facilitated the collection of vast amounts of user data – effectively the cost to social media users of using these services. Simultaneously supplied with ever more sophisticated graphic presentation tools, media outlets gleefully leapt on the opportunities provided by 'big data' to play this information back to the public in the form of infographics and other types of data visualisation. News organisations offered some of the most elegant examples.

In 2008, the US pollster Nate Silver launched FiveThirtyEight, as a polling aggregation website. From 2010 to 2013, it became a licensed feature of the New York Times online, after which it was taken over by the US sports broadcaster, ESPN. At its peak during the 2012 US presidential election campaign, as many as 20 per cent of visits to nytimes.com came through FiveThirtyEight (Tracey, 2012).

Following Nate Silver's departure, the New York Times launched its own 'data driven venture', The Upshot, in 2014. At its launch, David Leonhardt, the New York Times editor responsible, said 'We are trying to help readers get to the essence of issues and understand them in a contextual and conversational way . . . we will be using data a lot to do that . . . because it's a particularly effective way, when used in moderate doses, of explaining reality to people' (McDuling, 2014).

Such 'data driven journalism' is today commonplace in news reports to world over. As a natural consequence, PR practitioners' desire to provide news outlets with data driven content has driven the proliferation of infographics produced by PR agencies and departments, particularly within an industry as data-dependant as the pharmaceuticals. But how effective are these artefacts?

The effectiveness of pharmaceutical industry infographics

A number of frameworks have been created to analyse the potential or actual effectiveness of infographics, or as guides to their creation (e.g. Tufte, 1983; Mollerup, 2013; Kosslyn, 2006; Barnard, 2005; Stones & Gent, 2015b; Lima, 2017). Each of these frameworks has a different emphasis based on its purpose, ranging from Barnard, who defines the subject from the point of view of graphic design, to Stones & Gent who look at the effectiveness of information design as a tool for public health. However, the frameworks share some similarities in how they

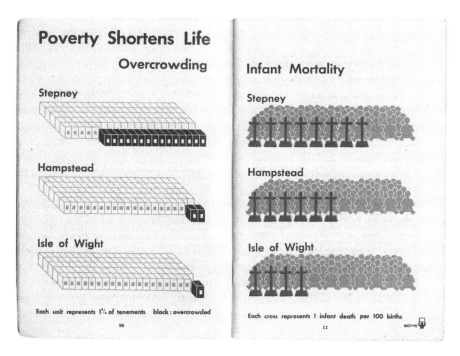

Figure 4.10 'Poverty shortens life': pages from Ronald Davison, Social security: the story of British social progress and the Beveridge plan. London: Harrap, 1943. Produced with the support of the Ministry of Information.

Used with permission: Otto and Marie Neurath Isotype Collection, University of Reading, UK.

choose to deconstruct and explore the subject matter – even if they employ different terminology. Common themes used in this brief analysis of two infographics by the British pharmaceutical company, GlaxoSmithKline (GSK) which are of relevance to healthcare PR campaigns include: persuasion, symbols and icons, communication goals and target audience.

In terms of assessing the potential effectiveness of these materials, our analysis is underpinned by the key stricture Isotype, where a unit value is assigned to a representative symbol and repeated as required.

In terms of persuasion, the adult asthma infographic incorporates a clear narrative, through which the viewer is 'led' by a brightly coloured line – almost literally the 'red thread' of fate found in East Asian legend. GSK's 'primary' orange colour is prominent throughout this and the Salford Lung Study infographics, perhaps used to draw the eye to statements or data believed to be the most persuasive. As with many infographics produced by the pharmaceutical industry in support of medicinal products, the aim in of the adult asthma infographic aims to draw attention to an 'unmet need' experienced by adults asthma sufferers. The aim of the Salford Lung Study infographic highlights the scale and collaborative nature of a major GSK-sponsored study into the effectiveness of a GSK-produced treatment for asthma and chronic obstructive pulmonary disease (COPD).

In terms of unmet need, the adult asthma infographic highlights the relative paucity of asthma education telling us that 'only one in three adults have an asthma action plan', and that 'more than 3 in ten adults are not taught how to recognize asthma symptoms'. While there is no further information about what an asthma action plan is or why it might be necessary or desirable, the wording and icons lead us to believe that such an action plan is important for asthma sufferers. Similarly, readers are likely to assume that a high proportion of adults unable to recognise asthma symptoms could lead to asthma attacks being missed. The asthma infographic also informs us that 'asthma levels are higher than ever', although the scale of the graph used to depict the 1.1% increase over nine years seems to exaggerate extent of this rise.

The Salford Lung Study attempts to convince the viewer of the large scale (and presumably therefore robustness) of a clinical trial, illustrating also how large numbers of health professionals and patients were involved. The likely outtake is that this is a high quality, well organised and meaningful trial which will yield correspondingly high quality and meaningful data.

Symbols and icons that are used within infographics range greatly but can be distinguished in the following ways; colour, contrast, repetition, graphic type, image, photography, language, typography, layout and compatibility. How each of these elements is used impacts greatly on how the infographic communicates its message. Isotype used signs and symbols as a pictorial representation for the infographic and while graphically successful, this oversimplification can sometimes lead to a loss of detail. Therefore striking the right balance between aesthetically pleasing (and possibly attention grabbing) embellishment, and hard data is important both to engage and persuade intended audiences. The GSK materials

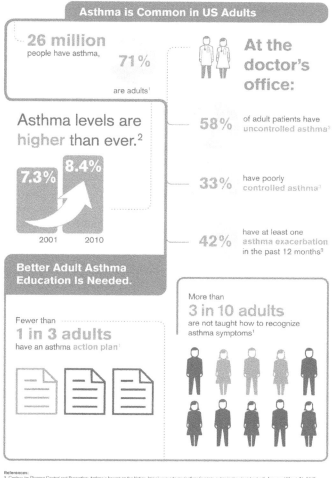

Figure 4.11 An infographic produced as part of a disease awareness campaign about adult asthma by GlaxoSmithKline. The company manufactures a range of asthma products including Nucala (mepolizumab), a targeted therapy for adults with severe refractory eosinophilic asthma. The infographic mimics Isotype's use of one figure to depict one unit of measurement, combining simple, corporately acceptable colours and clear, sans serif fonts for legibility across a range of digital platforms. The headline, logo and 'line' leading the viewer through the infographic are all coloured in orange, as part of GSK's intention – stated clearly within the company's corporate identity guidelines – to 'own' the colour orange: "We want to truly take ownership of the colour orange within our look and feel and we'll do this through the use of a vibrant and engaging orange in our communications. Orange is a dynamic colour with a real feel-good factor and a positive outlook. Amongst our competitors orange is different and disruptive, making it a strong identifier for GSK." (GSK, 2013).

clearly follow some of the recommended practices. Simply by following the strict GSK 'look and feel visual guidelines' (GSK, 2013), the adult asthma and Salford Lung Study Tweet incorporate 'harmony and simplicity' in colour usage (Shin, 2016, 18), while restricting use of colour, paying attention to careful 'alignment' of information and having a clear heading (Stones & Gent, 2015b, 18).

The *communication goals* of an infographic should closely affect decisions on the presentation of information using an infographic. The message must be made relevant and therefore presenting the right amount of information in an appropriate manner is paramount (Kosslyn, 2006, 6). For example, it seems likely that messages aimed at a health professional audience would prioritise data over 'attention-grabbing', but otherwise superfluous embellishment which would be more suitable for a general public audience with less inherent interest in the data and a greater requirement for arresting visual design. This entails careful consideration of the use of different graphic types (such as colour, contrast, repetition, graphic type, image, photography, language, typography) (Shin, 2016; Stones & Gent, 2015b) and the extent of embellishment (Barnard, 2005, 15) in order for the message to be accepted.

In addition, the GSK examples are designed to appear in different spaces and this impacts on the way that the data and graphic elements within each example has been applied – where elements have been applied at all. This in turn impacts on the communicative success of each piece. For example, the use of typography in the 'Salford Lung Study' Tweet has a clear hierarchy with minimal text and – through the use of colour and typography – priority given to numerical figures and icons. This piece only contains charts used purely as decorative icons, whereas the adult asthma infographic makes extensive use of charts mixed with decorative icons. According to most models of infographic production, further restricting colour (Stones & Gent, 2015a, 14) and reducing unnecessary elements that add little to the infographic's message are likely help the infographic achieve its communication goals by giving the symbols and icons used greater impact.

In terms of appreciating target audiences for these materials, Kosslyn (2006, 11) also highlights being mindful of 'capacity limitations' because 'people have a limited capacity to retain and to process information, and so will not understand a message if too much information [needs to] be retained or processed'. This needs to be achieved through understanding how to connect with a particular audience (Stones & Gent, 2015a, 5), the target audience's 'goals and interests' (Kosslyn, 2006, 3) and the 'understandability' of the infographic (Mollerup, 2013, 10). Therefore, making sure that the audience is going to have the appropriate knowledge and right capacity to be able to comprehend what is being presented is imperative to the success of an infographic.

Isotype has clearly had a large impact on all of the examples from GSK and broadly, many other pharmaceutical companies' infographics. However, there are some striking deviations from Isotype's strictures in the GSK examples. This is particularly true when looking at the use of decorative icons to represent an object *alongside* icons that are being used to represent a numerical value. The mixed use of 'decorative' and numerically representative iconography is a clear deviation from Isotype and only where there is a clear separation between the two elements can they both work on a single infographic to communicate a message quickly and succinctly.

Even this brief analysis indicates the importance of persuasion, symbols and icons, communication goals and knowledge of target audience to infographics produced by or for pharmaceutical PR campaigns. To produce an infographic requires a careful, considered, collaborative and knowledgeable approach that appreciates the history of the infographic and the context in which the infographic is to be viewed. It is important the infographic is given the attention and appreciation that it deserves in order to make sure that the message has the best chance of success.

Conclusions

In conclusion, far from being a purely contemporary phenomenon, data visualisation in support of pharmaceutical PR activity has a rich history linked to seminal developments in graphic communication practice. In addition, while the use of data visualisation in PR is often effective and ethically sound, materials that lack integrity or are produced without consideration for well-established, evidence-based principles may be uninteresting, misleading, inaccurate or unfit for purpose and therefore counterproductive to campaign objectives.

While there seems little evidence that the popularity of infographics and other forms of data visualisation is likely to wane in the near future, it seems likely that developments in the practice will continue to yield materials that vary in quality and effectiveness and that practitioners would be well advised to refer to thoroughly developed 'systems' such as Isotype in order to observe, appreciate and preserve the integrity of data visualisation in such a significant and important area.

Notes

1 For example: *Visual.ly*, Visualisingdata.com, Informationisbeautiful.net and Visualcom plexity.com
2 For example: *Piktochart* and *Easel.ly*
3 In 2012, a survey from the UK Department of Business, Innovation & Skills found that In some areas of England, around a quarter of adults have the numeracy skills of a 7 to 9 year old, or below (BIS, 2012)
4 Health literacy can be defined as 'the personal characteristics and social resources needed for individuals and communities to access, understand, appraise and use information and services to make decisions about health.' (WHO, 2015)
5 Although in recently years, Google has expressed some reservations about the quality and usefulness of many infographics.
6 Sponsorship of non-promotional education programmes which aim to affect healthcare professionals knowledge, understanding and attitudes towards disease states or influence prescribing habits (Moynihan et al., 2002)
7 Magazines and journals produced by pharmaceutical companies and incorporating cutting edge graphic design were popular communication tools between the 1950s and 1970s. In addition to Upjohn's *Scope*, titles including *Naturwissenschaft und Medizin* (*n+m*) published by Boehringer Mannheim (now integrated into the Roche Group following its sale to Hoffman La-Roche in 1997) with many covers designed by the influential Erwin Poell (b.1930) who later went on to design many stamps for the Deutsche Bundespost.

References

American Pharmaceutical Manufacturers Association. (1953). *Public Relations Primer for the Drug Industry*. Washington, DC.: American Pharmaceutical Manufacturers Association

Barnard, M. (2005). *Graphic Design as Communication*. Abingdon, UK: Routledge.

Bateman, S. *et al.* (2010). 'Useful Junk? The Effects of Visual Embellishment on Comprehension and Memorability of Charts.' *ACM Conference on Human Factors in Computing Systems (CHI 2010)*, Atlanta, GA, USA. 2573–2582.

Baur, D (2017) The Death of Interactive Infographics. Medium.com. Available at: https://medium.com/@dominikus/the-end-of-interactive-visualizations-52c585dcafcb [accessed 2 Oct 2017].

Benady, A. (2017). *A Brief History of Scheduling: Lessons in Scheduling from Aerospace, Pharma, Publishing and Politics: Chartered Institute of Public Relations Influence Magazine, Q2 2017*. London: Chartered Institute of Public Relations, 20–23.

BIS. (2012). 'Skills for Life Survey Reveals English and Maths Levels of Adults.' *BIS Press Release*. Available at: www.gov.uk/government/news/skills-for-life-survey-reveals-english-and-maths-levels-of-adults [accessed 14th June 2017].

Bucchi, M. & Saracino, B. (2016). '"Visual Science Literacy": Images and Public Understanding of Science in the Digital Age.' *Science Communication*, 38(6): 812–819.

Burke, C. (2009). 'Isotype: Representing Social Facts Pictorially.' *Information Design Journal*, 17(3): 211–223.

Burke, C. (2013). *Isotype: Design & Contexts 1925–1971*. London: Hyphen Press.

Burke, C. (2016) *Otto Neurath und die Wiener Methode der Bildstatistik*. In: Eisele, P., Ludwig, A. and Naegele, I. (eds.) Futura. Die Schrift. Verlag Hermann Schmidt, Mainz.

Bylykbashi, K. (2016). 'Why Healthcare PR Is More Important Than Ever.' *Gorkana Website*. Available at: www.gorkana.com/2016/05/opinion-why-healthcare-pr-is-more-important-than-ever/ [accessed 2nd April 2017].

Cairo, A. (2013). *The Functional Art: An Introduction to Information Graphics and Visualization*. Berkeley, CA: New Riders.

Cairo, A. (2016). *The Truthful Art: Data, Charts, and Maps for Communication*. Berkeley, CA: New Riders.

Consumers International. (2006). *Branding the Cure: A Consumer Perspective on Corporate Social Responsibility, Drug Promotion and the Pharmaceutical Industry in Europe*. London: Consumers International.

Dick, M. (2017). 'Developments in Infographics.' In Franklin, B. & Eldridge, S. (eds.), *The Routledge Companion to Digital Journalism Studies*, Abingdon, Oxon: Routledge, 498–508.

Donohue, J. (2006). 'A History of Drug Advertising: The Evolving Roles of Consumers and Consumer Protection.' *Milbank Quarterly*, De, 84(4): 659–699.

Dupin, C. (1826). *Carte figurativ de l'instruction populaire de la France*. Available at: https://fr.wikipedia.org/wiki/Carte_figurative_de_l%27instruction_populaire_de_la_France#/media/File:Carte_figurative_de_l%27instruction_populaire_de_la_France.jpg [accessed 2nd February 2018]

Dur, B. (2014). 'Data Visualization and Infographics in Visual Communication Design Education at the Age of Information.' *Journal of Arts and Humanities*, 3(5): 39–50.

Few, S. (2012). *Show Me the Numbers: Designing Tables and Graphs to Enlighten*. Burlingame, CA: Analytics Press.

Friendly, M. (2007). 'A Brief History of Data Visualization.' In Chen, C., Härdle, W. & Unwin, A. (eds.), *Handbook of Computational Statistics: Data Visualization, Vol. III: Ch. 1*. Heidelberg: Springer-Verlag.

Genesis Burson-Marstellar. (n.d.). 'Our History.' *Genesis Burson-Marstellar Website*. Available at: www.genesisbm.in/who-we-are/our-history/ [accessed 7th August 2017].

Greene, J.A. & Herzberg, D. (2010). 'Hidden in Plain Sight: Marketing Prescription Drugs to Consumers in the Twentieth Century.' American Journal of Public Health, May, 100(5): 793–803.

GSK. (2013). 'Our Look and Feel Visual Guidelines, v.1, October 2013.' *GSK Website*. Available at: https://cz.gsk.com/media/510676/gsk-new-brand-rules2013.pdf [accessed 23rd July 2017].

Guidry, J. *et al.* (2016). 'How Health Risks Are Pinpointed (or Not) on Social Media: The Portrayal of Waterpipe Smoking on Pinterest.' *Health Communication*, 3(6): 659–667.

Guidry, J. *et al.* (2017). 'Ebola on Instagram and Twitter: How Health Organizations Address the Health Crisis in Their Social Media Engagement.' *Public Relations Review*, in press. Available at: https://doi.org/10.1016/j.pubrev.2017.04.009 [Accessed 12th May 2017].

Hartle, J. (2017). 'Otto Neurath's Visual Politics: An Introduction to "Pictorial Statistics Following the Vienna Method.' *ARTMargins*, February 2017, 6 (1): 98–107.

Iliinsky, N. & Steele, J. (2011). *Designing Data Visualizations*. Sebastopol, CA: O'Reilly.

Janser, A. & Junod, B. (eds.). (2009). *Corporate Diversity: Swiss Graphic Design and Advertising by Geigy, 1940–1970*. Zurich: Lars Müller Publishers.

Johnson & Johnson. (1888). *Modern Methods of Antiseptic Wound Treatment*. New York: Johnson & Johnson. Available at: https://wellcomelibrary.org/item/b21212740#?c=0&m=0&s=0&cv=12&z=-1.0668%2C0%2C3.1336%2C1.6628 [Accessed 1st August 2017].

Kent, M. (2013). 'Using Social Mdialogically: Public Relations Role in Reviving Democracy.' *Public Relations Review*, 39: 337–345.

Kirk, A. (2012). *Data Visualization: A Successful Design Process*. Birmingham: Packt Publishing.

Klanten, R. (2008). *Data Flow: Visualizing Information in Graphic Design*. Berlin: Die Gestalten Verlag.

Klanten, R. (2010). *Data Flow 2: Visualizing Information in Graphic Design*. Berlin: Die Gestalten Verlag.

Kosslyn, S. (2006). *Graph design for the Eye and Mind*. New York, NY: Oxford University Press.

Krum, R. (2014). *Cool Infographics: Effective Communication with Data Visualization and Design*. Indianapolis, IN: John Wiley & Sons.

Lane, G. (2017). *Botox: Reading between the Lines: Chartered Institute of Public Relations Influence Magazine, Q2 2017*. London: Chartered Institute of Public Relations, 28–33.

Lankow, J., Ritchie, J. & Crooks, R. (2012). *Infographics: The Power of Visual Storytelling*. Hoboken, NJ: Wiley.

Lewine, A. (2014). 'Outside Voices: The Visual Web Is Changing Everything in Media and Advertising.' *Wall Street Journal*, 24th June.

Li, H. & Moacdieh, N. (2014). 'Is "Chart Junk" Useful? An Extended Examination of Visual Embellishment.' *Proceedings of the Human Factors and Ergonomics Society 58th Annual Meeting*. Los Angeles: Sage Publications.

Life Magazine (1960). 'New Way to Calm a Cat.' 18th April: 93–95.

Lima, M. (2017). *The Book of Circles: Visualizing Spheres of Knowledge*. New York: Princeton Architectural Press.

McCandless, D. (2010). *Information Is Beautiful*. London: Collins.

McCandless, D. (2014). *Knowledge Is Beautiful*. London: Collins.

McDuling, J. (2014). '"The Upshot" Is the New York Times' Replacement for Nate Silver's FiveThirtyEight.' *Quartz*, 10th March. Available at: https://qz.com/185922/the-upshot-is-the-new-york-times-replacement-for-nate-silvers-fivethirtyeight/ [accessed 3rd December 2016].

Mitman, G. (2011). 'The Color of Money: Campaigning for Health in Black and White America.' In Serlin, D. (ed.), *Imagining Illness: Public Health and Visual Culture*. Minneapolis: University of Minnesota Press.

Mollerup, P. (2013). *Data Design: Visualising Quantities, Locations, Connections*. London and New York: A&C Black Visual Arts.

Moynihan, R., Heath, I. & Henry, D. (2002). 'Selling Sickness: The Pharmaceutical Industry and Disease-Mongering.' *BMJ*, 324: 886–891.

Neurath, O. (1927). Statistik & Proletariat. In Neurath (1991) Gesammelte Bildpädagogische Schriften. Edited by Rudolf Haller & Robin Kinross. Vienna. Hölder-Pichler-Tempsky. pp 77 – 84. Cited in Burke (2009) 'Isotype: Representing Social Facts Pictorially.' *Information Design Journal*, 17(3).

Neurath, O. (1931). 'Pictorial Statistics Following the Vienna Method.' reproduced in *ART-Margins*, February 2017, 6u(1): 108–118.

Neurath, O. (1936). *International Picture Language (from Facsimile Reprint of the [1936] English Edition*. Department of Typography & Graphic Communication, University of Reading, 1980.

Neurath, M. & Kinross, R. (2009). *The Transformer: Principles of Making Isotype Charts*. London: Hyphen Press.

Nightingale, F (1858) Diagram of the causes of mortality in the army in the East in *Notes on Matters Affecting the Health, Efficiency, and Hospital Administration of the British Army*. Available at: https://commons.wikimedia.org/wiki/File:Nightingale-mortality.jpg [accessed 3rd December 2016]

O'Dwyer's PR Services Report. (1991). Profiles of Top Healthcare PR Firms, October 1991.

Patterson, R. (1939). 'Review of Health Education by Isotype by Otto Neurath, Ph.D., and H.E. Kleinschmidt, M.D. New York: Academic Public Health Association, 1939.' *American Journal of Public Health*, May.

Peraza, D. (2017). Interview with Deroy Peraza, Creative Director, Hyperakt Agency. Personal communication, 16 September 2017.

Phillips-Fein, K. & Zelizer, J. (2012). *What's Good for Business: Business and American Politics Since World War II*. Oxford: Oxford University Press.

Pines, W.L. (1999). 'A History and Perspective on Direct-to-Consumer Promotion.' *Food and Drug Law Journal*, 54: 489.

Playfair, W. (1786). *Commercial and Political Atlas: Representing, by Copper-Plate Charts, the Progress of the Commerce, Revenues, Expenditure, and Debts of England, during the Whole of the Eighteenth Century*. London: Corry. Re-published in Wainer, H. and Spence, I. (eds.) (2005). *The Commercial and Political Atlas and Statistical Breviary*. Cambridge: Cambridge University Press.

Playfair, W. (1801). *Statistical Breviary: Shewing, on a Principle Entirely New, the Resources of Every State and Kingdom in Europe*. London: Wallis. Re-published in Wainer, H. and Spence, I. (eds.) (2005). *The Commercial and Political Atlas and Statistical Breviary*. Cambridge: Cambridge University Press.

PRCA Census. (2016). Available at: http://prmeasured.com/wp-content/uploads/2016/06/PRCA-PR-Census-2016.pdf [accessed 1st September 2017].

PR Council. (2016). 'Healthcare.' Web Page. Available at: http://prcouncil.net/inside-pr/healthcare/ [accessed 1st September 2017].

Rendgen, S. (2012). *Information Graphics*. Cologne: Taschen.

Roberts, L. & Wright, R. (2017). *Can Graphic Design Save Your Life?* London: Graphic Design & Publishing.

Seale, C. (2003). *Media and Health*. Thousand Oaks, CA: Sage Publishing.

Shaoqiang, W. (2018). *Playful Data: Graphic Design and Illustration for Infographics*. Promopress. [Forthcoming].

Shin, H. (2016). *Epidemic and Risk Communication: An Analysis of Strategic and Graphic Characteristics of Infographics*. Electronic Thesis, Iowa State University, Ames, IA.

Smart, A. (2017). Interview with Andrea Smart, Marketing Director, Parker Design. Personal communication, 20 September 2017.

Stiff, P., Esbester, M. & Dobraszczyk, P. (2010). 'Designing and Gathering Information: Perspectives on Nineteenth-Century Forms.' In Weller, T. (ed.), *Information History in the Modern World: Histories of the Information Age*. Basingstoke: Palgrave MacMillan, 57–88.

Stones, C. (2014). 'Infographics Research: A Literature Review of Empirical Studies on Attention, Comprehension, Recall, Adherance and Appeal.' *Visualisinghealth.com*. Available at: https://visualisinghealth.files.wordpress.com/2014/12/lit-rev1.docx [Accessed 1st February 2017].

Stones, C. & Gent, M. (2015a). 'If the Guardian Can Do It, We Should Be Able to Do It!' *Examining Public Health Infographic Strategies Used by Public Health Professionals: Design 4 Health 2015 Proceedings*. University of Sheffield.

Stones, C. & Gent, M. (2015b). 'The 7 Graphic Principals of Public Health Infographic Design.' *Visualisinghealth.com*. Available at: https://visualisinghealth.com/design-guidelines/ [Accessed 15th May 2017].

Sweeney, M. (2017). 'Guardian and Observer to Relaunch in Tabloid Format.' *The Guardian* newspaper, 13th June. Available at: www.theguardian.com/media/2017/jun/13/guardian-and-observer-to-relaunch-in-tabloid-format [accessed 19th July 2017].

Tracey, M. (2012). 'Nate Silver Is a One-Man Traffic Machine for the Times.' *New Republic*, 6th November. Available at: https://newrepublic.com/article/109714/nate-silvers-fivethirtyeight-blog-drawing-massive-traffic-new-york-times. [accessed 20th June 2017].

Tufte, E.R. (1983). *The Visual Display of Quantitative Information*. Cheshire, CT: Graphics Press.

Twyman, M. (1975). 'The Significance of Isotype.' *Isotype Revisited Website*. Available at: http://isotyperevisited.org/1975/01/the-significance-of-isotype.html [accessed 2nd August 2017].

Von Debschitz, U. & Von Debschitz, T. (2013). *Fritz Kahn: Infographics Pioneer*. Cologne: Taschen.

Vossoughian, N. (2011). *Otto Neurath: The Language of the Global Polis*. Rotterdam: Nai Publishers.

Walker, S. (2017). 'The Contribution of Typography and Information Design to Health Communication.' In Tsekleves, E. & Cooper, R. (eds.), *Design for Health*. Abingdon, UK: Routledge.

World Health Organisation. (2013). *Effective Medicines Regulation: Ensuring Safety, Efficacy & Quality: World Health Organisation Policy Perspectives on Medicines*. Geneva:

World Health Organisation. Available at: http://apps.who.int/medicinedocs/pdf/s4921e/
s4921e.pdf [accessed 1st September 2017].
World Health Organisation. (2015). *7th Global Conference on Health Promotion: Track
Themes, Track 2: Health Literacy and Health Behaviour*. Available at: www.who.int/
healthpromotion/conferences/7gchp/track2/en/ [accessed 2nd December 2016].
Yau, N. (2011). *Visualize This: The Flowing Data Guide to Design, Visualisation, and
Statistics*. London and New York: Wiley.

Part 2

Spatial dimensions of public relations

5 Limits or opportunities for strategic communication?

The role of space and place in mediating #Demo2012

Simon Collister

In June 2012 the UK's national membership organisation for students in further and higher education, the National Union of Students (NUS), announced it would hold a national demonstration aimed at 'step[ping] up pressure on the coalition government' which had recently passed legislation removing funding for disadvantaged students, increasing university tuition fees, and opened up the higher education market to greater private competition (BBC News, 2010; Mulholland, 2010). The demonstration, held on 21st November 2012, marked an important moment for the NUS, and the UK student movement more generally, for two reasons. Firstly, the demonstration – named #Demo2012 – was the first national mobilization of students organized by the NUS since its initial demonstration in 2010 held to challenge the new government's higher education policy. This event arguably represented a watershed in student politics as, although the NUS organized march in central London went ahead as planned, a significant number of grassroots students deviated from the planned route, broke through police lines and occupied the national offices of the governing Conservative Party – which were subsequently vandalized and the scene of fighting between protestors and police.

This seemingly spontaneous eruption of vandalism and violence at an ideological and geographical landmark appeared to demonstrate a renewed force of feeling and motivation among students to 'fight back' against government policy (Hancox, 2011). Importantly, it represented the biggest show of student force for over a decade and proved to be a catalyst for a rejuvenated student movement which saw a wave of further protests, university occupations, vandalism and violence described by some as 'the Winter of Protest' (*ibid*).

#Demo2012 was additionally significant in that it could be interpreted as a test of the NUS's ability to impact future government higher education policy as well as demonstrate continued relevance to its members. Following on from the 2010 demonstration the NUS faced criticism from students who believed the organisation distanced itself from the unplanned and controversial grassroots student activism which led media and political condemnation but which appeared to galvanize student attitudes and action towards government policy (Landin, 2012).

In response to this, the NUS and its then new president, Liam Burns, saw #Demo2012 a platform with which to reinvigorate support for the NUS among student members and reassert its importance as a relevant political organisation aiming to 'promote, defend and extend the rights of students' in the UK (NUS, n.d.b). Indeed, the purpose of #Demo2012 is stated clearly by Burns in a speech uploaded to the film-sharing website, YouTube: 'In a year in which there are no votes in parliament and no legislation coming before politicians, it's about time we started setting the agenda' (NUS, 2012a).

This chapter will provide an analysis of the factors and forces mediating the narrative arising from the demonstration. It will argue that while strategic media management – both traditional mass media and online, grassroots social media – was deployed successfully in the build-up to the event, the physical spaces and places on the route of the demonstration become enrolled as active dimensions of the communication process and subsequently played a crucial role in shaping the way in which the event's narrative become mediated.

Analysis of these processes will focus, in particular, on the inter-relation between the different material and expressive components arising before, during and immediately after the event. The methodologies adopted in order to do this include content analysis of media produced around the demonstration;[1] follow-up interviews with key actors from the NUS involved in the strategic media management of the event as well as observational ethnography by the author during #Demo2012.

Drawing together this data it is possible to understand how the planned strategic communication techniques of the NUS shape the media narrative around the demonstration but how this narrative becomes influenced – and arguably re-shaped – by the behaviour and actions of participants interacting with the symbolic and material dimensions of physical places and spaces on the route of the demonstration.

Strategic media management: building the pre-event narrative

Taking into account the NUS's stated aims of using #Demo2012 to set the agenda on the future of higher education its initial actions suggest an effective start with consistent pre-event coverage of the demonstration featuring in both mainstream and social media. There are, however, a small yet significant series of challenges to the NUS and its agenda occurring predominantly within student media. While this represents a small proportion of pre-event coverage it, nevertheless, helps set the tone for a more widespread critical engagement and undermining of the NUS narrative as #Demo2012 unfolds. This section will identify and analyse a number of the material and expressive components mediating #Demo2012 in the days preceding – and morning of – the event and analyse their role in shaping mediation of the final event.

From the moment #Demo2012 was formally announced in April 2012, the NUS' communications team began developing a public relations strategy with a 'clear calendar of [media] actions' designed to raise awareness of the NUS' three key policy areas articulated by the demonstration's slogan, 'Educate, Employ, Empower' (NUS, n.d.a): 1) improve access to education; 2) improve graduate employment prospects and 3) empower students to have a stronger voice on issues that concern them (Hoyles, 2014).

The strategy additionally aimed to mobilise students to take part in the demonstration (Hoyles, 2014; Pool, 2014). Above all, such a strategy was designed and deployed to shape the media narrative around higher education in favour of the NUS' policy position supported by the massed demonstration to highlight the strength of the NUS' mandate and justify its position as a grassroots organisation 'which makes a real difference to the lives of students' (NUS, n.d.b).

Media content analysis and interviews with NUS employees managing the organisation's communication in the build-up to the demonstration strongly suggests media management tactics deployed across both traditional and social media played a significant part in shaping the media narrative around #Demo2012. For example, the focus of media coverage in national UK news outlets and on social media pre-demonstration was designed strategically to convey the NUS' policy position as well as provide practical information about #Demo2012 to mobilize participants. This was the result a range of strategic communications techniques, such as exclusive briefings, timely intervention in the professional news cycle and public opinion surveys to generate news-worthy headlines which ensured consistent and positive content was generated and placed in the period ahead of #Demo2012 (Hoyles, 2014; Pool, 2014).

The first coverage alerting the public and policy-makers to #Demo2012 appeared in the British national newspaper, *The Observer*, on the Sunday before the demonstration. The article provided background to the political context in which the demonstration was taking place and cited an NUS-commissioned survey that indicated pessimism among parents towards future education and economic prospects for their children. While leading with a policy-focused angle, the article also allowed the NUS to link this wider political situation to the forthcoming demonstration targeting current government policy, as NUS president Liam Burns asserted in the article:

'Students from across the country will be marching through London on Wednesday to protest against a government which has disempowered a generation by abdicating its responsibility to ensure access to education and employment'

(Boffey, 2012)

The Observer's Sunday coverage was a strategically planned tactic used by the NUS known as a 'Sunday for Monday' (Hoyles, 2014) whereby a story is given as an exclusive to a national Sunday news publication in order to alert other news outlets to the story in advance of their Monday copy deadline, thus increasing the likelihood of vital Monday coverage (Campbell, 2011; Dean, 2013, 123–124).[2]

As a result, *The Observer's* Sunday 'trailer' article is followed on Monday 19th November by a more substantial announcement and analysis of #Demo2012 in *The Observer's* sister-title, *The Guardian* (Walker & Clarke, 2012) as well as a shorter article revealing the event in *The Independent* newspaper (The Independent, 2012).

Coverage supporting the NUS continued to appear in *The Guardian* on Tuesday 20th November in the form of another PR-led, survey-based news story based on research findings from an NUS commissioned survey. Here public opinion research identified that nearly half of all UK students have considered dropping out of their course due to concerns about money. As with *The Observer*'s previous survey-led story, findings were strategically aligned with the NUS' policy agenda and again acted as a bridge to trail the demonstration as 'a chance for students to convey their feelings to the government and call on politicians to offer a better deal' (The Guardian, 2012a).

This was a further example of the deployment of NUS commissioned surveys as a tactic to strategically manage the news agenda by ensuring a variety of stories receive coverage in the run up to the event. The use of such a tactic was confirmed by Hoyles who revealed that the approach was necessary as, unlike the previous 2010 demonstration ahead of a major political vote, this time the NUS lacked a big story around which to hang the #Demo2012 coverage and so used surveys to create lots of smaller ones (Hoyles, 2014).

Given the lack of a substantial news story to underpin #Demo2012 the NUS adopted further news management techniques, such as offering exclusive briefings on forthcoming stories to selected journalists on outlets likely to be sympathetic to the NUS' position (*ibid*). Such a strategy of 'information subsidy' (Gandy, 1982) is adopted, ostensibly, to maximise the likelihood of media coverage by alleviating the problems of resource scarcity and time-sensitivity of the new-gathering process.

On the day of the demonstration the NUS' strategic management of the mainstream media narrative continued with the national news broadcast network, *ITV News*, publishing a series of preview articles online likely managed through media embargoes – a formal news management technique used to control the distribution or reporting of a story until a specific time (*ibid*).

Consistent with the use of an embargoed press release the ITV News content included substantial references to NUS key messages found consistently in pre-demonstration coverage. For example, the initial *ITV News* coverage featured an NUS prediction of 10,000 participants on the demonstration – a figure acknowledged by Hoyles (2014) as being officially confirmed to the media by the NUS to make the event more news-worthy – and sets out the NUS' formal policy position on higher education funding (ITV News, 2012b).

Subsequent *ITV News* coverage focused on NUS President, Liam Burns', comments that students feel 'a sense of desperation for their future' (ITV News, 2012a) and predictions of an "epidemic of dropouts" (ITV News, 2012) – all messages drawn from NUS funded surveys and identical to those expressed in coverage earlier in the week.

At 08:21am on the day of the demonstration *The Guardian* published its lead piece on the demonstration which included content strategically aligned with, and reinforcing, earlier coverage, including NUS predictions of 10,000 participants and students' desperation for their future and further exclusive findings from a new NUS-commissioned survey.

At 09:29am *The Guardian* also published an official route map of the demonstration and launched its 'live-blog' – a novel and hybrid approach to news-reporting that blends 'conventional reporting with curation, where journalists sift and prioritise information from secondary sources and present it to the audience in close to real time, often incorporating their feedback"'(Thurman & Walters, 2013, 83)

Although more autonomous that conventional news stories as a result of its curatorial function and reliance on user-generated content drawn from social media, *The Guardian*'s live-blog arguably still operated within the NUS media management strategy given that the NUS had agreed to help promote and share its content via its social media channels (Pool, 2014). The live-blog also arguably plays a more significant role in mediating the demonstration through its ability to report live and direct from specific places on the route. This – significant – attribute will be examined in further detail later in the chapter.

The strategic management of the media narrative ahead of #Demo2012 by the NUS was not only restricted to mass media. The NUS' communications team was also active in attempting to shape the online conversations emerging from networks of formal and informal media actors in social media.

Specifically, the NUS' social media strategy saw their communications team develop a range of 'on message' content tailored for targeted third-party support-ers. Pool (2014) asserts that the NUS spent time 'looking at different audiences and putting out different articles based on different policy areas and how they would affect different people'. Based on this strategic planning 'different strands of content' were created, for example, 'membership facing content [. . .] was about fighting the argument – what was happening in terms of government and policy, updates with what was happening with the demo and ideas and tips on how to mobilise and support volunteers' (*ibid.*).

This carefully targeted content was then distributed to a range of third-party groups and online networks – both affiliated or ideologically aligned with the NUS and more general, lifestyle groups. For example, Pool acknowledges that ahead of the demonstration the NUS' 650 member unions were provided with training to help mobilise individual students to promote the event through social media and charities, trade unions and supporters were approached 'to contribute to [the NUS'] social media work as well' (*ibid*). In addition to 'friendly' networks, the NUS also contacted more consumer groups which the NUS 'felt the [#Demo2012] issues would have affected' (Pool, 2014), such as the influential online parenting forum, *Mumsnet*', to help promote #Demo2012, although this had limited impact (*ibid*).

This strategic management of social media by the NUS appears to have been effective in terms of shaping the online narrative around #Demo2012. Content analysis of a sample of Twitter data[3] gathered from 16th November to 11.00am on 21st November (the official start time of #Demo2012) indicates that the overall tone of Twitter conversations is overwhelmingly supportive of the demonstration.

Approximately two-thirds (45 per cent) of tweets published contain personal expressions of support, anticipation and excitement about Demo2012 (See: Mac-Doo, 2012; NextGenLab, 2012; Peters-Day, 2012; Woodburn, 2012); share logis-tical information (See: NUS_LGBT, 2012; Sewards, 2012); provide formal legal advice for those on the demonstration (See: Day, 2012; GBCLegal, 2012); quote key NUS policy messages (Peltz, 2012) and share supportive media coverage (Alice, 2012).

Supporting Pool's assertion of a planned NUS social media strategy 'on message' Twitter content is predominantly generated by official NUS representatives – both as individuals and groups. Moreover, these formal NUS actors represent the most active Twitter users ahead of the demonstration responsible for 41 per cent of all tweets published in the pre-event period.

Although tweets supporting the NUS dominate Twitter ahead of the demonstration, criticisms of the NUS, its policies and leadership are also voiced from a range of left and right-wing ideological positions (See Bastani, 2012; Collins, 2012; Grant, 2012; Morgan, 2012; Shorthouse, 2012). While representing a minority (34 per cent) of total pre-demo Twitter content, these critical tweets are significant in that the theme and source of the tweets further reinforce the apparent disconnect between the NUS as an institution and its grassroots members – a trait also identified in pre-demonstration coverage in student media. The largest single theme of Twitter criticism (35 per cent of all negative tweets) discusses and links to an image of a contentious chant sheet containing potentially offensive lyrics promoted by the NUS Vice President (Stace, 2012).

Evidence of the NUS' strategic management of the social media narrative continues to be found in an analysis of blogs. Of the 25 blog posts published between 16th November and 11.00am on 21st November 52 per cent express support for the NUS. Many blogs reference or directly re-produce NUS material, such as mainstream media coverage (Anticuts, 2012e, Defend The Right To Protest 2012); publish expressions supportive policy analysis (Wright, 2012); sharing practical and logistical information, such as the route map and rendezvous points (Central Students Union, 2012a); and issuing 'call outs' to mobilise readers to attend the demonstration (Angela, 2012; BellaCiao, 2012f). As with Twitter content, pro-NUS content is published on blogs managed by student unions, trade unions and anti-cuts campaigning groups, again, supporting the likelihood that such material was generated through the NUS' strategic approach of targeting affiliated members or ideologically aligned groups (Pool, 2014).

Conversely, 28 per cent of blog posts published in the same timeframe are critical of the NUS and #Demo2012. Negative coverage includes further repetition of the stories dominating student media, such as the offensive chant sheet issued by the NUS (EditorLibertine, 2012) and a story featuring accusations of a student union bribing studemnts to take part in the demonstration (Monnery, 2012). Politically motivated criticism is also present, with right-wing, pro-market critiques of NUS policy (Crossley, 2012) and left-wing critiques of the NUS' failure to offer a radical alternative to pro-market reforms of higher education (Margeson, 2012; Sampson, 2012).

#Demo2012 event analysis: space and place as catalysts for critical expression

As demonstrated above, the NUS' adoption of strategic media management techniques largely succeeded in ensuring that the mass and socially mediated narratives ahead of #Demo2012 supported its objectives of setting the political agenda around higher education policy (NUS, 2012a). Next the chapter will turn its attention to the role played by space and place in shaping #Demo2012's media narrative.

As has been shown, the days and hours ahead of #Demo2012 strategic media management by the NUS establishes a mass and social media narrative which supports the organisation's aims and agenda.[4] Within minutes of the march officially assembling, however, the hitherto pro-NUS media narrative becomes much more critical towards the organisers. Crucially, it can be argued that the material domains of space and place through which the demonstration passes play a significant role in shifting the tone of this narrative.

First, however, it is necessary to understand how the physicality – that is, materiality – of spaces and places can be operationalised as an analytical function. For Endres and Senda-Cook (2011), place is a 'particular location' constituted by 'a combination of material and symbolic qualities' (Endres & Senda-Cook 2011, 259) while 'space' is the 'more general notion of how society and social practice are regulated (and sometimes disciplined) by spatial thinking' (*ibid*). Understood as such, places and spaces can be interpreted as accounting for how the 'confluence of physical structures, locations and bodies can function rhetorically' (*ibid*, 261). Applying such a reading to social movements and protest events, Endres and Cook argue that place and space exert 'a fluid tension between materiality and symbolism'"(*ibid*, 262) that can 'have a variety of results beyond the intent of protest organisers' (*ibid*).

This perspective on the communicative role of place and space, can be adopted to account for the complex confluence between the material environment and #Demo2012 participants which functions spontaneously in ways that surprised the NUS organisers; ultimately making the media harder to manage and reshaping the media narrative around the event. Central to this is the widespread use of internet-enabled smartphones and social media apps (specifically Twitter in the case of #Demo2012) that allow people to share experiences and opinions through text as well as richer, audio-visual media thus mediating of the physical world in real-time.

This locative form of communication (Evans, 2015; Frith, 2015) forms an important component in changing the hitherto pro-NUS media narrative as the demonstration unfolds. Firstly, it specifically allows participants on the demonstration to express their opinions, share content and interact with other demonstrators in the same or nearby locations, thus catalyzing the media narrative in particular directions. Secondly, the interpolation of this location-based media content into wider mass media reporting is made possible by an innovative news gathering and reporting format, a live-blog, deployed during the demonstration by a leading British newspaper which exploits the largely real-time and unfiltered mediation afforded by locative media, such as Twitter.

Turning again to the demonstration and the route selected by the NUS for #Demo2012 was designed fundamentally to avoid politically significant locations, such as Parliament Square, or other focal points for the violence and property damage seen during the previous student protests, such as The Conservative Party headquarters on Millbank and other central London locations targeted during anti-austerity protests, e.g. government administration buildings such as The Treasury on Whitehall (Hoyles, 2014). This fact is further is acknowledged by NUS president, Liam Burns, when he asserts that in planning the demonstration, the NUS has 'done everything [it] can to negate violence,' and that NUS members 'are quite clear about this being a peaceful demonstration. I think we've set the tone right' (Sheriff, 2012a).

As a result of this strategic planning, instead of adopting the traditional route for political protests through London, taking in the politically symbolic locations of Trafalgar Square, Whitehall (the home of the British government's administrative function) and the Houses of Parliament in Parliament Square (the home of British democracy), the #Demo2012 route deliberately avoided them. For example, the route bypassed Whitehall by running in parallel with it down the Victoria Embankment alongside the River Thames before passing Parliament Square on its southern edge. Rather than entering Parliament Square, the route then crossed the Thames heading away from Parliament towards south London where it ended in a rally in Kennington Park, some way from the political and symbolic heart of central London (see Fig. 5.1).

Such a route, some argued, would lead to an 'ineffective' demonstration away from the UK's centre of political power (Sheriff, 2012b). Indeed, as Hind (2012) asserts: every major protest has traditionally taken its

> route *north* of Westminster Bridge, not over it to the south, because every protest has wanted to face the House of Parliament for the longest period possible, before heading along Whitehall to Downing Street. Every march I've been on slows down on this bend as people take a good old look at it, shout a lot and generally increase their rowdiness!
>
> (Hind, 2012) [italics in original]

Such a statement highlights how significant – both symbolically and physically – place can be on a demonstration such as Demo2012.

For example, the materiality of the route approaching the Houses of Parliament acts to physically slow down the protestors and present them with the symbolic centre of UK political power – usually the place against which demonstrators are focusing their attention, or 'rowdiness' in Hinds terms (*ibid*). Such a phenomenon is ideal for an event such as Demo2012 given its aim to set the government's agenda (NUS, 2012a).

Despite this intent, however, the NUS coordinated with London's Metropolitan Police Service in planning what can be argued is a contentious route:

> There was no way of getting [#Demo2012] through Parliament with the police. There'd have been no demo at all. We had to go to an end point: not Hyde Park as that was ruled out after the TUC event due to the Fortnam & Mason incident [occupation by anti-austerity protestors following a trade union demonstration]. The only choice we had in terms of getting police say so for it was to go to the [Kennington] Park
>
> (Hoyles, 2014)

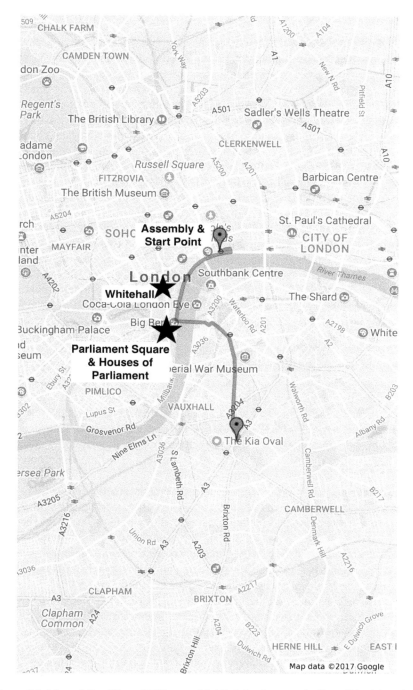

Figure 5.1 Map of the #Demo2012 route highlighting key symbolic political locations and landmarks.

(Map data: Google)

Moreover, on the day of the demonstration London's Metropolitan Police Service was involved in enforcing restrictions through the use of Section 12 Public Order laws, which gives police the right to confer specific requirements on public assemblies (NUS, 2012b). This legislative form of spatial management was implemented to minimize deviation from – and disruption on – the pre-agreed route. Furthermore, this spatial management was augmented through the use of rolling road-blacks and cordons to guide and control participants along the route with reinforced police lines and crowd-control barriers at significant and symbolic landmarks or flashpoints, such as outside the Houses of Parliament (Author's notes).

Such evidence suggests that both the NUS and the Metropolitan Police recognised the potential of the material environment to influence the physically disruptive potential of #Demo2012 and sought to manage it accordingly. However, accepting the rhetorical significance of space-place-body interactions during #Demo2012 which, according to Endres and Cook, can to generate 'a variety of results beyond the intent of protest organisers' (*ibid*, 262) it can now be argued that by attempting to strategically manage the physical environment of the demonstration, the NUS (with the Metropolitan Police) created a set of material conditions that significantly transformed the mediation and representation of the event from the earlier positive, pro-NUS media narrative to a negative one shifting critical attention from the Government's higher education policy – the over-arching aim of #Demo2012 – to the NUS and its leadership.

From the outset of #Demo2012, the NUS' choice of location for demonstrators to congregate pre-march represents a deliberate use of the demonstration's physical environment. As the NUS's communication manager at the time of the event confirmed: the choice of a small 'assembly space' was intentional 'so it felt like a massive demo' for participants while the presence of '[television] cameras and people hanging banners on the bridge overlooking the assembly space and speeches on megaphones''was designed to create a sense of power and build excitement ahead of the march (Hoyles, 2014).

Once underway, however, demonstrators were continually directed along the route and encouraged to keep moving in order to prevent a critical mass of participants from congregating and initiating the type of disruption seen during the 2010 demonstration (Walker & Paige, 2010). This containment tactic – implemented through coercion by NUS stewards and subsequently by the threat of arrest by police for participants trying to slow the march down or stop it is initially met with little resistance by the majority of the participants Author's notes).

One reason for this might be that the early part of the demonstration passes along the Victoria Embankment, a historically symbolic landmark for political demonstrations (Hind, 2012). It also acts as a physical space channeling demonstrators into a long-column of banner-waving and chanting mass crowd thus offering a somewhat iconic representation of the solidarity and strength of the movement (Albury, 2012; Parker, 2014).

As the demonstration arrives at the end of the Embankment it meets a fork in the road which leads either right towards the politically symbolic space of the Houses of Parliament and Parliament Square or left across Westminster Bridge towards the official NUS rally destination in South London. Despite the police cordon managing the space along the route and NUS stewards directing participants across Westminster Bridge a number of demonstrators began to congregate in front of the police barriers blocking entrance to Parliament Square (Author's notes and Kenny, 2012) in a show of dissatisfaction as to their inability to gain access to Parliament.

At this point in the demonstration two significant events occur: firstly a group of around 150 protestors (Owen, 2012: entry at 12:56pm) attempt to break through police lines into Parliament Square. This results in 'scuffles' with police (NatSam, 2012) and leads to a stand-off between police and demonstrators (Author's notes). Secondly, when this attempt to reach Parliament Square fails, another group of demonstrators initiate a sit-down protest at the entrance to Westminster Bridge in an attempt to prevent the march from continuing on its route (TheFounder, 2012). This group articulates the argument that the end destination of the march is politically ineffective and urge demonstrators to remain at Parliament to have its voice heard – the stated aim of #Demo2012 (Owen, 2012). These occurrences – the interaction between demonstrators and Parliament's physical presence as a politically significant place – have a pivotal effect on the way #Demo2012 is mediated.

As Endres and Senda-Cook assert (2011, 262): place exudes 'a fluid tension between materiality and symbolism' and it is the oscillation between these two properties that impact on the #Demo2012 frame. For example, on the one hand Parliament is significant to demonstrators as a symbolic place of political power, on the other it also operates as a physical place where demonstrators can congregate, display the strength of their movement and express their opposition to the government's policies. Moreover, the location operates physically *and* symbolically as a place where historic student protests have gathered to protest to parliament (Walker & Paige, 2010).

Making sense of these overlapping interpretations and significances of place, Parkinson (2009) argues that:

> public space[5] does convey meanings and can have behavioural effects, but those meanings are socially constructed, the effects socially mediated, dependent on narratives as well as physical factors.
>
> (Parkinson, 2009, 8)

If we read Parliament's significance through the lens suggested by Parkinson – that is, as a physical space interpretable only through a narrative socially constructed by protestors – it can be argued that Parliament becomes a symbolic political landmark central to #Demo2012, but which the police, the NUS and the route itself prevent demonstrators from accessing.

Having been initially imbued with a sense of physical solidarity created by the NUS' strategic choice of assembly space, combined with the politically symbolic march along the Embankment, the actions of the NUS and police in preventing access to the ultimate politically symbolic space of Parliament any perceived political power possessed by the demonstrators.

In response to this physical disruption and political frustration demonstrators act spontaneously by, firstly, attempting to break through barricades into Parliament Square and, secondly, initiating a sit-down protest on Westminster Bridge in an attempt to force participants to remain at Parliament to continue protesting and seeking a way through to Parliament Square rather than continuing to the politically impotent rally location in Kennington Park (Author's notes).

It is at this point in the demonstration that many of the participants begin to recognize that the demonstration route, turning away from Parliament, is likely to be of limited efficacy in achieving the NUS' stated aims of empowering students to make their voices heard by the government. As a result, it can be argued that the initial solidarity and anger against government policy accrued among the grassroots student and education activist movement begins to be refocused on the NUS and its leadership's apparent complicity with the police and political authorities in holding an emasculated demonstration.

The events at Parliament and Westminster mark a turning point in attitude among grassroots students towards the NUS. For instance, based on an analysis of communicative content expressed – both textually and visually – by participants on the march[6] it becomes clear that by a small margin a majority is critical of the NUS (53 per cent), with the strongest negativity arising as demonstrators 'live-tweet'[7] anti-NUS sentiment in increasing volume via Twitter.[8] Dominant themes expressed by participants include criticism of NUS leadership and efficacy as a grassroots organisation for the organi'ation of #Demo2012; the absence of politically symbolic landmarks on the route; the demonstration's climax in a seemingly insignificant and remote part of South London and the perceived collusion between the NUS, its stewards and the Metropolitan Police in selecting and managing the demonstration's route.

It's also possible to draw a more quantitative inference as to the significance of the Parliament/Westminster Bridge events in shifting the expressive narrative. Analysis of Twitter data gathered for the duration of the demonstration indicates that the frequency of tweets published gains momentum at times consistent with the events discussed.

This suggests that during the Parliament stand-off and Westminster Bridge sit-down protest that took place between approximately 12.50pm and 1:30pm the quantity of content generated is greater than at other points during the demonstration. This suggests that the physical, spatial environment at key moments on the demonstration played decisive roles – both qualitatively (i.e. generating negative expressive content) and quantitatively (i.e. velocity and volume of expression) – in the mediation of the event.

Such an argument is also supported by an analysis of tweets, YouTube films and images shared by reporters from the media outlet, *East London Lines*. This data plotted geographically further demonstrates that larger volumes of negative or anti-NUS content is expressed at key flashpoints on the route. These locations (circled) represent both the stand-off at Parliament and sit-down protest on Westminster Bridge and events at the final rally at Kennnington Park (see Fig. 5.2)

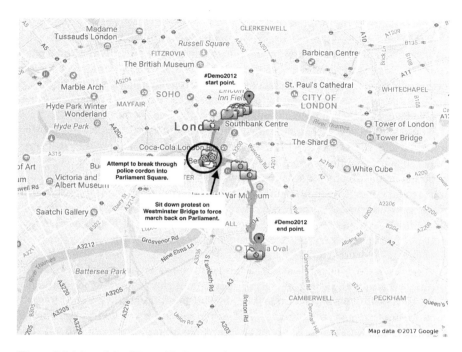

Figure 5.2 Map of the #Demo2012 route showing locations that generated increased volumes of social media content during the demonstration.

(Map data: Google)

Read as such, it becomes clear that these specific aspects of the route's physical environment operate as key material components in the construction of the #Demo2012 frame-as-assemblage.

The Guardian's #Demo2012 live-blog

The ramifications of the physical environment on the mediation of #Demo2012 can be seen if we consider how this spatially-influenced narrative generates socially mediated expressive content from participants in the demonstration, which, in turn, is enrolled into mass media coverage of the event. Central to this mediation process was the use of an emerging reporting format, a 'live-blog', by the UK's national newspaper, *The Guardian*.

Although an emerging and under-researched area of media (Thurman & Walters, 2013, 82–83), live-blogs can be described as 'live conversation[s] around a big story incorporating breaking news and verified facts with eyewitness material and audience opinion from social media channels' (Newman et al., 2012, 14). Thurman and Walters add further clarity to the concept by articulating a live-blog as a: 'single blog post on a specific topic to which time-stamped content is progressively added for a finite period – anywhere between half an hour and 24 hours' (Thurman & Walters, 2013, 83).

The adoption of live-blogs by institutional media organisations enables news gathering and production to respond to the dynamics of a digitally mediated environment. Such an environment can be said to be characterized by rapidly evolving communication structures which consist of heterogenous networks of formal as well as *informal* media actors, for example ordinary people using their internet-enabled smartphones to produce and report events 'live' as they occur.

This results in news production and gathering oriented around a complex 'information cycle' (Chadwick, 2013) emerging from a variety of sources in real-time, rather than the traditional top-down editorially planned approach to news as demonstrated in the first half of this chapter where the NUS carefully and strategically managed the media agenda. In this new media environment, narratively conventional news stories are superceeded by stories that are oriented around the non-linear flows of digitally networked information (Manovich, 1999) generated by a range of formal and informal actors structured by the logic of databases (*ibid*) and data streams (Manovich, 2012).

As a result, live-blogging acts as a format for news organisations to make use of the 'unstructured data, coming in fragments of raw, unprocessed journalism from both professionals and the public' by shifting journalistic practice towards 'a more iterative and collaborative approach in reporting and verifying the news' (Hermida, 2012, 665). Thus, it can be argued, live-blogs are more dynamic and inclusive of alternative narratives and news sources when compared to other forms of mediation.

This is evidenced by *The Guardian*'s live-blog reporting of the demonstration as it actively seeks out and covers alternative issues outside of the NUS-Government's binary news agenda that dominated the event build-up and early stages of the demonstration as a result of the NUS' strategic news management. By identifying the social media content being generated by participants on the demonstration and using it in its live-blog, *The Guardian* is able to report #Demo2012 using the 'raw, unprocessed journalism' (Hermida, 2012, 665) emerging outside of the NUS' media management, which in turn exposes the other agendas and perspectives arising – in particular, the negative expressions towards the NUS outlined above.

Owing to the format of live-blogs the information critical of the NUS is organised and absorbed into the wider news agenda in as close to real-time as possible. As #Demo2012 unfolds *The Guardian* is able to provide a more diverse account of the event's narrative but also has a commercially competitive edge in breaking and shaping how events are mediated live during the demonstration.

This is significant in determining the over-arching media narrative of the event because, as demonstrated above, the key moments that catalyse negative opinions about the NUS, such as the stand-off and clashes with police at Parliament and the sit-down protest on Westminster Bridge, are rapidly identified and used as hooks for follow-up news stories by *Guardian* journalists. Moreover, this real-time mediation of events then creates and validates news stories for other media outlets that go on to use *The Guardian*'s breaking accounts as the source for post-event coverage of #Demo2012.

For example, *The Guardian* is the first mainstream news outlet to break the stage invasion story (Owen, 2012) and approximately an hour after it happened the first fully articulated news story appears in *The Guardian* (*The Guardian*, 2012) leading with mobile phone footage uploaded to the video-sharing platform, YouTube, of hecklers at the rally, a detailed description of the stage invasion and inclusion of the chant dominating latter stages of the demonstration: 'NUS, shame on you. Where the fuck have you brought us to?' (Author's notes).

Within hours other news outlets ran similar stories adopting the same angle, re-using *The Guardian*'s video footage and citing the anti-NUS chant. Coverage critical of the NUS and #Demo2012 appeared across both right and left-wing media, with The Daily Mail (Duell, 2012) and The Independent (Rawlinson, 2012) while the Guardian publishes an extended follow-up article reporting that the NUS president 'Liam Burns, has been pelted with eggs and fruit at the conclusion of a march in London, which was marked by a low turnout and widespread anger over the perceived failure of the organisation to fight the trebling of university fees' (Malik & Ratcliffe, 2012).

Of the immediate news coverage, only the BBC provides a post-event account of the demonstration which downplays both events at Parliament/Westminster Bridge and at the rally, merely reporting '[t]here was a small stand-off between protesters and police at Westminster. But the protest passed off peacefully, ending with a rally in Kennington'. (BBC News, 2012).

Taking into account the mass mediated coverage of #Demo2012 it is possible to draw a link between the 'spatial narrative' and the shift of the event's narrative against the NUS. Firstly, as already discussed, the physical environment of Parliament and Westminster Bridge helped initiate dissatisfaction among participants towards the NUS leadership and the route, which was galvanised by the strategically planned spatial practices of the anti-NUS Imaginary Party. Such moments during the march can be quantitatively and qualitatively linked to the shift in expressive sentiment.

The Guardian's live-blog, tracking, assessing and reporting on this narrative shift in real-time, subsequently is able to break the first major post-event 'story' focusing on the stage invasion and growing anger towards the NUS among grassroots students which in turn sets the news agenda for subsequent mass media coverage of the event. The significance of *The Guardian*'s live-blog is further reinforced in comments made by the NUS' Press Officer who asserts that one of the live-blog journalists approached him for an interview with Liam Burns immediately after the egging.

Despite giving a 15 minute interview, the Press Officer reveals that the journalist:

> barely used any of it and wrote a very critical story about issues unrelated –
> [the stage invasion and general student anger towards the NUS] [. . .] and
> *The Guardian* continued to use it [. . .] despite it being an insignificant issue.
> I managed to talk it down with most people [. . . for] the BBC it become a

footnote in what they wrote about rather than a big thing. The Guardian surprised us, really, by running it

(Hoyles, 2014)

This would suggest that traditional media management was adopted in an attempt
to control the fall out of the stage invasion and – while it seemingly worked with the
BBC's coverage – *The Guardian*, taking its lead from the socially mediated content
expressed by #Demo2012 participants, was able to articulate a counter-narrative.

Crucially, it was *The Guardian*'s counter-narrative that continued to shape the
majority of other post-event mass media coverage to the extent that it prevented
the NUS' strategically planned post-event narrative from receiving wide coverage.
For example, the NUS' Press Office discusses how the organisation had briefed
journalists and placed an exclusive story with both the Guardian and the Independent to run after the demonstration (Hoyles, 2014). This story, featuring the
NUS' proposal for a new system of postgradate loans as a solution to the current,
unsatisfactory fees arrangement, gained no further coverage beyond its exclusive
placements despite offering a relevant follow-up story for the NUS' #Demo2012
narrative.

Due to the 'spatial narrative' created by the physical and symbolic environment
on the route and the material practices of an activist group the socially mediated
expressed narrative shifted against the NUS, becoming enrolled in *The Guardian*'s
live mediation of the event and subsequently going on to set the news agenda post-
#Demo2012. Such spontaneous, planned and contingent material and expressive
elements become inculcated in such a way that generates a stabilising effect on
the master frame-as-assemblage to the extent that it successfully undermines the
NUS' earlier strategically managed frame and transforms it into an entirely critical
narrative of the demonstration.

Conclusions

This chapter has argued that the material realms of the physical environment – such
as the domains of space and place – can be increasingly understood as relevant
in influencing processes of mediation and the ability to effectively plan and manage communication strategically. Drawing together the diverse range of material
and communicative factors operating together – from the strategically planned
and managed organisational narrative of the pre-event build-up, to the real-time
mediation of events by grassroots participants influenced by place and space and
the subsequent reporting of #Demo2012 by the mass media – a set of concluding
observations can be made.

These hopefully point towards an original reading of strategic communication
in which previously unseen forces, such as place and space, become enrolled in
the mediation process due the rise of digitally-enabled grassroots communication using locative media as well as the increasing adoption of innovative news
gathering and reporting formats, such as the live-blog, by institutional news media
as a way to express the "raw, unprocessed journalism" (2012, 665) arising from

place-space-body interactions. From the case study, it can be seen how the material domains of the everyday world can potentially have a much greater significance in shaping and influencing effective communication than has previously been considered by media and communication scholars (although some scholarship is beginning to address these issues (see for example: Gillespie, Boczkowski, & Foot, 2014; Revers, 2015).

Such a reading also has implications for an applied understanding of strategic communication and communications management. For instance, ahead of the demonstration the NUS' communications team deployed a range of media relations techniques which meant it was able to manage both traditional mass media coverage of the demonstration as well as the narrative arising from the largely autonomous networks of digitally-empowered stakeholders emerging around the event. As a result, it was able to effectively manage the mediation of the demonstration and the news and political agenda surrounding the event in order to achieve a largely favourable narrative ahead – and during initial stages – of #Demo2012.

However, once the demonstration reached the politically symbolic locations of Parliament Square and Whitehall, the materiality of space and place becomes key determining factors in the communication and mediation of the event.

Such spaces and their symbolic interpretation by demonstrators initiate a series of spatial practices: firstly in the form of attempts by participants to break through police lines into Parliament Square and secondly a sit-down protest that blocks the route of the demonstration forcing demonstrators back on Parliament.

Recognising that the material environment can interact with physical locations and human bodies to act rhetorically (Endres & Senda-Cook, 2011, 261) it possible to connect such phenomena with a quantitative increase in volume and a qualitative change towards an anti-NUS narrative that occurs at this point in the demonstration. By recognising the role played by the material domain in influencing the mediation and subsequent narrative around the demonstration it can be argued that the limits of strategic communication management – in focusing on the expressive dimensions of communication – be glimpsed.

Alternatively, it can be asserted that the boundaries of what scholars have conventionally understood as strategic communication need to be re-thought. For example, to what extent would influencing the choice of route to strategically include politically symbolic landmarks (while maintaining safety and public order) have helped the NUS manage the mediation and communication during the demonstration? Would a greater understanding of the technological infrastructure, routines and needs of real-time digital news publishing, such as *The Guardian*'s live-blog, and the ways in which it interacts with and shapes events have helped the NUS manage the mediation of demonstration more effectively? While the planning and management of place, space and spatial practices are not traditionally considered part of a strategic communicators role, the rise of digitally-enabled, location-based and real-time communication tools increasingly bring the physical world into the mediated one – and thus, it can be argued, the realm of the strategic communicator.

Notes

1 The timeframe was selected based on a macro-analysis of media data generated around the event. There was little media coverage or social media interaction concerning the event outside of the dates chosen.
2 Conventionally, Monday is traditionally seen as the optimum day to launch 'news' given its position at the start of the week and potential to accommodate the fullest development of a story as well as achieve the longest possible uninterrupted exposure. The 'Sunday for Monday' tactic achieves both two rounds of news coverage (i.e. both Sunday and Monday) as well as securing premium Monday coverage – the most prominent news moment in the week, thus ensuring significant agenda-setting impact for a story.
3 Given the high volume of Twitter data gathered during the research timeframe (16th-26th November 2012) a longitudinal and randomized sample of 10% of the data was taken for detailed analysis. All analysis and discussion of Twitter data in this section is drawn from this dataset.
4 There is some minor criticism of the NUS within mass and social media ahead of #Demo2012, but this was limited to right-wing critiques of the NUS' policy position on higher education or more 'sensationalist' criticisms, such as allegations student groups were 'bribed' to attend and the use of 'offensive chants' in official NUS documents.
5 The interpretation of the terms space and place tend to vary between scholars or scholarly fields. Here Parkinson refers to 'public space' as "space that is public because it used for public purposes. This might be space like major town squares or the grounds of legislatures where the '*demos*' gathers to influence public decision making, perhaps through demonstrations" (Parkinson, 2009, 5). This is comparable to Endres and Cook's notion of place (2011), rather than space *per se*.
6 Analysis of communications content during the demonstration is based on a timeframe of 11:00–16:00 – that is, from the official assembly time for the demonstration (see: www. demo2012.org.uk/?page_id=22) until the crowds had dispersed and the demonstration had wound down (see Owen, 2012 and author's notes).
7 The use of Twitter to report on an event or issue in a real-time or 'live' fashion.
8 Compared to Twitter, other media publishes very little expressive content during the march. What does appear is either 'pre-packaged' information strategically planned or coincidentally published during the 'live' demonstration period (for example see: www. itv.com/news/update/2012-11-21/students-protest-against-university-fees-and-lack-of-jobs) or peripheral stories not directly related to key events during the demonstration, (for example see: www.impactnottingham.com/2012/11/false-start-to-nus-demo-2012 and www.nouse.co.uk/2012/11/21/nus-playing-around-with-politics).

References

Albury, James. (2012). Twitter. Retrieved 20th May, 2014, from https://twitter.com/alburyj/status/271226493529628672
Alice, Samantha. (2012, 21st November). Retrieved 21st March, 2014, from http://twitter.com/SamanthaAlice19/statuses/271184007234977792
Angela. (2012, 19th November). National Student Demonstration 21 November 2012. Retrieved 21st March, 2014, from http://ouactivists.wordpress.com/2012/11/19/national-student-demonstration-21-november-2012/
Anticuts. (2012, 21st November). See You again on #Dec5: Free Education, Living Grants, Abolish the Debt! Retrieved 21st March, 2014, from http://anticuts.com/2012/11/21/see-you-again-on-dec5-free-education-living-grants-abolish-the-debt/
Bastani, Aaron John. (2012, 20th November). Retrieved 21st March, 2014, from https://twitter.com/AaronBastani/status/271013445166567424

BBC News. (2010). Tuition Fees Vote: Plans Approved Despite Rebellion. *BBC Politics News Website*. Retrieved 22nd May, 2014, from www.bbc.co.uk/news/uk-politics-11952449

BBC News. (2012). Students March in London Protest. *BBC News Website*. Retrieved 20th May, 2014, from www.bbc.co.uk/news/education-20412792

BellaCiao. (2012, 20th November). Student Demo 2012 Organized by NUS Spread the Word. Retrieved 21st March, 2014, from www.bellaciao.org/en/spip.php?article22323

Boffey, Daniel. (2012). NUS Survey Reveals Parents' Fears for Young People. *The Guardian*. Retrieved from www.theguardian.com/politics/2012/nov/18/nus-survey-parents-fears-young-people

Campbell, Alastair. (2011, 20th June). A New Version of an Old Cliff Richard Song Could Be Biggest Feelgood Dampener Yet. Retrieved from www.alastaircampbell.org/blog/2011/06/20/a-new-version-of-an-old-cliff-richard-song-could-be-biggest-feelgood-dampener-yet/-sthash.RUkWYsfy.dpuf

Central Students Union. (2012a, 20 November). #Demo2012. Retrieved 21st March, 2014, from http://centralsu.wordpress.com/2012/11/20/demo-2012/

Chadwick, Andrew. (2013). *The Hybrid Media System: Politics and Power*. Oxford: Oxford University Press.

Collins, Thomas. (2012, 20th November). Retrieved 21st March, 2014, from https://twitter.com/ThomasDCollins/status/271160083050795008

Crossley, Alexander. (2012, 21st November). The #Demo2012 Student Protests Are Misinformed, Misguided and Contradictory. Retrieved 21st March, 2014, from http://alexander-crossley.com/2012/11/21/student-protests-are-misguided-misinformed-and-contradictory/

Day, Rebecca. (2012, 21st November). Retrieved 21st March, 2014, from https://twitter.com/beckyday89/statuses/271183520783802369

Dean, Malcolm. (2013). *Democracy under Attack: How the Media Distort Policy and Politics*. Bristol: The Policy Press.

Defend The Right To Process. (2012, 21st November). Trade Unionists Support Student Protests Today. Retrieved 21st March, 2014, from www.defendtherighttoprotest.org/trade-unionists-support-student-protests-today/

Duell, Mark. (2012). Huge Student Rally against Tuition Fee Hike Ends in Chaos as Union President Is Heckled Off Stage after Being Pelted with Eggs . . . and a Satsuma. *Daily Mail Website*. Retrieved 20th May, 2014, from www.dailymail.co.uk/news/article-2236484/Liam-Burns-Huge-student-rally-tuition-fee-hike-ends-chaos-NUS-president-heckled-stage.html-ixzz2uQm7Mrs0

EditorLibertine. (2012, 20 November). NUS Chants: Chair's Statement. Retrieved 21st March, 2014, from http://lylibertine.wordpress.com/2012/11/20/nus-chants-chairs-statement/

Endres, Danielle, & Senda-Cook, Samantha. (2011). Location Matters: The Rhetoric of Place in Protest. *Quarterly Journal of Speech*, 97(3), 257–282.

Evans, Leighton. (2015). *Locative Social Media: Place in the Digital Age*. Houndmills & New York: Palgrave MacMillan.

TheFounder. (2012). Twitter. Retrieved 20th May, 2014, from https://twitter.com/rhulfounder/status/271239384941068288/photo/1

Frith, Jordan. (2015). *Smartphones as Locative Media*. Cambridge: Polity Press.

Gandy, Oscar H. (1982). *Beyond Agenda-Setting: Information Subsidies and Public Policy*. Norwood, NJ: Ablex.

GBCLegal. (2012, 21st November). Retrieved 21st March, 2014, from https://twitter.com/alexpday/statuses/271187290821365760

Gillespie, Tarleton, Boczkowski, Pablo J., & Foot, Kirsten A. (Eds.). (2014). *Media Technologies: Essays on Communication, Materiality, and Society*. Cambridge, MA & London, England: The MIT Press.

Grant, Alan. (2012, 16th November). Retrieved 21st March, 2014, from https://twitter.com/alangrantuk/statuses/269368384074960896

Hancox, Dan (Ed.). (2011). *Fightback: A Reader on the Winter of Protest*. London: OpenDemocracy.

Hermida, Alfred. (2012). Tweets and Truth. *Journalism Practice*, 6(5–6), 659–668.

Hind, Sam. (2012). March Dynamics: Why Place Matters. *The Semaphore Line Blog*. Retrieved 20th May, 2014, from http://thesemaphoreline.wordpress.com/2012/11/22/march-dynamics-why-place-matters/

Hoyles, Will. (2014, 12th February). Interview with the author.

ITV News. (2012, 21st November). NUS Warns of 'Epidemic of Dropouts'. Retrieved 17th March, 2014, from www.itv.com/news/update/2012-11-21/nus-warns-of-epidemic-of-dropouts/

ITV News. (2012a, 21st November 2012). Students Feel 'Sense of Desperation'. Retrieved 17th March, 2014, from www.itv.com/news/update/2012-11-21/students-feel-sense-of-depression-for-their-future/

ITV News. (2012b, 21st November 2012). Students to Protest over Funding Cuts. Retrieved 17th March, 2014, from www.itv.com/news/update/2012-11-21/students-to-protest-over-funding-cuts/

Kenny, Alan. (2012). Twitter. Retrieved 20th May, 2014, from https://twitter.com/alankennyswp/status/271242592593776640

Landin, Conrad. (2012). NUS: Don't Let Us Down This Time. *Guardian Comment Is Free Website*. Retrieved 22nd May, 2014, from www.theguardian.com/education/2012/nov/19/studentpolitics-students

MacDoo, Rosey. (2012, 21st November). Retrieved 21st March, 2014, from https://twitter.com/RoseyMacdoo/statuses/271164958656577536

Malik, Shiv, & Ratcliffe, Rebecca. (2012). Student March Ends in Eggs, Fruit and Anger. *Guardian Website*. Retrieved 20th May, 2014, from www.theguardian.com/education/2012/nov/21/student-march-eggs-anger

Manovich, Lev. (1999). Database as Symbolic Form. *Convergence: The International Journal of Research into New Media Technologies*, 5(2), 80–99.

Manovich, Lev. (2012, 27th October). Data Stream, Database, Timeline: The Forms of Social Media. Retrieved 24th March, 2014, from http://lab.softwarestudies.com/2012/10/data-stream-database-timeline-new.html

Margeson, James. (2012, 19th November). #Demo2012: Why Bother Marching? Retrieved 21st March, 2014, from http://mnafc.wordpress.com/2012/11/19/demo2012-why-bother-marching/

Monnery, Neil. (2012, 21st November). The NUS Are Undertaking #Demo2012 Today but Why Are the University of Manchester Strong-Arming Societies and What Good Will It Do? Retrieved 21st March, 2014, from http://neilmonnery.co.uk/2012/11/21/nus-undertaking-demo2012-today-su-officials-blackmailing-su-societies-good-do/

Morgan. (2012, 21st November). Retrieved 21st March, 2014, from https://twitter.com/morgan_____/statuses/271207524814962688

Mulholland, Hélène. (2010). Tuition Fees: Government Wins Narrow Victory as Protests Continue. *Guardian Website*. Retrieved 22nd May, 2014, from www.theguardian.com/education/2010/dec/09/tuition-fees-vote-government-wins-narrow-victory

NatSam. (2012). Twitter. Retrieved 20th May, 2014, from https://twitter.com/Gnat2009/statuses/271261638605283328

Newman, Nic, Dutton, William H, & Blank, Grant. (2012). Social Media in the Changing Ecology of News: The Fourth and Fifth Estates in Britain. *International Journal of Internet Science*, 7(1), 6–22.

NextGenLab. (2012). Retrieved 21st March, 2014, from https://twitter.com/NextGenLab/status/271186594487218177

NUS. (2012a). Liam Burns Announces Date for National Student Demonstration. *YouTube Website*. Retrieved 22nd May, 2014, from www.youtube.com/watch?feature=player_embedded&v=qwQrjOhV09E!

NUS. (2012b). Section 12 on Today's Route. *Demo2012 Website*. Retrieved 20th May, 2014, from www.demo2012.org.uk/?p=278

NUS. (n.d.a). About. *#Demo2012 Website*. Retrieved 21st May, 2014, from www.demo2012.org.uk/?page_id=18

NUS. (n.d.b). What We Do. *National Union of Students' Website*. Retrieved 21st May, 2014, from www.nus.org.uk/en/who-we-are/what-we-do/

NUS_LGBT. (2012, 20th November). Retrieved 21st March, 2014, from https://twitter.com/NUS_LGBT/status/270869316776390657

Owen, Paul. (2012). Students Protest at Demo2012 – As it happened. *The Guardian* website. Retrieved 5th February, 2018, from https://www.theguardian.com/education/2012/nov/21/student-protests-demo-2012-live-blog.

Parker, Robin. (2014, 20th May). Twitter. Retrieved 20th May, 2014, from https://twitter.com/R_J_Parker/status/271235782407225344

Parkinson, John. (2009). Symbolic Representation in Public Space: Capital Cities, Presence and Memory. *Representation*, 45(1), 1–14.

Peltz, Adrienne. (2012, 20th November). Retrieved 21st March, 2014, from https://twitter.com/adi_peltz/status/270928329761239040

Peters-Day, Alex. (2012, 21st November). Retrieved 21st March, 2014, from https://twitter.com/alexpday/statuses/271187290821365760

Pool, Lisa (2014, 14th March). Interview with the author.

Rawlinson, Kevin. (2012). Angry Student Protests Return to the Streets of London. *Independent Website*. Retrieved 20th May, 2014, from www.independent.co.uk/news/uk/home-news/angry-student-protests-return-to-the-streets-of-london-8340801.html

Revers, Matthias. (2015). The Augmented Newsbeat: Spatial Structuring in a Twitterized News Ecosystem. *Media, Culture & Society*, 37(1), 3–18.

Sampson, Tony D. (Tony D. Sampson, 19th November). Students to Protest over Funding Cuts and Employment Prospects. Retrieved 21st March, 2014, from http://viralcontagion.wordpress.com/2012/11/19/students-to-protest-over-funding-cuts-and-employment-prospects/

Sewards, Mark. (2012, 20th November). Retrieved 21st March, 2014, from https://twitter.com/MarkJSewards/status/270817864225796096

Sheriff, Lucy. (2012a). NUS President Liam Burns Concerned #Demo2012 Student Protests Will Turn Violent. *Huffington Post Website*. Retrieved 20th March, 2014, from www.huffingtonpost.co.uk/2012/11/06/nus-president-liam-burns-worried-student-violence-demo2012_n_2081976.html

Sheriff, Lucy. (2012b). NUS Releases Route of Demo 2012, the Student Protest Planned for November. *Huffington Post Website*. Retrieved 20th March, 2014, from www.huffingtonpost.co.uk/2012/10/15/nus-releases-route-of-student-demo-2012_n_1966294.html

Shorthouse, Ryan. (2012, 21st November). Retrieved 21st March, 2014, from https://twitter.com/RyanShorthouse/status/271186240123052032

Stace. (2012). Retrieved 21st March, 2014, from http://twitpic.com/bev7i0

The Guardian. (2012). Demo 2012: Student Rally Disrupted by Hecklers. *Guardian Website.* Retrieved 20th May, 2014, from www.theguardian.com/education/2012/nov/21/demo-2012-student-rally-disrupted-by-hecklers

The Guardian. (2012a). NUS Warns of 'Epidemic of Dropouts'. *The Guardian.* Retrieved from www.theguardian.com/education/2012/nov/20/nus-warns-of-epidemic-of-dropouts

The Independent. (2012). Students March over Lack of Jobs. *The Independent.* Retrieved from www.independent.co.uk/news/education/education-news/students-march-over-lack-of-jobs-8327507.html

Thurman, Neil, & Walters, Anna. (2013). Live-Blogging: Digital Journalism's Pivotal Platform? *Digital Journalism, 1*(1), 82–101.

Walker, Peter, & Clarke, Rebecca. (2012). Students to Protest over Funding Cuts and Employment Prospects. *The Observer.* Retrieved from www.theguardian.com/education/2012/nov/18/student-protest-funding-employment-prospects

Walker, Peter, & Paige, Jonathan. (2010, 9th December). Student Protests – as They Happened. *Guardian Website.* Retrieved 20th May, 2014, from www.theguardian.com/education/blog/2010/dec/09/student-protests-live-coverage

Woodburn, Tom. (2012, 21st November). Retrieved 21st March, 2014, from https://twitter.com/tom_woodburn/statuses/271188967699927041

Wright, Mark. (2012, 19th November). Students Back on the Streets This Wednesday, Join the Demo against Fees and Cuts. Retrieved 21st March, 2014, from http://markwrightuk88.blogspot.co.uk/2012/11/students-back-on-streets-this-wednesday.html

6 The communicative function of public spaces

Noureddine Miladi

The study of urban spaces has attracted increasing attention over past decades partly due to the symbolic role attached to them and their use by social movements. City squares and other prominent urban spaces are becoming sites of resistance in an attempt from the public to reassert their political power (Rovisco and Ong, 2016). Unlike cities themselves, which can be viewed as spaces of transition, city squares and public spaces at large remain places of interaction and communication. Through their monuments, statues, street art and images they signify memorable glories which evoke responses with, debates about and interactions by the public.

In this chapter, I examine the communicative functions attributed to public spaces. I look at the role town and city squares, public gardens, museums and art galleries play in developing social relations, establishing connections and building friendships. Drawing on the French philosopher and sociologist, Henri Lefebvre, whose work on the critique of everyday life, the right to the city and the production of social space provides a challenging insight into the symbolic and significant role of the social production of space. I analyse the symbolic meanings of public spaces and the extent to which the communicative functions of such spacesare being recreated.

Lefebvre's development of the theory of space in his *Le Droit a la Ville* (Right to the City) (1968) provides a conceptual underpinning for the symbolic power of public spaces and their social and political significance. Furthermore, I argue here that the significance of this phenomenon emerges in large part from its incorporation of town/city squares and street walls as part of spatial strategies to build tactics of resistance. These strategies further emanate from Lefebvre's understanding that "any space implies, contains and disseminates social relationships . . . a space is not a thing but rather a set of relations between things (objects and products)" (1968: 82–83).

Defining public space

One may define a public space as a meeting point for social gatherings, celebrations, or simply for daily interaction between citizens. A thriving public space is that which facilitates interaction among people and safeguards security, diversity and neighborliness. This description may include town markets, waterfronts, town squares, museums, plazas, parks and shopping centres. Public places differ in terms of their prestigious status in any given country. All over the world, certain places qualify as great spaces while others are of less importance.

Public spaces also earn their significance from the historical events they embodied. They reflect the local historical atmosphere which leaves its mark on passersby and visitors. In this sense, such spaces may serve as places of inspiration or contemplation to visitors. Modern public spaces also provide interesting visual experiences which incorporate murals, statues and other instances of public art and usually appear welcoming to visitors from various ethnicities and backgrounds.

It is also important to understand public space as an everyday counter-space where counter-publics strive for change. Following this line of argument, certain public spaces may earn their significance because they are places of dissent or political activism. Some of the most enduring symbols of public space related to political dissent include Trafalgar Square in London, Tahrir Square in Egypt, Tiananmen Square in Beijing, Taqsim Square in Istanbul and Kasba Square in Tunis owing to the fact they have become synonymous with free speech, anti-war movements and pro-democracy protests. Such spaces are barometers with which to measure public opinion and dissatisfaction – and on which governments and the media keep a close eye.

Debates about public spaces consider the extent to which they are viewed as sites of free interaction and free speech or spaces which signify the hegemonic order of the state (Mitchell, 1995, 2003). However, such spaces, significant as they may be, are normally shaped and constructed through an official planning process as well as through an organic course of action which often involves local communities and various stakeholders. Therefore, an ideal public space in which no preconditions exist does not practically exist.

In his work, *The Production of Space*, Lefebvre (1991) posits that because space is historically a key site of public interaction it gets defined and redefined by citizens who engage with each other in that space. It is through spatial practices, such as celebrations, protests, vigils, and other gatherings that spaces develop social meanings and historical significance. Symbols and images related to spaces remain in the social memory and get inherited from a generation to another. The symbolic meaning of space is also mediated through cultural practices. History books, cultural products like paintings, people's stories and other human practices, all produce and reproduce space along with associated meanings such as hierarchies of class, justice, control and freedom.

It is helpful to explore some of these factors using Trafalgar Square in London, the capital city of the United Kingdom, as a vivid example of a public space that buzzes with communicative sites and symbols. The statue Nelson's Column is surrounded by four bases which have statues of military figures placed on three of them. The fourth has been authorized by the Mayor of London to be used as display of art. In her study on public spaces, Blazwick (2013) contends that the Mayor allowed temporary use of this platform by the public for one hundred days in 2013, A total of 2,100 people selected from hundreds of thousands of applicants from all over the UK, each spent one hour on the plinth. Each person displayed a unique cultural exercise, from art displays to dancing and singing. Some people chose nudity for their one hour. As a result, thousands visited the square and the event was televised by the satellite television channel, Sky Arts, which enabled the initiative to be communicated to and witnessed by millions of viewers around the world.

However, this project is not just about displaying one's own work of art but about communicating the values of a civil society. It empowers people to express their aspirations in a pluralistic language. In this sense, public art stands as a form of communication and participation which recognises that people bring their own unique identities. It embraces people and their cultural diversity where streets and public spaces become the spheres for a participatory culture.

Thus, a key characteristic of a communicative public space is to be participatory, inclusive and democratic. Public spaces are socially produced and reproduced over the decades and centuries; their significance gets inherited over various generations through the activities which take place in them.

The availability of shared, democratic and freely accessible physical spaces, democratic and freely accessed, are pivotal to the healthy development of communication and engagement among communities (Fraser, 1992). Among faith communities one may refer to the role of religious places/centres as illustrations of strong and united communities. Churches, Mosques, Synagogues, Gordwaras and Buddhist temples can be viewed not only as places of worship but multi-functional social arenas. A multitude of social affairs tend to take place in such religious centres like marriage ceremonies, celebrations, funeral prayers and educational gatherings. In many cases, such places also serve as temporary shelters for the homeless and travelers as well as sources of daily meals for the needy.

Privately owned public spaces

The above functions of public spaces are coming under threat due to the increased trend of privatisation of spaces usually known to be freely-accessible. By privately-owned public spaces, it is meant spaces that are available for public access or intended for public use but in which the public are very restricted in what they can do. For example, in such spaces actions such as organizing gatherings, protests and even filming or taking photographs can be restricted. A documentary produced by the United Kingdom's *Channel 4 News* (2016) highlighted the upsurge of this phenomenon across modern urban cities in the United Kingdom. It gave various examples across the country where public spaces are becoming increasingly privately owned and therefore less and less public.

Around City Hall in London, for instance, which is the offices of the Mayor of London, a green square appears like a public space that can be accessed by ordinary people. It is, however, privately owned by the Samaritans Property Corporation of Kuwait which bought it for 1.7 billion pounds in 2013. Another space near St Paul's Cathedral in central London is owned by the Mitsubishi Estate Company of Japan. Public access to these squares is often denied – such as in 2011 when a court injunction was used to prevent the Occupy London movement from attempting to assemble in it.

In a different example, Schmidt and Németh (2010: 454) speak about the challenges faced by the traditional functions of parks, plazas and sidewalks due to the increased privatization of the management of such spaces. Firstly, the provision and management of public space has become increasingly privatized, with developers, property managers and local business associations taking the lead in providing and maintaining parks, plazas and atriums. For instance, in the city of New York, hybrid ownership involving both public and private sectors. Public parks including New York City's Bryant Park and Central Park, while owned by the City of New York, are both managed by the privately-funded Bryant Park Restoration Corporation and the Central Park Conservancy, respectively (*ibid*).

This co-ownership may help provide funds to maintain those spaces. But in return, it can reduce free access to members of the public. In response to this increasingly privatized environment, policy-makers may argue that such spaces have been purchased by developers because they were derelict lands and now transformed into well-maintained spaces. Also, the 'proponents of privately owned or operated spaces argue that the efficiency of the private sector in distributing public goods outweigh any potentially negative social impacts' (Schmidt and Németh, 2010: 454).

Do public spaces have communicative functions?

This chapter considers public spaces and urban architecture not merely as steel and stone but through the prism of communication; it locates communicative activity and the potential for interactivity in those environments. The concept 'communicative space' serves here as a critical lens through which we can understand the role of public sites, such as squares, monuments and parks, beyond simply being made of concrete or trees and plants. Sculptures, artefacts and installations do not exist for a trivial reason, argue Drucker and Gumpert (2009: 65), but they 'invoke a kind of collective consciousness'. Cities thrive and develop with communication and they '. . . speak through stone, steel, structures and shapes' (*ibid*).

Over the past decades, a thread of academic scholarship has developed around the issue of public spaces and urban architectural environments. Cities are usually considered for their beauty of architectural buildings, gardens and museums. What attracts passers-by and tourists, in most cases, is the aspect of beauty. People, for instance, are fascinated by the shapes, colours and age of both modern and historical buildings – a visual persuasion reflected in tourism brochures and magazines. The marketing of a city focuses on the gaze. Yet beyond visual persuasion there exists another layer of meanings embedded in those shapes, colours and history of buildings and monuments: this is their communicative function.

Memorials and monuments

Public spaces and memorials planted in them reflect complex negotiations and sometimes a power struggle process or lobbying between city planners, historians, policy makers and the public. To this end we should understand that the placement of the Statue of Liberty for instance is not a mere act of embellishment to the city of New York but a sophisticated choice that emerged as part of a carefully measured decision to serve a political vision and reflect a key value of American society.

This social value is associated with freedom, equality and emancipation. The same can be said about other cities around the world. The immense statue of Jesus Christ overlooking Rio de Janeiro, on Mount Corcovado, southeastern Brazil, the Sphinx and Pyramid of Giza, Egypt, Peter the Great Statue in Moscow, Sendai Daikannon in Japan, The Spring Temple Buddha in the Zhaocun township of Lushan County, Henan, China, Mother Motherland or The Mamayev Monument in Mamayev Kurgan in Volgograd, Russia among many others around the world are of great symbolic meanings. They all represent carefully designed and structured monuments to signify cultural/religious values and political/social ideals pertinent to where they belong.

Mitchell (2003: 128) contends that public spaces are organized areas in urban cities where often citizens or travellers, specifically whom he calls the 'properly behaved' often 'might experience the spectacle of the city'. Here spaces are considered as controlled and ordered in specific ways, according to a planned setting. They are also decorated with monuments which reflect the will of hegemonic powers in society. As such, the 'properly behaved' citizens as termed by Mitchell enjoy a preplanned and pre-organized urban space of interaction. Moreover, nowadays these citizens communicate and interact in heavily monitored spaces controlled through security camera systems.

In fact, similar to the communication function of the print media in Europe during the eighteenth- and nineteenth-century, as proposed by Habermas (1989: 225), it can be argued that monuments and statues encourage communication and debate among citizens in urban public spaces. Across the world, public spaces – in particular town squares – are synonymous with power struggles and collective communication by citizens in order to seek social or political change.

Such spaces also constitute arenas where citizens gather to celebrate national days and commemorate important historical events. Central public spaces such as Trafalgar Square in London, Tiananmen Square in China, Taksim in Turkey, Al Kasba Square in Tunis, Green Square in Tripoli (Libya), Pearl Square in Manama (Bahrain), Tahrir Square in Cairo (Egypt), Valias Square in Tehran (Iran) Central Park in New York, among many others around the world mark the central nerve of every country's population for communication and engagements.

This understanding of public spaces has been developed by Habermas as somewhere people can meet and where various forms of activities can take place including communication. These 'democratic' spaces facilitate discussion as a form of political engagement in the traditional sense. For Habermas (1989) the public sphere is what cafés, pubs, clubhouses and community centres offer – but it also exists in parks, town squares and other public spaces. Hence what makes a city and public space communicative are also the interactions, encounters and experiences which take place in such spaces and their rhetorical functions.

Moreover, public spaces remain epicenters of historic political events in which revolutions took place, civil disobedience started and victories achieved. Such

Figure 6.1 Tahrir Square in Cairo, Egypt became a focal point for political dissent during
the Arab Spring uprisings in 2011.

places also shape history and have remained for centuries emblematic to citizens,
generation after generation. This is why various central public spaces in towns and
cities become of significant importance.

Trafalgar Square in central London, for instance, commemorates the historical
Battle of Trafalgar (in Cape Trafalgar, Spain) on 21st October 1805 when the British Navy was victorious over the French and Spanish navies in the Napoleonic
Wars. Nelson's Column, placed in the epicenter of Trafalgar Square, was erected in
memory of Vice Admiral Horatio Nelson's bravery and service to the country. Nelson died in the Battle of Trafalgar and is still remembered for his victorious battles
for the British Empire. Especially from the nineteenth-century onwards, the square
became a significant landmark in London and indeed across the whole of the United
Kingdom. It hosts major national celebrations, public events, political demonstrations such as the anti-war protests and Christmas and in recent years Eid celebrations.

War memorials

Another example worth looking at in terms of its communicative function are
war memorials. Placed sometimes in central parks or city squares, war memorials
tend to signify symbolic meaning and they are often part of the design of a city,
as established by authorities in a country. One may argue that they symbolize a
glorious past especially when considering the great wars such as, World War I and
World War II.

Such memorials are erected partly to 'make sense of the past, make peace with it, and bring us into the future. And maybe in order to heal, a war memorial needs to invoke public discussions and controversies' (War Memorials 2007). However, their *raison d'être* may differ from one country to another. In countries where despotic regimes rule, dictators tend to plant statues to themselves in every public place. Key roundabouts and government buildings turn into displays for their statues. Saddam Hussein, Hafed al Assad of Syria, Ben Ali and Bourguiba former presidents of Tunisia, Kamal Ataturk shaper of modern Turkey, North Korea's Kim Jong-un and China's Communist leaders among scores of other present and past world leaders, all construct statues of themselves in every key public space in order to dominate public consciousness and further inculcate fear and control in the hearts and minds of their subjects.

However, in other parts of the world, memorials get erected to commemorate the achievements of the country's commander in chief and remind the generations to come about their service or their concerted efforts to establish justice and peace. Human rights activists, political leaders or army generals are often revered for their great works. Abraham Lincoln's statue in the West Virginia State Capitol in the United States, Winston Churchill's statue in Parliament Square in London, Nelson Mandella's statue in Ramallah, Palestine and Mahatma Ghandi's statue in London's Tavistock Square are examples of world leaders or human rights activists who have been commemorated for their struggles; their memorials – among others – stand as reminders for what they did.

Thanks to the existence of these memorial and artifacts embellishing city squares and parks, civic engagement and public interaction thrive. Gehl (1987) has explored how public spaces and urban planning can be of great importance in enhancing citizen's interactivity and fashioning chances for public gatherings. Public spaces, which include statues and murals can be considered one of the oldest means of communicating messages to citizens.

Parks as means for visual influence

Parks and public gardens are becoming increasingly in demand nowadays, especially in cities where there is a need for open spaces for public interaction and entertainment. People tend to escape the hassle and bustle of busy urban environments and resort to parks for relaxation and leisure. Central parks often also embody grand cultural events like circuses and exhibitions. On the whole, parks can serve as places of substantial socializing opportunities between inhabitants (Jolé, 2002). In parks professionals retreat from the crowds during lunch-breaks, weekends or holiday periods. In busy cities like London, for instance, professionals tend to resort to public green spaces to enjoy their lunches away from their high-tech offices and steel buildings. Such spaces during sunny weather become vibrant and vivacious with people as meeting spaces or transit nodes.

In *Beyond Buildings*, Ragsdale (2014) looks at the potential of visual persuasion for designed public spaces. By analysing green public spaces such as parks, he considers the way such spaces influence the viewer. Ragsdale argues that parks, public gardens and squares are not mere gathering arenas but they have a function and social influence. Building on theories of visual communication and persuasion he further argues that parks are designed to affect the viewers and have a social impact on passers-by in such a way that they trigger a discussion or raise questions about a historical era. Tourists can be one of the social groups to whom such sites appeal most. They visit historical places specifically to learn more about local history and culture. They also find fascination in old statues, old walls and memorials planted in large parks and carefully designed green spaces.

Moreover, Ragsdale (2014) argues that public buildings such as museums are also planned to have a central presence in urban cities for an intended visual impact in the eyes of the viewers. According to him the built environment presents important elements of architectural design. It is interesting to note, for instance, the symbolic placement of the Louvre in Paris: 'the location of the Louvre at one end of the grand axis known as the Champs Élysées, as well as the museum's centrality in the city of Paris, are both elements which contribute powerfully to the visual power of the building. The grounds of such palaces as Versailles and Schönbrunn equally illustrate the visual power of the site' (Ragsdale, 2014: xiv).

However, beyond parks and green spaces, ancient civilisations developed other means for social interactivity and entertainment. Fagan (2002) for example explored the Roman public bathing experience and Roman Bath Houses as places for public bathing. Ancient Rome developed them as sites of public entertainment and characteristic of the Roman civilization. Such spaces served as communal social hubs which facilitated conversation and debates. Public baths, constituted central public spaces where Roman people meet up daily. The real motive from this exercise was not necessarily to bathe but to meet friends, drink and socialize with people from the opposite sex.

On another level, public spaces, such as town squares, may serve as sites for political activism. In his study regarding the political function of such spaces, Oldenburg (1989) maintains that public places provide significant spaces for grassroots politics. Namely in countries where large public spaces are under tight control by despotic regimes, cafes, restaurants and public gardens and town squares become the arenas where political action may galvanize. Also, this is where disenfranchised social groups find solace and support from friends and like-minded people. In a study on Polish immigrants in Phoenix (USA) and how they negotiate the social space in the city, Jolanta and Thomas (1998) suggest that 'Phoenicians navigate the complexities of modern urban space with multiple identities . . . people negotiate cultural identity largely through specialization of their experience' (1998: 25).

In some cases, public spaces around the world can be employed as settings for reinventing and consolidating citizenship and national unity. For that purpose, city planners invest concerted efforts to energise their cities with music concerts and cultural events. Music events organized by city authorities or civil society organization are nowadays significant activities not only for tourism attraction but as expressions of cultural identity. Also, traditional music festivals are in some parts of the world employed as a way to enhance economic development and cement the bond between cities' inhabitants.

Such spaces can also be made every year sites for national celebrations, commemoration and remembrance days. Their roles are usually assigned by policy-makers where certain spaces are designated for official commemorations, for instance, and others designated for national days, while others still are the settings for annual remembrance days for certain groups, such as the victims of World War I and II. In short, and considering Henry Lefebvre's contention that any space has a cumulative social history, which makes it what it is. Moreover

> 'Every social space is the outcome of a process with many aspects and many contributing currents signifying and non-signifying, perceived and directly experienced, practical and theoretical. In short, every social space has a history, one invariably grounded in nature, in natural conditions that are at once primordial and unique in the sense that they are always and everywhere endowed with specific characteristics'
>
> (Lefebvre, 1968: 110)

The communicative function of public spaces may also face various attempts to disrupt it. Authoritarian control can be one such example where dictatorships squash dissent through the total control of central public spaces/squares. The Tiananmen Square protests of 1989 in Beijing, China, where a student led protests grew into a significant movement known as the '89 Democracy Movement'. The protests were ruthlessly suppressed by army tanks and the events turned into bloody massacres. Another more recent example televised live around the world and on social media was the Rabaa massacre on 14th August 2013 in Cairo. Egyptian security forces and army tanks raided Rabaa al-Adawiya Square in central Cairo to disperse millions of supporters of elected president Mohamed Morsi who had been imprisoned after a military coup led by General Abdelfattah Sissi. The events marked a turning point in Egypt's democracy movement and a total disruption to the role of public spaces for free social and political movements after the 2011 Egyptian revolution.

Another example about the harmful disruption to the communicative function of public spaces are concrete walls constructed to physically divide neighborhoods and communities. A global peace project titled 'Painting for peace' (Bramley, 2016) highlights the danger of dividing communities and disrupting their communication using physical walls or barriers. Whether it is about the walls in Belfast, which divide Protestant and Catholic communities in Northern Ireland, or walls separating rich and poor in São Paulo, Brazil, or the separation wall erected by the Israeli government separating East Jerusalem off from the rest of the West Bank, or the three mile wall built by the American army in central Baghdad creating the 'green' or 'safe zone', all of these landmarks divide communities.

Such obstructions damage community relations and isolate groups of people across religious and ethnic lines. In a vivid description of how damaging a dividing wall can be to community communication and community relations, Wendy

Pullan, who has studied the detrimental effect of such walls, argues that what makes these walls so damaging is that they are

'often in a place where no one would have expected a wall, they divide the urban fabric – they cause spatial discontinuities. If you get that, you usually get social discontinuities as well – it cuts the normal flow of movement in a city, it means that people never encounter each other, or very rarely'

(Pullan cited in Bramley, 2016)

Reporting on the drastic impact on community relations of the 'Separation Wall' in East Jerusalem a documentary by the news organisation Al Jazeera English argues that 'it matters little what they are called – whether walls, barriers or fences – the intention is the same: to redefine human relations into 'us' and 'them'. (Al Jazeera English, 2016).

Spaces of transition versus spaces of communication

The above analysis about public spaces stands in disagreement with Westermann (2006: 190) and others' suggestions that modern public spaces have been turned into 'spaces of transition and much less into spaces of communication, a development that has become faster since mobile technology entered city spaces. It seems that people transit the modern city spaces in 'bubbles' of private spaces'. This transformation has been reinforced by social media and the ownership of smart phones. The impact of social media use in public spaces will be further discussed later on in this chapter in light of the social changes and the perception of space, but it is worth noting at this stage that the notion of space has according to them become problematic.

On the one hand and according to Nawratek (2011: 8), the term 'public space' is becoming too vague to 'effectively describe the phenomena of contemporary urban spaces'. Town squares and shopping centres as places of public interaction are according to him nearing virtual (i.e. quasi-public) spaces (*ibid*). Also, today we cannot talk anymore of the equal and universal citizen, but we rather speak of a 'multi-public' or 'counter-public'. So, modern public spaces should rather be understood as 'spaces of social interaction' instead of being proper public spaces.

On the other, different scholars have expressed their concerns about the worrying trend in public spaces embodied in the 'commodification' process that is taking place (Madanipour, 1996). This is about the dominance of entertainment and consumption in the modern shopping malls. In contemporary urban spaces, it is enough for capital and information to circulate. The conventional reason to deter from public spaces as locale for human interaction and civic involvement does not seem to matter anymore (Dean, 2009). In urban environments, modern city planners mainly consider cities as business enterprises.

This entrepreneurial approach has meant an emphasis on marketing an image of cities based on entertainment and consumption. This image-enhancing task adds to the commercial focus of public spaces and has meant that contemporary urban public spaces are becoming places of transition and less and less places of gathering or meeting. This applies to town squares and boulevards surrounded by big malls and entertainment venues which do not connect people with people, but rather people with consumption.

In a detailed study on urban commercial centres, Bauer (2004) looks at the symbolic development of Tokyo-Shibuya Crossing. This commercial district, he argues, represents a sophisticated space where entertainment, digital advertising seize peoples' attention. Visitors are bombarded with commercial messages forced on them by advertising companies. The public in this environment are monopolized and they do not seem able to influence their environment. Examples where public spaces have become sophisticated displays of commercial brands is New York Time Square, Piccadilly Circus in London, Lake Town Outlet in Japan, Les 4 Temps in district La Défense, Paris, Mall of Qatar (Doha) and The Dubai Mall in Dubai, UAE. Display screens containing publicity for global conglomerates or entertainment material has shaped the character of these places and turned public attention towards display technologies rather than what goes on in the physical space itself.

This phenomenon is arguably not restricted to the above 'mega consumption' spaces, but is characteristic of hundreds of shopping malls across urban spaces in cities around the world. Such developments have become the new face of public spaces congested with the use of technologies for communication. In such

Figure 6.2 Shibuya Crossing in Tokyo, Japan as a heavily commercialised public space.

cosmopolitan and urbanised cities, clogged with technological presence, contemporary public spaces seem to target the publics as 'consumers' more than citizens of a city.

In this sense, city squares earn their significance since they represent the centres of commerce and the locus of power in various countries. As a result of this growing commercially-driven urban environment, few critics speak about the loss of authentic public spaces even before the technological revolution in internet use and social media networks (Hannigan, 1998). The new public spaces are not anymore central parks or historical public places and memorial places but commercial centres buzzing with sophisticated advertising and consumption-driven environments. Others further question the existence of public spaces in the first place. Tonnelat (2010: 5) argues that 'more and more, commercial centers cater to specific income brackets, which means that a class selection operates seamlessly to separate the population and reproduce in the commercial realm the divisions already observed in the residential one. So where are the true public spaces?'

As an antidote to this critique, one may consider the value of public space and the monuments planted in them as a public good. Who does benefit from these spaces and who does not? How about the homeless and the disfranchised people in society? Are these spaces and monuments available to all public and enjoyed by all citizens or are they only elitist? What do they mean after all to the poor and homeless who find in these spaces only a temporary shelter? Are they primarily made for the touristic gaze as part of the modern urban infrastructure or aimed at benefiting the widest spectrum of society?

The proliferation of social media uses nowadays in public spaces and the analysis of the emerging culture of virtual communication and interaction may offer some explanations to the above questions and the problematics of conceptualizing the speedy changes of the role of public spaces and their communicative functions.

Zoning in public spaces

There has been a growing literature regarding public space and its communicative roles, especially given the growing impact of mobile technologies and how people interact in urban public spaces. The widespread embrace of internet technologies and the use of smartphones have become visible in every sphere of urban life and public squares, parks and malls are no exception.

The perception of public space and people's experiences of what goes on in those spaces is no longer confined nowadays to physical settings but social media networks have become across the world alternative virtual spaces for connectivity and interaction. Online activities on social media platforms now challenge the way we consider traditional physical spaces as key to social engagement. Studies on Facebook, Twitter, WhatsApp, Instagram, Snapchat and other virtual platforms argue that group discussions, debates and connectivity can thrive in the virtual world without people's physical meetings.

Graham (2004) discusses the extent to which electronic devices have been transforming social relations in the urban cities. Since 2004 he has observed that 'saturation of the city with mobile phones and other personal mobile ICT technologies heralds a reconstruction of the way city spaces are used, appropriated and mediated' (2004: 133). It can also be argued that new technologies, especially smart phones have nowadays fashioned new uses for public spaces in which interactivity have become less face-to-face and in favour of a virtual one. Unlike in the past when people meet and talk in public spaces, new technologies have facilitated a state of physical presence with virtual engagement linking people in various parts of the world. This has given rise to the detached individual instead of the socially engaged citizens.

Furthermore, the increasing use of smart phones in public spaces increases the zoning of those spaces where people build a type of 'mobile box', which isolate them from one-another while they are in public. Public spaces in this case seem to have fostered new roles, which are about facilitating virtual interactivity while segregating individuals into private zones. They form both physical spheres for people's interaction as well as imagined ones where individuals get isolated in virtual spheres (Aurigi and De Cindio, 2008). This amounts to a form of substitution of the physical world with the imagined or virtual 'reality'.

However, in spite of the dominance of social media as virtual platforms for communication nowadays, physical public spaces remain crucial in the lives of citizens in both urban and rural areas. Although face-to-face communication competes with online interaction and socialization, physical interaction in the real world remains the most trustworthy and consistent. For instance, for social activism and political resistance, physical spaces remain crucial and most significant. In various parts of the world large public spaces have been transformed into sites of resistance and political activism. In Rojo's words 'contemporary social movements have changed spatial forms of gathering and have claimed urban public spaces as sites of resistance. Through these new patterns, they have created and extended physical and political spaces in the power of the citizen can asserted' (2014: 584).

Conclusion

The critical approach to understanding the role of public spaces in modern urban environments is not a new trend. Various scholarly efforts by geographers, environmentalists, historians, sociologists and communication scientists have all pioneered the study of social movements and social developments in relations to public spaces.

The right to an open space in the city where people can communicate and interact freely had been heralded by the French sociologist Henri Lefebvre in his *Le Droit a la Ville* (Right to the City) (1968). The basic human right of freedom that the city should embody has been also extended by other scholars such as Hamelink (2004) who proposed the concept of the 'communicative city'. Public spaces, they argue, should be organised in a way that facilitate a link among citizens in order to enhance communication and interaction. Hamelink (2004: 298) contends that 'the right to the communicative city brings together a whole set of other human rights, such as the right to free association, to privacy and to participation in cultural life.'

The free association builds a social order where communities thrive and a healthy social bond is created between people which Castells (1989) speaks about as the development of cities as processes. In those communicative cities, public space becomes meaningful insofar as it is actively used by all citizens, albeit depending on the quality of activities which take place in it and where freedom of expression remains a decisive accompanying value.

However, as argued earlier in this chapter there appears to be a growing criticism towards the way public spaces are being transformed in connection with modern urban changes, technological developments and the way they are consumed in urban cities. This trend of thought contends that urban environments are heavily controlled and regulated nowadays through surveillance systems and systems of communication. This begs a redefinition of contemporary public spaces from spaces of social engagement and free interaction to spaces of social control and consumption.

Also, the growing paradox in these spaces leads to the emergence of a dialectic tension between the physical conception of a public space and the various activities which it traditionally embodies, like celebrations, political and social protests, and the power of market forces in turning these spaces into spaces of consumption rather than spaces of communication. Finally, the increasing concentration of virtual zoning that is taking place through these spaces due to the use of new communication technologies like smartphones is increasingly producing a binary opposition between existing in a given, physical space while being detached from people. In other words, being physically part of a public setting while belonging to a virtual or imaginary 'community' of people who are not part of that setting. Another aspect discussed in this chapter is the debate about the perceived loss of the traditional meaning of public spaces. Public spaces have become synonymous with shopping centres and entertainment venues where everything is oriented towards consumption both material and semiotic and not for encouraging debate or interaction.

In sum, the communication flows of contemporary urban environments are crucial in understanding their communicative function. In this flow then, cities are not only about buildings and urban designs, but fundamentally about people; at the core of what makes urban spaces communicative is the space where people meet and interact. So, what makes certain public spaces attractive and others off-putting? Public spaces do not develop by chance. People avoid bleak and steel buildings and look for vibrant spaces with greenery and water for relaxation. By engaging in the public space and making themselves visible people assert their right to that space and to the city itself.

Research about public spaces will keep evolving due to the significance of both urban planning and what citizens attribute to place. To this end, vibrant public spaces are necessary for a communicative city. They enhance economic growth, attract tourists, increase property value and help communities thrive. They are, also, associated with a safe environment and good public health. Social media's transformative power in shaping how we perceive public spaces and how we interact in those spaces will keep attracting even more attention due to the rapid social and technological changes and their potential impact in this area.

References

Al Jazeera English (2016). Walls of Shame: West bank separation. *Wall, TV Documentary Broadcast on July 23, 2016*. Retrieved from www.youtube.com/watch?v=3jcxFxtToF0. Accessed 28 April 2017.

Aurigi, Alessandero. and De Cindio, Fiorella. (eds.) (2008). *Augmented Urban Spaces, Articulating the Physical and Electronic City*. Hampshire: Ashgate.

Bauer, D. (2004). *The Real Time City Has Arrived* (urbane potenziale durch mobile netz-werke). Austria, Graz: Technical University of Graz.

Blazwick, Iwona. (2013). Art in public space. Lecture at TEDExAthens 2013. Retrieved from www.youtube.com/watch?v=60ETgVrHUR0. Accessed 4 April 2017.

Bramley, Ellie Violet. (2016). *Painting for peace: Global mural project highlights the walls that divide our cities*. Retrieved from www.theguardian.com/cities/2016/sep/21/inter national-peace-day-murals-painting-city-walls-separating-communities. Accessed 22 March 2017.

Castells, Manuel. (1989). *The Informational City: Information Technology, Economic Restructuring, and the Urban-Regional Process*. New York: Blackwell.

Channel 4 News (2016). *Selling space – Britain's public spaces going private*. 12 February 2016. Retrieved from www.youtube.com/watch?v=8yMuZ6m9MeE. Accessed 7 April 2017.

Dean, Jodi. (2009). *Democracy and Other Neoliberal Fantasies: Communicative Capital-ism and Left Politics*. London: Duke University Press.

Drucker, Sarah J. and Gumpert, Gary. (2009) Freedom of Expression in Communicative Cities, *Free Speech Yearbook*, 44:1, pp. 65–84.

Drzewiecka, Jolanta. and Nakayama, Thomas N. (1998). City Sites: Postmodern Urban Space and the Communication of Identity, *Southern Communication Journal*, 64:1, pp. 20–31.

Fagan, Garrett G. (2002). *Bathing in Public in the Roman World*. Ann Arbor: University of Michigan Press.

Fraser, Nancy. (1992) 'Rethinking the Public Sphere: A Contribution to the Critique of Actually Existing Democracy', in Calhoun, C. (ed.), *Habermas and the Public Sphere* (pp. 109–142). Cambridge, MA: MIT Press.

Graham, Stephen. (ed.) (2004). *Cybercities Reader*. London: Routledge.

Habermas, J. (1989). *The Structural Transformation of the Public Sphere: An Inquiry into a Category of Bourjeois Society*. Boston: The MIT Press.

Hamelink, Cees. (2004). *Human Rights for Communicators*. New York: Hampton.

Hannigan, John. (1998). *Fantasy City: Pleasure and Profit in the Postmodern Metropolis*. London and New York: Routledge.

Jolé, Michèle. (ed.) (2002). *Espaces publics et cultures urbaines (Public Spaces and Urban Cultures)*. Paris: CERTU.

Lefebvre, Henri. (1968). *Le Droit à la ville (Right to the City)*. Paris: Anthropos (2nd ed.). Paris: Ed. du Seuil, Collection Points.

Lefebvre, Henri. (1991). *The Production of Space*. Oxford, England: Blackwell.

Madanipour, Ali. (1996). *Design of Urban Space*. New York: John Wiley & Sons.

Mitchell, Don. (1995) The End of Public Space? People's Park, Definitions of the Public, and Democracy, *Annals of the Association of American Geographers*, 85:1, pp. 108–133.

Mitchell, Don. (2003). *The Right to the City: Social Justice and the Fight for Public Space*. New York: Guilford Press.

Nawratek, Krzysztof. (2011). Rejecting the Communicative Paradigm of Public Space, *International Journal of Humanities and Social Science*, 1:4. Retrieved from www.ijhss net.com/journals/Vol._1_No._4;_April_2011/2.pdf. Accessed 22 March 2017.

Oldenburg, Ray. (1989). *The Great Good Place: Cafés, Coffee Shops, Community Centers, Beauty Parlors, General Stores, Bars, Hangouts, and How They Get You through the Day*. New York: Paragon House.

Ragsdale, J. Donald. (2014). *Beyond Buildings: Designed Spaces as Visual Persuasion*. Newcastle upon Tyne: Cambridge Scholars Publishing.

Rojo, Luisa Martin. (2014). Occupy: The Spatial Dynamics of Discourse in Global Protest Movements, *Journal of Language and Politics*, 13:4, pp. 583–598.

Rovisco, Maria. and Ong, Jonathan Corpus. (eds.) (2016). *Taking the Square: Mediated Dissent and Occupations of Space*. London: Rowman and Littlefield.

Schmidt, Stephen. and Németh, Jeremy. (2010). Space, Place and the City: Emerging Research on Public Space Design and Planning, *Journal of Urban Design*, 15:4, pp. 453–457.

Tonnelat, Stéphane. (2010). The Sociology of Urban Public Spaces. Wang, H., Savy, M. and Zhai, G. (eds.), *Territorial Evolution and Planning Solution: Experiences from China and France*. Paris: Atlantis Press.

Townsend, Anthony. (2004) Digitally Mediated Urban Space: New Lessons for Design, *Praxis*, 6. Retrieved from www.anthonymobile.com/wp-content/uploads/townsend-praxis.pdf. Accessed 24 March 2017.

War Memorials (2007). *Functions of memorials*. https://warmemorial.wordpress.com/2007/02/07/functions-of-memorials/. Accessed 22 March 2017.

Westermann, Claudia. (2006). Who Plays the Nightingale? Ascot, R., *Engineering Nature: Art and Consciousness in the Post-Biological Era* (pp. 189–194). Bristol: Intellect.

7 A time and place

The Las Vegas Mob Museum's experiential public relations

Jessalynn Strauss

It only took one dollar. For $1 – perhaps the least well-known but most important dollar spent during the development of Las Vegas, Nevada as a tourist destination – the City of Las Vegas secured possession of an old courthouse and post office that had outlived its federal duties. Today, located in the same building that housed some of the very events it recreates, the National Museum of Organised Crime and Law Enforcement – or, as it is more colloquially known, the Mob Museum – plays a pivotal role in Las Vegas's ongoing reinvention as a multifaceted tourist destination.

In its first four years of operation, the Mob Museum welcomed over one million visitors and earned a spot on numerous top-10 lists for Las Vegas tourists (Awards and Accolades, 2017). Located in the city's downtown Fremont Street neighborhood, this venture started as a bit of a gamble: While the downtown area housed many of Las Vegas's early casinos in the first half of the twentieth century, the neighborhood faded as megaresorts built up along the well-known Las Vegas Strip, about three miles away. But in 2002, then-Mayor Oscar Goodman purchased the former federal building (Figure 7.1) for the purpose of developing the Mob Museum, which would ultimately open on February 14, 2012 (Green, 2013; Skolnik, 2008).

This chapter examines the role of the Mob Museum as a crucial component in the public relations and marketing efforts of the city of Las Vegas. In the wake of the 2008 global recession, the city changed its marketing strategy considerably in order to emphasize non-gambling aspects of the popular tourist destination. Museums (the Neon Museum or 'Boneyard' is also included in this effort) added a cultural/heritage component that could be promoted alongside other elements such as dining, shopping, live entertainment and, of course, gambling.

The museum focuses on one of the most notorious elements of Las Vegas's history: the organized crime figures who were involved in the casino industry through the middle part of the twentieth-century. The Mob's direct involvement in casinos seems pretty far in Las Vegas's rearview mirror by now: By the time Steve Wynn opened his megaresort Mirage in 1989, kicking off the modern era of Las Vegas's economic development, organized crime in Las Vegas had largely been eradicated. But the early years of the city's history were littered with the names of well-known mobsters such as Bugsy Siegel, Meyer Lansky, and Moe Dalitz, all of whom are represented in the museum.

Figure 7.1 This former federal courthouse building, which now houses the Mob Museum, was purchased by then-mayor of Las Vegas Oscar Goodman for $1.

The Mob Museum serves as a key site for the modern development of Las Vegas as a tourist destination. As a museum, its exhibits construct an image of Las Vegas's past that will inevitably impact the way that tourists and visitors perceive the city. By examining the museum's historical context and the way that its collection communicates with the museum visitor, this chapter will show how the development and operation of the Mob Museum have played an important role in the public relations and marketing efforts of the city of Las Vegas and will consider how a place can communicate with audiences as part of a larger strategic plan.

Literature review

The following literature review first provides a brief introduction of concepts in museum theory that are relevant to the case at hand. The literature review next looks more specifically at the case of Las Vegas's Mob Museum and the role that its development has played in successfully completing the city's efforts to promote itself as a multifaceted tourist destination.

Key concepts in museum theory

The contemporary U.S. museum shares little in common with its historical forbears outside of the name. Throughout history, museums have served a number of purposes: They have promoted religions through the exhibition of artifacts, provoked deep thought and contemplation of art, and housed the valuable artifacts of an era under the watchful eye of a guide or curator (Alexander & Alexander, 2007). History museums in particular have, in some ways, written the history of the state in a way that supports the goals of democracy by creating an educated citizenry (Gable, 2006). Recently, the focus of museums has shifted to the education and experience of their audiences (Alexander & Alexander, 2007; Low, 2004), often in the name of public service (Weil, 2004).

Additionally, evidence has shown that museums can be successful drivers of economic growth or redevelopment (Iorio & Wall, 2011; Plaza, 2000; Tufts & Milne, 1999). However, the idea of the museum as an economic entity alienates its allegiances somewhat from both the traditional purview of museums (collection, preservation) to the more contemporary role of education. Museum funding always comes with a price, whether from a government that seeks to advance an ideology or redevelop an urban area, a corporation that seeks to brand itself as socially responsible, or a foundation that seeks to promote its own mission or goals (Marstine, 2006). Seeking funding through the tourist dollar may be a more palatable option for a museum, although it may have to simplify or 'dumb down' label text in order to capture a more mainstream audience (Marstine, 2006).

While we commonly consider museums authoritative, objective institutions, Marstine (2006) points out that this impression is vastly oversimplified:

> Decisions that museum workers make – about mission statement, architecture, financial matters, acquisitions, cataloguing, exhibition display, wall texts, educational programming, repatriation requests, community relations, conservation, web design, security and reproduction – all impact on the way we understand objects. Museums are not neutral spaces that speak with one institutional, authoritative voice. Museums are about individuals making subjective choices
> (2006: 2)

By making these choices – which items are to be included in the collection and how they are to be displayed, among others – museums have the ability to create an image or identity, which is affected by the curation of the exhibit (Gable, 2006). This includes not only the choice of objects, but also the prominence with which certain artifacts are displayed, the flow and order of the museum exhibits, and the text on labels used to identify and provide context for the items in the collection (Alexander & Alexander, 2007; Roberts, 2004).

In cultural/heritage museums, this interpretive choice can affect the way that audiences perceive a particular native group (Minghetti, Moretti, & Micelli, 2000). Weaver (2011) defines heritage tourism as 'visited spaces deemed, usually by experts, to constitute or contain the heritage of a destination' (p. 249). Many audiences, especially tourist publics, seek out heritage opportunities to escape from their own reality and the complexities of the modern world (Chhabra, 2008; Harrison, 1997).

> [Tourists] look for cultural diversity and authenticity. Local museums can provide a point of entry to such cultures by exhibiting and thereby authenticating

aspects of the culture which [sic] tourists are seeking to discover. They introduce visitors to local heritage or, at least, to what has been selected to represent local identity

(Iorio & Wall, 2011: 4)

Heritage tourism has become contested territory lately, with concerns that heritage sites can create artificial distinctions of 'others' or portray history in an inherently political way (Poria & Ashworth, 2009). History museums, in particular,
often misrepresent the very history they claim to portray in ways that have significant, unintended consequences (Loewen, 1999).

Additionally, because many of these museums exist as economic growth drivers and as such depend on attendance to succeed in that mission, their messages
must be palatable and uncontroversial to the potential visitor. This highlights a
critical disconnect in the use of museums in this dual economic/educational role:
In order to attract visitors, museums must accentuate their 'localness,' even if it
is done in a trivial or overly simplified, superficial manner that confirms tourists'
perceptions. However, in order to perform a truly educational role, museums must
challenge incorrect assumptions even if it detracts from the "enjoyment" function
of the museum (Harrison, 1997).

Keeping in mind that 'musing and amusement are interrelated' (Alexander &
Alexander, 2007: 4), it should come as no surprise that recently, museums have
begun to take on characteristics of entertainment. Perhaps due to the need to capture the attention of the elusive tourist dollar, "the museum has borrowed from
the cinema and the theme park to become a spectacle that engages all the senses,
whether staged to evoke an aesthetic experience, a historical context, or an interactive learning environment" (Marstine, 2006: 13).

The use of traditional advertising and marketing techniques to promote museums
to a mass audience has only served to further this conception of museum-as-product:

Banners and billboards on museum fronts indicate how close the museum has
moved to the world of spectacle, of the popular fair and mass entertainment.
The museum itself has been sucked into the maelstrom of modernization:
museum shows are managed and advertised as major spectacles with cal-
culable benefits for sponsors, organizers, and city budgets, and the claim to
fame of any major metropolis will depend considerably on the attractiveness
of its museal sites.

(Huyssen, 1995: 21)

Thus, the tourist-centered museum, described by Huyseen as a 'mass medium'
(1995: 14), serves an important communicative role: Because out-of-town visitors
largely comprise its audience, it conveys an important message about the city's history and image to those who might not have a pre-existing notion about the location.

This concept seems especially salient in the case of Las Vegas's Mob Museum
because of the historical link between the city's image and the museum's subject,
organized crime. The carefully controlled narrative of the city's image has long

been institutionalized in its marketing strategy; 'what happens here, stays here' is more than just an advertising slogan as far as Las Vegans are concerned (Green, 2013). Popular myth amplifies the role of mobsters, such as Benjamin 'Bugsy' Siegel, in the development of Las Vegas's casinos (Gragg, 2010) despite the fact that most of the city's early casinos were built by a combination of businessmen, primarily from Los Angeles (Lillisview, 2011; Schwartz, 2012). For years, Las Vegas tried desperately to refute these myths and eliminate the public's association of the city with organized crime (Strauss, 2015) – which is probably why Mayor Goodman's decision to build the Mob Museum came as such a surprise to many.

Building the Mob Museum

The timeline of the Mob Museum, from conception to construction, fell during a unique period in the city's and the nation's history. The museum was originally proposed in the first half of the 2000s, when Las Vegas's Strip was experiencing unprecedented growth and financial success. The older Downtown area, however, has struggled to compete since the Strip developed its larger hotel-casinos, and later mega-resorts, in the latter half of the 20th century (Trejos, 2013). In the mid-1990s, the casinos in the Downtown area banded together to build the Fremont Street Experience, a pedestrian mall with a big-screen video canopy that was billed as a 'sky parade' (History, n.d.). (Figure 7.2) Despite updates to the video display in 2004, visitor traffic to the downtown casinos declined, and the

Figure 7.2 The Golden Gate Hotel-Casino, seen here, has been operational in some fashion since 1906 and sits at the end of the Fremont Street Experience, a canopy (seen top left) that turns into a screen for nightly video and music shows.

area's development was further stymied when a planned extension of the city's monorail, which would have linked the Strip with Downtown, never came to fruition (Roembke, 2004).

The Mob Museum's concept first became public in the late 2000s with an Associated Press article (2007: 1) detailing plans to build 'a museum about some of [Las Vegas's] founding fathers and most influential figures – guys with names like Bugsy, Lefty and Lansky.[1] Market research showed that tourists would support such a museum, but the idea met with considerable controversy from the Las Vegas community (Skolnik, 2008). Influential board members recruited to support the development of the museum included a casino executive, a former senator, a local television news director, and even a former FBI agent who once headed the Las Vegas office. The product secured federal funding and traded on its historic building to build support from outside Las Vegas (Waiser, 2010).

But the Mob Museum's timing, much like the lives of those it profiles, was ill-fated. From a high of nearly 40 million tourists in 2007, the number of visitors to Las Vegas dropped nearly 8% over the next two years as the global recession caused potential tourists to tighten their belts (Historical Las Vegas Visitor Statistics, 2017). Large Strip casinos saw their revenues plunge and lowered room rates in order to remain competitive (Wells, 2009), pricing out the once-cheaper hotel options in the Downtown area. The museum's attempts to procure funds through the federal government's American Recovery and Reinvestment Plan, more commonly known as "stimulus" funds, raised the ire of federal legislators who derided both the museum's focus and its purported ability to stimulate Las Vegas's flagging economy (Friess, 2009).

Then-mayor Oscar Goodman, an ardent promoter of the Mob Museum project, fought back against government criticsand pushed forward with plans for the museum (Skolnik, 2009a). Rehabilitation of the building and development of the museum's collection continued apace, with the acquisition of important artifacts such as the brick wall involved in the St. Valentine's Day Massacre, an infamous mob shooting in Chicago (Katsilometes, 2009). (Figure 7.3)

The museum acquired the needed federal monies as well city and state funds from cultural budgets and sales taxes (Toplikar, 2009; Velotta, 2010); ultimately, the project procured a total of $42 million in public funds (Johnson, 2012). Dennis Barrie, co-creator of well-known tourist-centered museums in Cleveland (Rock and Roll Hall of Fame) and Washington, D.C. (International Spy Museum), was hired to curate the museum's exhibits, describing the museum as 'engaging and exciting and entertaining, but it also has a serious story to tell' (Toplikar, 2010).

With an originally forecast completion date of 2010 (Associated Press, 2007), the Mob Museum finally opened its doors on February 14, 2012. During its lengthy birthing process, the museum met with significant challenges; as the subhead from a newspaper article about the museum proclaimed, 'Planners find it's not easy promoting high-profile project while keeping it serious' (Skolnik, 2009b). The museum's image suffered significantly from its entanglement with the discourse over government spending, with one local editorial proclaiming two days before its opening, 'The Mob Museum has become synonymous with pork-barrel spending

Figure 7.3 The museum's key acquisition of the St. Valentine's Day Massacre wall, shown here, fueled its development. The wall, which still bears bullet holes and blood stains, served as the backdrop for the execution-style murders of seven Irish gang members by hired killers linked to the legendary Al Capone.

and irresponsible government in a time when many families are struggling to make ends meet' (Johnson, 2012).

By the time the museum opened in 2012, however, Las Vegas *needed* the Mob Museum. Although visitor numbers had risen somewhat since the recession, visitors were spending less on gambling, Las Vegas's traditional source of income (Nagourney, 2013). Dining and shopping had successfully assumed a place alongside the traditional tourist options of gambling and live entertainment, but the city was seeking to expand those options to attract an even wider range of potential visitors. The Mob Museum was, at the same time, both a natural and an odd choice to fill this void: Natural, because the city's history is inextricably intertwined with the elements of organized crime in its past, and odd, because Las Vegas spent many years trying to rid itself of the appearance of organized crime ties, primarily for the purpose of gaining corporate investment in its casino gaming industry (Strauss, 2015).

Opening in 2012, the Mob Museum also played a timely role in grassroots efforts to revitalize the downtown/Fremont Street neighborhood, once the hub of Las Vegas's economic activity. As Las Vegas grew in the 1950s and 1960s, enterprising casino owners realized the economic benefits of building outside the city lines, and what we now know as 'the Strip' developed an unincorporated area south of Downtown that would come to be known as the town of Paradise. As the

Strip thrived through the end of the twentieth century, the downtown area decayed (Heathcote, 2012). The building of the Mob Museum, however, held promise for community-based efforts to revitalize Las Vegas's urban core, as cultural museums are shown to benefit the business in the surrounding neighborhoods (Iorio & Wall, 2011).

As host of community events such as lectures and blood drives, the Mob Museum has clearly had a positive intangible impact on the downtown community (Carter, 2013); the direct economic impact has so far been unclear. The success of the museum itself has been more apparent – the museum paid back the first of four annual $1.5 million re-payments to the city in a symbolic suitcase full of cash, a cleverly done publicity stunt that was dutifully recorded in the local newspaper (Press, 2014). Regularly mentioned in discussions of Downtown's burgeoning redevelopment efforts (Schwartz, 2013; Shine, 2013), the museum continually seeks to improve upon its already-respectable visitor numbers.

The decision to pin the hopes of Las Vegas's economic resurgence on the Mob Museum signals quite clearly that, rather than running from its 'mobbed-up' past, Las Vegas is embracing it with open arms. But it bears considering whether a Mob Museum is really the kind of cultural/heritage tourism that the city should be programming, and what implications such a museum might have for tourist perceptions of Las Vegas.

This chapter addresses two research questions:

> RQ1: How has the Mob Museum used public relations tactics including more traditional efforts (media relations and special events) and less conventional ones such as space and exhibition?
>
> RQ2: How can space and place contribute to a public relations effort or campaign?

Method

This examination of the Mob Museum draws from two primary sources: articles in the popular press (local newspapers the Las Vegas *Sun* and Las Vegas *Review-Journal*, in addition to national newspaper coverage of the museum) and the museum itself, including its collection, the text on exhibit labels, and the physical building.

News articles were collected by searching for the term 'mob museum' on Google and Lexis-Nexis Academic. Although the full name of the museum is 'The National Museum of Organized Crime and Law Enforcement,' the shorter name is used more frequently in news articles due to the unwieldy length of the full name.

Observations of the museum, as well as photographic records, were collected during trips to the museum in April 2013, June 2014, and May 2016. These collection opportunities allowed the researcher to delve deeply into the material and view a variety of exhibits. Photos used in this chapter were taken during the May 2016 visit.

During the second visit, the research made careful observations in the specific elements of museum exhibition identified by Alexander and Alexander (2007):

- Concept/message
- Story line
- Objects displayed as part of the exhibit(s)
- Setting, which may include elements of the building created for the museum and layout of the museum

While performing observations in the museum, the researcher also heeded Marstine's (2006) suggestion that museum exhibits needed to be critically viewed by '[looking] at what museums don't say – what is implicit – as well as what they do state – what is explicit' (p4).

Information gathered from the newspaper articles and from observations in the museum are discussed in the next section. These results are separated according to their ability to answer one of the two research questions posed in the previous section.

Results

The museum as public relations technique

Museum exhibits are, by their nature, communicative (Alexander & Alexander, 2007). While many museums have adapted to fit modern market pressures by reorienting their focus on audiences and employing traditional marketing techniques to increase their patronage, this chapter considers the Mob Museum as an example of a museum that was developed for the purpose of fulfilling a larger strategic communication goal: The overall promotion of the city of Las Vegas as a tourist destination with a diverse range of entertainment options for visitors. This section considers the answer to the first research question by looking at the use of media relations by the Mob Museum, its engagement in community relations, and its use of special events to establish and maintain relationships.

Traditional public relations

A number of factors contributed to the prominence of the Mob Museum as a local news story. The ten-year timeline from the building's purchase to its opening date established the Mob Museum as a long-term, ongoing project in the community. When the Mob Museum's use of federal stimulus funds for development reached the national news, the museum suddenly catapulted into the national spotlight. The museum's unique focus, and the historical association of Las Vegas with organized crime, established it from the start as a story with a good news hook for travel and historic preservation publications as well as lifestyle programming in national media outlets.

Even before its opening, however, the Mob Museum scheduled a number of media-friendly opportunities to engage with local and national reporters in an active media relations campaign. Two and a half years before the museum even opened, a news conference to announce the beginning of the building's internal construction featured supportive Mayor Oscar Goodman and revealed a key piece of the museum's collection, the wall from the St. Valentine's Day Massacre, had been obtained (Katsilometes, 2009). Less than a year later, the mayor participated in a media tour of the still-under-construction museum, giving museum directors an opportunity to describe both the proposed content of the museum as well as its educational/experiential goals (Katsilometes, 2010).

Later media-friendly events included a briefing of the Las Vegas Convention and Visitors' Authority by the museum's executive director in October 2010 (Velotta, 2010) and finally, the museum's lavish grand opening in 2012 (Wingert, 2012). As mentioned previously, the Mob Museum has taken strategic advantage of even mundane events such as loan paybacks to hold events and cultivate a relationship with reporters so that it might receive recognition in the local and national press (Press, 2014). Prior media relations campaigns have successfully attracted the attention of national press to Las Vegas (Evans, 1999) and the Mob Museum has effectively carried on this tradition, serving a larger purpose of reaching wide audiences of potential visitors and informing them of this new addition to Las Vegas's stable of tourist attractions.

Although it was designed to target out-of-town visitors, the Mob Museum's organizers realized early on that the museum would not be able to survive alone on tourists for revenue. After all, it's unlikely that even a fraction of a percentage of Las Vegas's nearly 40 million yearly visitors intentionally planned their trip in order to check out the city's museums, and the Mob Museum (and other cultural opportunities) was forced to compete with a host of other entertainment options for tourists, including the historical draw for visitors to Las Vegas – gambling.

Mob Museum staff have dedicated considerable effort to building relationships with the community of Clark County, where Las Vegas is located, which recently passed the 2 million mark in population. A writer from local magazine *Vegas Seven* described the museum's success in attracting a community audience:

> This museum has cracked the event-programming code, persuading crowds from the full demographic spectrum and far corners of the Las Vegas Valley to forego their sitcoms and social clubs for an evening, drive Downtown and sit on hardwood benches for an hour listening to people talk about history – an accomplishment that, in the long run, is worth a hundred Travel + Leisure endorsements.
>
> (Kyser, 2013: 5)

As this writer indicates, the substantial population of retirees in the Las Vegas area is a boon for the museum, as these demographics tend to have more free time and participate more frequently in community events.

While many of the museum's events have an educational focus, it also sponsors events that are more social, such as its celebration of 'Repeal Day,' described as 'a booze-soaked blowout in honor of the end of Prohibition' (Kyser, 2013: 11). This variety of events allows the museum to attract all adult members of the community and cross demographic lines that often prove challenging to museums. However, the Mob Museum's subject matter presents a challenge in connecting with the community; its description of organized crime, while somewhat sanitized, is not exactly child-friendly, thus preventing the kinds of community partnerships with schools that traditionally boost museums' community relations efforts.

Although it operates as a nonprofit entity, the Mob Museum's media prominence has supported the city's efforts to attract tourist dollars. Even before its opening, it provided the opportunity to attract media attention both locally and internationally, with newspapers in far-flung places like Canada and Ireland profiling the museum and its strange tie to the city's history (Coughlan, 2013; Pratt, 2012). Its events have engaged the local community with the museum's efforts, and this combination of public relations events has created communication with both local and tourist publics. The next section looks at the physical space of the museum itself and considers the potential contributions of its exhibitions to the effort to promote tourism in Las Vegas.

The space and place of the Mob Museum

The building's setting is one of its advantages. Built in the former Federal Courthouse that served Las Vegas from 1933–2002, the Mob Museum uses the building itself as an artifact that ties into Las Vegas's history of organized crime and law enforcement. It is an imposing brick structure, and as one walks up the marble steps to the entrance, one can imagine how many of Las Vegas's most notorious figures took the same walk on their way to federal hearings or criminal trials.

Locating the Mob Museum in the courthouse allows the museum to accentuate one of its strengths: providing an authentic and realistic experience. Restored elements of the courthouse, such as the elevators, add to the scene. The objects in the museum's collection enhance this sense of authenticity. The museum's centerpiece object, the wall featured in the 1929 St. Valentine's Day Massacre, is joined by a vast collection of memorabilia from law enforcement, casinos, and organized crime history. Various rooms in the museum are decorated to invoke the time period of organized crime's heyday and piped-in music further enhances the immersive mood.

In one elaborately staged exhibit, visitors view a multimedia presentation of the Kefauver Hearings on Organized Crime. This presentation features audio and video recreations of the hearings, which occurred when then-U.S. Senator Estes Kefauver tried to root out organized crime and corruption in various American cities during the years 1950–1951. Visitors view this presentation 'in the very room' where the Las Vegas hearing occurred in 1950 – and the 8-minute film reminds you of this three times. (Figure 7.4)

All of these touches make it all the more surprising when the visitor exits a room showing a film about movie portrayals of the mob – darkened and decorated in plush red velvet featuring seating at cabaret-style booths – into the museum's gift shop. In addition to the traditional gift-shop paraphernalia – mugs, t-shirts – the

Figure 7.4 This room housed the Las Vegas hearing for the Kefauver Committee on Organized Crime in the 1950s. The multimedia presentation shown in this room puts
the visitor in a very particular physical and temporal space by recreating the
testimony of organized crime figures – many of whom were also early casino
owners.

store features organized crime related items of both an educational (books and
DVDs) and memorabilia nature. Organized crime's past ties to bootlegging are
represented by flasks and 'non-alcoholic moonshine'; its violent heritage is evoked
in a coffee mug with brass knuckles for a handle. There are sheriff's badges, among
other items, to represent the museum's secondary focus on law enforcement.

Alexander and Alexander (2007) discuss the museum's ability to tell visitors
a story, and in this light the Mob Museum delivers a very interesting message
through exhibit text and multimedia presentations. The museum's exhibits begin
with 'The Mob in America,' an exhibit that looks at the early days of organized
crime, which it locates primarily in ethnic immigrant communities in New Orleans,
New York and Chicago. A film ties the mob's start to anti-immigrant sentiment in
'slums' and 'ghettos' and describes the actions of organized crime operatives as an
attempt to take 'a shortcut to the American Dream.' In this film, mob members are
shown in contrast to the stereotypical immigrants of the early 1900s who earned
the 'American Dream' of success through hard work.

Although the museum presents a history of both organized crime and law
enforcement efforts, the placement of exhibits seems to give preference to the
former. (The museum gives visitors very clear instructions on how to proceed
through the exhibits, beginning with the history of the Mob and continuing through

a history of Las Vegas's establishment as a haven for gambling and vice.) By number, a large majority of the museum's exhibits focus on organized crime, not law enforcement, although considerable attention is given to the law's attempts to fight the mob, including an exhibit called 'America Fights Back.'

The title of this exhibit is especially interesting given other exhibits' association of organized crime with immigrant populations. Although unintentional, this juxta-position leaves a somewhat xenophobic aftertaste, where mobsters are portrayed as immigrants trying to achieve 'great wealth with no work' (in the words of mobster Lefty Rosenthal) and law enforcement officers are seen as enforcers of the hard work and rule-following required to legitimately achieve the American Dream.

Discussion

Over 40 million visitors per year come to the town of Las Vegas, and another 2 million live permanently in the Las Vegas area. From a business perspective, this represents a powerful market potential for any museum; the constant influx of tourists is especially attractive because this population is continually changing. As Las Vegas directs its marketing efforts at an increasingly diversified population, the Mob Museum offers a new cultural opportunity to a visitor base increasingly interested in activities other than gambling.

This research considered the use of the museum as a public relations tactic in two ways. By utilizing traditional public relations strategies such as media relations and community relations, the Mob Museum has established its pres-ence in the Las Vegas community and its prominence as a cultural institution in a place that, to the tourist or outside observer, seems to be lacking in such things. Due to bad timing, the Mob Museum's receipt of federal funding briefly drew it into a larger media discourse about federal spending. However, the majority of news coverage of the museum has been positive, and its global reach has helped the museum fulfill its ambitions of driving Las Vegas tourism. Clearly, the Mob Museum has contributed to the city of Las Vegas's efforts to go outside its tradi-tional playbook – gambling and the 'what happens in Vegas, stays in Vegas' ethic of adult freedom – to broaden its appeal.

In addition to the public relations efforts undertaken to promote the Mob Museum to local customers and tourists alike, the museum itself serves as com-municative vehicle that sends messages to visitors through its use of space, place, and experience. An analysis of the space itself shows a heavy prioritization of organized crime while the law enforcement element of the museum is somewhat downplayed. In addition, the discussion of organized crime with respect to immi-grant communities has potential implications of xenophobia, which is concerning in a city that has an extremely high population of illegal immigrants (Lapan, 2012).

The museum's topical focus, as well as the messages delivered by its exhibits, leave no doubt in the mind of the visitor that the connection between Las Vegas and organized crime is a strong one. This helps to cement the representation of Las Vegas as a 'tough little town,' the title of an exhibit that tells the story of Las Vegas's early days. (Figure 7.5)

Figure 7.5 The introductory text to this exhibit on Las Vegas history reads, in part, "What were the odds? A city sprouts in the desert and becomes a global capital of adult entertainment and extravagance – a place where anything seems possible." This slightly more elaborated image of Las Vegas goes beyond its historical image as an "adult playground" and creates an image of an underdog fighting against long odds in a place of infinite possibilities.

The stories of organized crime figures such as Meyer Lansky, Bugsy Siegel, and Moe Dalitz, intertwined with Las Vegas's history, portray these men as leading figures in the community. In this way, the city of Las Vegas plays a key role in a recurring 'bad-boy-gone-good' narrative that shows gangsters transformed into legitimate businessmen.

The decision made by then-Las Vegas Mayor Oscar Goodman to build a 'mob museum' was certainly a controversial one. In addition to questioning whether the museum could succeed financially, the museum's opponents suggested that the city should not be tying its image to organized crime when it had previously tried to downplay or even deny this association. In fact, the city's casinos long struggled to obtain corporate investors because of the perception that they were associated with organized crime.

But ultimately, including the city's organized crime history via the exhibits of the Mob Museum has allowed Las Vegas to advance a richer, more complex history and narrative to potential visitors. With the expansion of gambling into neighborhoods across the United States, the city's initial draw – legalized casino gambling – no longer exerts the same pull on potential visitors. By enabling the city to broaden the scope of Las Vegas's appeal, the exhibits housed in the Mob Museum – and even the building itself – help to elaborate the city's image by offering experiences to visitors that bring Las Vegas's mob history to life.

Future research

So far, over 1 million people have visited the Mob Museum. Future research could address these visitors directly, assessing whether they have changed their perceptions about Las Vegas's affiliation with organized crime, both historical and contemporary. Research could also determine to what extent they have received the museum's vaguely xenophobic message about the immigrants who comprised many of the early mob organizations, and whether it may have affected their perception of immigrants.

Future research could also compare the Mob Museum in Las Vegas to other museums that address their own location and history. Perhaps, despite its salacious title and topic, the Mob Museum is not much different from other local history museums throughout the world.

Conclusion

In just over 100 years, the city of Las Vegas has seen a lot of changes. Once merely a stop on the railroad, Las Vegas has become one of the world's top destinations for both leisure and business. As modern market pressures force Las Vegas to diversify its tourist options, the Mob Museum has stepped in to provide a new historical and cultural opportunity for both the city's tourists and its more than two million residents.

When compared to museums that showcase the progress of human history or tackle weighty issues such as the Holocaust or civil rights, the focus of the National

Museum of Organized Crime and Law Enforcement might seem a little superficial. However, the history of Las Vegas is inextricably intertwined with modern American history. Rather than denying or downplaying the connection, the Mob Museum has stepped up to own it. In doing so, the museum has controlled the narrative about organized crime in for Las Vegas visitors and residents alike, becoming a defining authority on organized crime's role in the casino industry.

Moreover, the museum has contributed to the redevelopment of Las Vegas's downtown and helped evolve the city's relationships with tourists by providing a story for national media to cover. By providing an opportunity to promote media relations at the local and national level, and by engaging in the community, the Mob Museum is not merely fulfilling former mayor Goodman's dream of attracting tourists to Las Vegas's mob heritage; it is also promoting relationships with a number of stakeholder publics. In this way, the museum serves as an innovative public relations tactic for the city both through traditional means such as media relations and through its ability to convey messages experientially to its visitors.

Note

1 Goodman was no stranger to pushing back against government opponents: When President Barack Obama suggested that Las Vegas was an unsuitable business travel location for "responsible" businesses, especially those receiving federal bailout funds, Goodman publicly called out the president, saying the comments were "harmful" to the city's attempts to extricate itself from a perilous financial situation in a town where convention attendance accounted for a large percentage of visitors. (Causey, 2014).

References

Alexander, E. P., & Alexander, M. (2007). *Museums in Motion: An Introduction to the History and Functions of Museums*. Lanham, MD: Rowman Altamira.

Associated Press. (2007, December 10). Las Vegas plans to open Mob Museum. *Msnbc. com*. Retrieved from www.nbcnews.com/id/22187515/ns/travel-destination_travel/t/las-vegas-plans-open-mob-museum/

Awards and Accolades. (n.d.). *The Mob Museum*. Retrieved April 7, 2017, from http://themobmuseum.org/awards-and-accolades/

Carter, G. (2013, January 13). Married to the Museum. *Vegas Seven*. Retrieved from http://vegasseven.com/2013/01/31/married-museum/

Causey, A. K. (2014, January 26). Is modern Las Vegas really 'Sin City'? *Las Vegas Review-Journal*. Retrieved from www.reviewjournal.com/

Chhabra, D. (2008). Positioning museums on an authenticity continuum. *Annals of Tourism Research, 35*(2), 427–447.

Coughlan, F. (2013, June 1). VIVA LOST VEGAS: This glittering city in the Nevada desert is a blur of casinos, but there is a lot more to be found if you bother to look, says Frank Coughlan. *Irish Independent*. Retrieved from https://www.independent.ie/life/travel/viva-lost-vegas-29312524.html

Evans, K. J. (1999, February 7). Maxwell Kelch. *Las Vegas Review Journal*. Retrieved from http://www.lvrj.com

Friess, S. (2009, January 10). Stimulus money for a Mob Museum: Got a problem? *The New York Times*. Retrieved from www.nytimes.com/2009/01/10/us/10mob.html

Gable, E. (2006). How we study history museums: Or cultural studies at Monticello. In J. Marstine (Ed.), *New Museum Theory and Practice: An Introduction* (pp. 109–128). Malden, MA: Blackwell Publishing.

Gragg, L. (2010). Promoting post-war Las Vegas: The live wire fund, 1945–1950. *International Journal of Arts and Sciences, 3*, 9–16.

Green, M. (2013). How the Mob (Museum) was won: Building a history of organized crime in the U.S. *UNLV Gaming Research & Review Journal, 17*(2), 101–105.

Harrison, J. (1997). Museums and touristic expectations. *Annals of Tourism Research, 24*(1), 23–40.

Heathcote, E. (2012, April 28). Gamble to revitalise the city's downtown starts to pay off: Postcard from . . . Las Vegas. *Financial Times (London, England)*, p. 8.

Historical Las Vegas Visitor Statistics (1970–2016). (2017, February). *Las Vegas Convention and Visitors Authority (LVCVA)*. Retrieved from www.lvcva.com/includes/content/images/media/docs/Historical-1970-to-2016.pdf

History. (n.d.). *Fremont Street Experience*. Retrieved from www.vegasexperience.com/#/about/

Huyssen, A. (1995). *Twilight Memories: Marking Time in a Culture of Amnesia*. New York, NY: Routledge.

Iorio, M., & Wall, G. (2011). Local museums as catalysts for development: Mamoiada, Sardinia, Italy. *Journal of Heritage Tourism, 6*(1), 1–15.

Johnson, D. (2012, February 12). Taxpayers get whacked at Mob Museum. *Las Vegas Review-Journal*. Retrieved from www.reviewjournal.com/

Katsilometes, J. (2009, August 4). Goodman marks Mob Museum progress – Las Vegas Sun News. *Las Vegas Sun*. Retrieved from www.lasvegassun.com/

Katsilometes, J. (2010, May 25). Goodman tours Mob Museum, says 'there is no competition'. *Las Vegas Sun*. Retrieved from www.lasvegassun.com/

Kyser, H. (2013, June 25). Cracking the code of cultural cred. *Vegas Seven*. Retrieved from http://vegasseven.com/

Lapan, T. (2012, March 12). Looking at immigrant populations and immigration enforcement laws by state. *Las Vegas Sun*. Retrieved from www.lasvegassun.com/

Lillisview, M. (2011, June 7). Guy McAfee credited with branding the Strip. *Las Vegas Review-Journal*. Retrieved from www.lvrj.com/

Loewen, J. W. (1999). *Lies across America: What our Historic Sites Get Wrong*. New York, NY: The New Press.

Low, T. (2004). What is a Museum? In G. Anderson (Ed.), *Reinventing the Museum: Historical and Contemporary Perspectives on the Paradigm Shift* (pp. 34–47). Lanham, MD: Rowman Altamira.

Marstine, J. (2006). *New Museum Theory and Practice: An Introduction*. Malden, MA: Blackwell Publishing.

Minghetti, V., Moretti, A., & Micelli, S. (2000). 'Intelligent' Museum as value creator on the tourism market: Towards a new business model. In *Information and Communication Technologies in Tourism 2000* (pp. 114–125). Vienna: Springer.

Nagourney, A. (2013, July 31). Crowds return to Las Vegas, but gamble less. *New York Times*. Retrieved from www.nytimes.com/

Plaza, B. (2000). Guggenheim museum's effectiveness to attract tourism. *Annals of Tourism Research, 27*(4), 1055–1058.

Pratt, T. (2012, October 19). What Happens in Brooklyn Moves to Vegas. *The New York Times*. Retrieved from http://www.nytimes.com/2012/10/21/magazine/what-happens-in-brooklyn-moves-to-vegas.html

Poria, Y., & Ashworth, G. (2009). Heritage tourism – current resource for conflict. *Annals of Tourism Research, 36*(3), 522–525.

Press, A. (2014, April 17). Mob Museum makes huge payment in cash, mafia style – Las Vegas Sun News. *Las Vegas Sun*. Retrieved from www.lasvegassun.com/

Roberts, L. C. (2004). Changing practices of interpretation. In G. Anderson (Ed.), *Reinventing the Museum: Historical and Contemporary Perspectives on the Paradigm Shift* (pp. 144–162). Lanham, MD: Rowman Altamira.

Roembke, J. (2004). The Las Vegas monorail: First in its class. *Mass Transit, 30*(6), 36–43.

Schwartz, D. G. (2012, November 8). The Columbus of highway 91: How Thomas Hull pitched camp outside city limits, built the El Rancho and invented the Las Vegas strip. *Vegas Seven*. Retrieved from www.vegasseven.com/

Schwartz, D. G. (2013, February 7). Mobbing the Mob Museum. *Vegas Seven*. Retrieved from http://vegasseven.com/

Shine, C. (2013, February 14). Director has no beef with Mob Museum's first year in business. *Las Vegas Sun*. Retrieved from www.lasvegassun.com/

Skolnik, S. (2008, August 17). Oh, the irony: The former mob lawyer gets FBI support for Mob Museum. *Las Vegas Sun*. Retrieved from www.lasvegassun.com/

Skolnik, S. (2009a, January 12). Mayor returns fire over Mob Museum funding – Las Vegas Sun News. *Las Vegas Sun*. Retrieved from www.lasvegassun.com/

Skolnik, S. (2009b, February 3). Mob Museum walks on public tightrope. *Las Vegas Sun*. Retrieved from www.lasvegassun.com/

Strauss, J. (2015). *Challenging Corporate Social Responsibility: Lessons for Public Relations from the Casino Industry*. Abingdon, UK: Routledge.

Toplikar, D. (2009, November 18). Las Vegas Mob Museum continues to move forward. *Las Vegas Sun*. Retrieved from www.lasvegassun.com/

Toplikar, D. (2010, March 25). Downtown museum to tell story of mob in Las Vegas, elsewhere. *Las Vegas Sun*. Retrieved from www.lasvegassun.com/

Trejos, N. (2013, November 1). It's all coming up aces in Downtown Las Vegas: A hip, happening neighborhood arises from once-seedy area. *USA Today*, p. 4D.

Tufts, S., & Milne, S. (1999). Museums: A supply-side perspective. *Annals of Tourism Research, 26*(3), 613–631.

Velotta, R. N. (2010, October 13). Tourism officials updated on progress of Mob Museum. *Las Vegas Sun*. Retrieved from www.lasvegassun.com/

Waiser, L. (2010, July 23). Las Vegas Mob Museum takes shape in former courthouse. *National Trust for Historic Preservation*.

Weaver, D. B. (2011). Contemporary tourism heritage as heritage tourism. *Annals of Tourism Research, 38*(1), 249–267.

Weil, S. E. (2004). From being about something to being for somebody: The ongoing transformation of the American Museum. In G. Anderson (Ed.), *Reinventing the Museum: Historical and Contemporary Perspectives on the Paradigm Shift* (pp. 170–190). Lanham, MD: Rowman Altamira.

Wells, J. (2009, September 1). MGM Mirage's CEO 'playing offense'." *CNBC.com*. Retrieved January 8, 2014, from www.cnbc.com/id/32642315

Wingert, G. (2012, February 15). Vegas opens museum to examine its mobbed-up past. *Las Vegas Sun*. Retrieved from http://www.lasvegassun.com/

Part 3

Researching visual and spatial public relations

8   A visual history of BP's use of public relations after Deepwater Horizon

Nick Lovegrove

Introduction

This chapter outlines the development of a visual research methodology based on a series of rhetorical pieces of design that explored how graphic design's techniques of persuasion could be used to expose and critique the PR industry. This methodology was adopted and used to undertake a critical investigation of BP's crisis management of the Deepwater Horizon accident. Using the firm's own press releases, commissioned imagery and publicly available digital data a one-off publication was produced that acted as a timeline charting the company's response to the disaster as well as its wider socio-cultural representation in the media. By attempting to explain the nature, history, practices and ethics of the PR industry through drawing attention to the way organisations attempt to control and manipulate their public image these proposed research methods initiate the process of visualising the profession from an activist's perspective.

Background

The respective worlds of graphic design and public relations rarely seem to engage, yet there is much common ground. With *communication* as their core function, their traditional position as a mediated link between an organisation and its audience means that (within a commercial context, at least) they are often used by a client simultaneously. Although PR's origins within the field of communications result in a disparate vocabulary, many definitions of PR could also be applied to graphic design. Phraseology such as 'controlling flows of information', 'influencing stakeholders' and 'strategic communication processes' are equally relevant to the common understanding of the role a graphic designer performs. They might, perhaps, be viewed as two sides of the same coin.

   This paper examines those correlations, the development of visual research methodologies on the subject of public relations and how graphic design's techniques of persuasion could be used to expose and critique the PR industry. It assumes the reader is more than aware of the impact design has in the communication process but perhaps has little previous knowledge of graphic design history and theory. Descriptions of a series of visual case studies aim to draw attention to the way organisations attempt to control and manipulate their public image.

Designer as reporter

Although defining any commercial activity or academic field is fraught with potential semantic discord, both disciplines have followed loosely similar paths of development and now claim hugely influential positions within the modern world. As industries, both have their origins in the 19th Century development of branded consumer goods and services; before developing a more coherent identity and some degree of public recognition during the Western post-war boom. Meggs and Purvis write:

> William Addison Dwiggins arrived at the phrase graphic design in 1922, but it was rarely used until after World War II – until then graphic designers were called "commercial artists." The field expanded dramatically in the last decades of the twentieth century, with technology playing an increasingly critical role
>
> (2011: 7)

As a researcher relatively new to the field of public relations, it has been easy to draw parallels between the debates happening within the world of PR and those surrounding graphic design. After a heady period of growth, both are currently engaged in a period of self-reflection and epistemological dialogue – with similar discussions regarding identity, technology and ethics. For example, the implications of the democratisation of technology, the active or passive role of the professional within the communication process and issues of diversity and representation.

The development of 'critical PR' in the 1990s is mirrored by the expansion of the application of critical theory within graphic design at the around the same time. L'Etang writes:

> Critical work in public relations has blossomed in the last decade. It has challenged current assumptions, defined and critiqued a "dominant paradigm" (and thus in the process defined itself and marked new boundaries), applied critical theory (especially those who have been influenced by media sociology) and critiqued policy and practice
>
> (2005: 522)

Critical theory also influenced writing on design, resulting in a body of work that questioned the scope of design practice. Many writers and design practitioners, contributing to the influential 'First Things First' manifesto (1999) questioned the role of a graphic design as a profession, and challenged designers to think beyond that of communicating the needs of a client.

> We propose a reversal of priorities in favour of more useful, lasting and democratic forms of communication – a mind shift away from product marketing and toward the exploration and production of a new kind of meaning
>
> (Adbusters et al., 1999)

In the mid 1990s Katherine McCoy wrote: 'Designers must break out of the obedient, neutral, servant-to-industry mentality, an orientation that was particularly strong in the Reagan/Thatcher 1980s. Design is not a neutral, value-free process. A design has no more integrity than its purpose or subject matter'(McCoy, 1994: 111)

Along with Rick Poynor and Ellen Lupton, Michael Rock popularised the idea of 'graphic authorship'. In his 1996 essay 'The Designer as Author he wrote 'Authorship may suggest new approaches to the issue of the design process in a profession traditionally associated more with the communication rather than the origination of messages. He clarified his position in a 2009 essay titled 'Fuck Content':

> In *Designer as Author* I argued that we are insecure about the value of our work. We are envious of the power, social position and cachet that artists and authors seem to command. By declaring ourselves "designer/authors" we hope to garner similar respect. Our deep-seated anxiety has motivated a movement in design that values origination of content over manipulation of content.

These widely-read and deliberately provocative texts resulted in a meme loosely based on the prefix 'Graphic Designer as . . .' which developed into a dialogue between designers and commentators. One of these responses, a 2001 essay titled *The Designer as Reporter* Poynor proposed that graphic designers had the creative, technical and intellectual skills to be able to explore issues in the same spirit that an investigative journalist might.

> What if the designer was to function more like a journalist? In other words, develop a sphere of knowledge and expertise, select a subject, conduct research, gather material, then create an appropriate final form, using all the resources of design, both words and images, to communicate the story or argument.

As a designer who had been working in the industry for a decade, notions of exploring what graphic design practice has the potential to be, away from the constraints of client-based practice, appealed greatly when I was studying for a Masters in the subject in 2012. Whilst searching for a field of study, I wanted to explore how graphic design's techniques of persuasion could be used to critique, or potentially change, an issue I believe warranted attention.

One of the areas under consideration was public relations, a subject of which i had little prior knowledge but did have first-hand experience of (what I later found out) was termed 'media relations'. My first job after graduating was working in a regional office of a large UK broadcaster. Within months I had a full-time job designing graphic elements for local news bulletins. Located within the newsroom, collaborating closely with journalists and editors, I quickly became aware of the origins of the work I was being asked to visualise. The job invariably meant watching a lot of local television news and, thanks to my 'behind the scenes' role, it became clear how many of the stories, presented as independent journalism were actually sourced from PR companies. The fax machine would receive a nearly constant stream of press releases from companies, public sector organisations, protest groups and charities, all attempting to influence the news agenda.

As an idealistic, inquisitive young designer I was fascinated by the way companies could use the public's trust in journalism to promote their own messages. I wondered why the term 'PR' was so widely known but there seemed to be so little public awareness or consideration regarding what PR agencies actually do – and their indirect influence on society. It also made me consider what the public perception of *news* really is (in this case, the often peculiar world of 'regional' news), how this affected my understanding of various communication theories and most importantly the lack of public visibility of what was clearly a very influential industry.

This lack of *visibility* was a crucial reason why the field of PR was an interesting choice for me to study using visual means. Designers rely on semiotic theory on a daily basis, trying to predict the chosen audience's interpretation of a set of signs to influence their reading of the piece. Whether it's the choice of typeface, colour scheme, paper type or the cropping of image, designers have a multitude of decisions to make every time they create something. Over the last century or more this has resulted in a shared set of individual signs, accepted readings and common visual languages that the public are remarkably familiar with, even if they know little about the subject.

Most professions have a set of visual signifiers that a designer can assemble to create syntagmatic relationships, yet public relations doesn't seem to have its own paradigm to draw upon. The lack of visually distinct working environment, professional uniform or discernible product contribute to this amorphous state. Therefore, the industry's image is built on public figures. In the UK, that may include 'professionals' such as Max Clifford or Alastair Campbell or fictional characters including Bridget Jones, Malcolm Tucker and Edina Monsoon.

I would now argue that this absence of visual identity has been a conscious if not deliberate decision by the PR industry. From the move away from the term 'propaganda' to the far more ambiguous 'public relations', the "unseen mechanism" (Bernays, 1928: 9) can perform more effectively when it manifests itself as a transparent vessel. By contrast, the advertising industry, which is similar in many ways, has arguably a far higher public profile and unashamedly talks of its own importance.

When starting a graphic design project on public relations, one of the immediate challenges was to construct a visual language that is connected to the subject and one that an audience can decode, engage with and create their own meaning – yet there seemed to be very few cultural signifiers to work with. Creating a consistent new visual identity to critique a subject, in what was likely to become a variety of designed outcomes, was an interesting challenge in its own right. This body of work will be described in this essay, with particular attention given to 'Crisis Communication' – a piece of visual research exploring BP's response to the accident on the Deepwater Horizon oil rig in the Gulf of Mexico in 2010.

Visual research

The popularity of research methods using visual materials has grown rapidly over recent years (Rose, 2014: 22) and can refer to the gathering, analysing, and presenting visual data (Margolis and Pauwels, 2011: xix). In addition to primary methods of gathering information such as photojournalism, drawing and filmmaking; the internet and digital technology has allowed researchers to easily access a vast archive of information and imagery.

Noble and Bestley (2016: 11) describe about three models for graphic design research, one of which, called 'research through design' refers to subjects outside of the design sphere.

> Research through design involves the development of new artefacts of which the goal is to visually communicate new knowledge, but the practice is not at the centre of the whole research process. The use of graphic design as an instrument for investigating and articulating a particular subject area, which may lie outside of the field of design – as such, this model of design research would include mapping, information design, and editorial approaches to visualizing and categorizing data.

Possibly the most common and conventional way that graphic design is used in research is in the creation of data visualisations. Whether created by researchers (with no formal training in design) or specialists using more advanced techniques – quantitative data presented visually can be used to manipulate the way data is understood, emphasise or suppress certain findings, compare datasets and potentially create new hypotheses that wouldn't have been found otherwise.

With an initial research question of '*How do commercial organisations use the public relations industry to influence UK news journalism?*' I attempted to find an existing set of data that I could visualise. I was granted access to the raw data gathered during Cardiff University's School of Journalism, Media and Cultural Studies' investigation into 'churnalism' (Davies, 2008), which was featured in the book Flat Earth News. Notoriously, the study found that only 12 per cent of stories could be said to be sourced entirely by the journalist who wrote the story (Lewis et al., 2007). After initial tests, it was clear that the only way a visualisation of this data would answer my question was in the form of a series of simple pie-charts, I devised my own visual research project.

On 14th June 2012, I purchased two newspapers – one from the quality press (*The Times*) and one tabloid (*The Sun*). I selected key sentences, which contained a distinctive or unusual series of words, from every article featured in both papers. Using a variety of online research sources, including Google, news-wire services and the website, Churnalism.com, I searched for these sentences to give an indication if sections of the text had been repeated elsewhere.

If they had been, the press releases containing the original source of the text were often easy to find, either via news-wire services or the media section of company websites. Each article was categorised into either a) definitely containing PR-generated material; b) likely to contain PR-generated material (but no direct evidence of the original source) or c) articles written as a result of original reporting or from news wire services. Distinctions were also made to separate press releases likely to be written on behalf of commercial clients, against those written by political parties.

The layout of each page was then visualized and organised into diagram, representing every double page spread (Figures 8.1 and 8.2). The articles were then colour-coded, mapped against their respective categories. Although this was a very quick and far from rigorous experiment, the result is two diagrams which clearly show the extent that journalists rely on press releases. The diagrams make it easy for the viewer to see the structure of each newspaper and also make comparisons between the two titles. They confirm that there is more original reporting in *The Times*, and that the middle sections of each paper are the most likely place to find PR-generated articles. None of these findings will

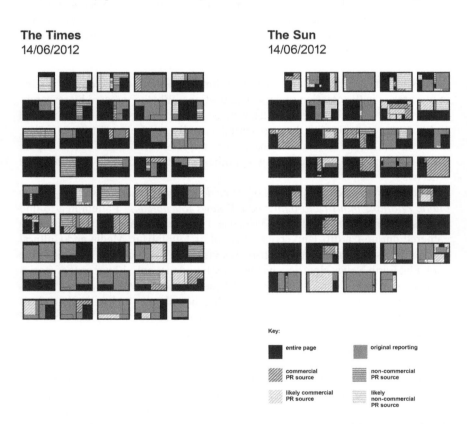

The Times
14/06/2012

The Sun
14/06/2012

Key:

entire page

original reporting

commercial PR source

non-commercial PR source

likely commercial PR source

likely non-commercial PR source

Figure 8.1 and 8.2 Visualisation of PR-generated material versus original reporting (i) and (ii)

be a surprise to those with an interest in journalism or PR but the use of visual methods does create what perhaps could be termed a more powerful, if not accurate, piece of communication.

Although graphs are common in many kinds of research, the way they are designed is just as open to interpretation, debate and manipulation as the data they present. Despite attempts to keep the design as simple and objective as possible, my position as a designer attempting to draw attention to the issue means that an unbiased outcome is impossible.

This 'rhetoric of neutrality' (Kinross, 1985: 18), formed out of the modernist ideals of the Bauhaus, was at odds with my aims and intentions for this body of research. If I wanted to raise awareness of the practices that the PR professionals employ on a daily basis, as well as the frequency that the public absorbs PR-generated material – a more persuasive, rhetorical approach was required. The provocative vocabulary of the revised research question '*How can graphic design be used as a tool to critique and expose the Public Relations industry?*' clarified my objectives and moved the rest of the project away from a data-led approach to more of a campaigning, activist-led methodology.

There is a rich history of graphic art being used as a propaganda tool to address social and political issues. Whether created by someone who may refer to themselves as a graphic designer or not, for many centuries words and images have been combined to create powerful pieces of communication. From work commissioned by official sources such as political parties and charities; to the more underground, unofficial world of hand-painted protest banners, flyposters to photocopied zines – there are many ways in which graphic design can be used to attempt to create change.

Whilst public relations as a whole may seem like an unlikely focus for a piece of 'graphic agitation', the more I read about the subject the more I believed that a critical response was necessary. Beyond my first-hand experience of 'media relations' (or perhaps 'churnalism') in a television news room, the field of public relations and the sub-categories within it have much less public-visibility and potentially much greater influence on society. Although 'greenwashing' has become a commonly used term, and individual cases of bad practice may become public; areas such as public affairs, crisis management, civic marketing and the management of Corporate Social Responsibility (CSR) programmes are rarely considered as a whole by those outside the field. The vast scale of the industry, with thousands of professionals seeking to advance the political, economic and cultural authority of the corporations has largely avoided being the subject of criticism in a visual form.

Although PR is commonly perceived by the public in a negative way, with an awareness largely based around media relations activities (White & Park, 2010: 319), terms such as "public relations gimmick" and "public relations nightmare" (*ibid*), trivialise and simplify what could be viewed as a deeply manipulative industry which distorts public understanding of almost any issue. The wider political issue surrounding the 'manufacture of consent' lies at the heart of my research and deserved to be explored visually.

Critical graphic design

Jan van Toorn "one of the most distinguished and provocative figures in an excep-
tional generation of Dutch graphic designers" (Poynor, 2004) is known for his
work exploring social and political issues. Rather than a more direct, conventional
approach of creating work on behalf of charitable organisations or generating self-
initiated projects "his approach had much in common with that of a campaigning or investigative journalist, except that his medium of expression was design
and the image, rather than the written word." (Poynor, 2007: 185). Van Toorn,
influenced by Brecht (Poynor, 2008: 96) developed a reflexive perspective and a
commitment to demystifying communication. 'In his work since around 1970, Van
Toorn has attempted wherever possible – and not always with complete success, as
he admits to – to make viewers of his designs aware of the mechanics of manipulation. He has always returned to this idea . . . always insisting on this aim as a
basic condition of honest, open, democratic communication.' (Poynor, 2008: 97).
This aligns closely with critiques of public relations. L'Etang (2005: 521) writes:

> Critical Theory is thus not a single theory but an interdisciplinary approach
> which seeks to define assumptions which are taken-for-granted with a view
> to challenging their source and legitimacy. It aims to transform those social,
> political and economic structures which limit human potential. It seeks to
> identify, challenge, and debate the strategies of domination that are implicit
> in such structures. Such investigation and debate have the potential to raise
> awareness and act as a catalyst for change. There is thus an implicit political
> motivation behind Critical Theory and the research that it inspires.

Mirroring this, Poynor (2014) – adapting Dunne and Raby's description of critical design applied to products (2014) – states that critical graphic design "uses
speculative design proposals to challenge narrow assumptions, preconceptions and
givens about the role graphic communication plays in everyday life." This type of
critical theory, influencing the notion of the 'Designer as Reporter' (Poynor, 2007:
185) lead to my self-initiated brief *"create a series of rhetorical pieces of graphic
design that explain the nature, history, practices and ethics of the PR industry to
the public."*

In his essay 'Research and Destroy: Graphic Design as Investigation' Daniel van
der Velden states 'When not defined by problem-solving, graphic design is able
to occupy a (dialectical) position' adding "'The true investment is the investment
in design itself, as a discipline that conducts research and generates knowledge –
knowledge that makes it possible to seriously participate in discussions that are
not about design.'

Establishing a visual language

As discussed earlier in this essay, the lack of visual signifiers associated with the
profession presents a challenge for a designer. After rejecting an overtly political

visual style for this yet-to-be-designed body of work, a new visual language was needed to create the right tone of voice and bring a consistent feel to the various outcomes.

Using various visual research methods, I conducted various short case studies into the ways one press release is disseminated and mediated by journalists. These included Kelloggs' sponsorship of an initiative to encourage more children to swim, British Airways' announcement of their sponsorship of a public viewing area at the London 2012 Olympics and a survey to promote a manufacturer of weight loss tablets. This research revealed that despite being a largely written or spoken text-based activity, the media commonly illustrates PR-generated stories either with images supplied by the agency or stock library photography. Additionally, press releases, now usually distributed digitally, almost always use one of Microsoft's system fonts (for example Arial, Tahoma, Times New Roman or Verdana). These two tropes formed a core part of my methodology, creating a new almost anti-design aesthetic and thus became the visual foundation for all the practical work I would undertake during the rest of the project.

These three fonts, rarely used by graphic designers and are sneered at within typographic circles because of their perceived ugliness, or more likely because of their ubiquity. Originally designed as a (cheaper) replacement for Helvetica "among the design community, Arial retains bad blood." (Garfield, 2010: 82). When, in 2009 IKEA chose to replace Futura with Verdana for the main typeface used their catalogues, it was jokingly dubbed 'Verdanagate' by the New York Times (Garfield, 2010: 222). Garfield writes:

> Verdana, on the other hand, despite being a superb font, designed by Matthew Carter, is linked to something modern and commonly reviled: Microsoft. Verdana is thus available on almost every PC and Mac, and is one of the most widely used fonts in the world. Along with a handful of other prominent typefaces, it has been directly responsible for a homogenization of the public word: a sign over a cinema looks increasingly like one over a bank or hospital, and magazines that once looked original now frequently resemble something designed for reading online.

Likewise, stock photography is also the subject of mocking derision by the design community – despite being used widely. Lupton and Miller (1999: 121) write 'this kind of photography is not the award-winning sort commissioned by leading art directors, nor is it a heartfelt grass-roots expression. It is, instead, a kind of corporate vernacular that fuels a vast amount of graphic design practiced in both amateur and professional settings.' Whether the journalist or picture editor chooses to use 'commissioned' imagery or searches within a stock library, both types have a similar aesthetic – relying on high-quality cameras, classic compositional techniques, representation of stereotypes and unsubtle metaphors. They continue 'stock photography is most often used straightforwardly in consumer contexts, but is has been used ironically and analytically.'

Designing a new typeface

One of the most widespread practices in public relations is repeating of a message by multiple trusted sources to build a manipulated form of consensus: Bernays' infamous 'engineering of consent'. Using this metaphor, I started experimenting with how overlapping transparent layers could create a new 'truth'. Rather than arbitrary shapes, I started using letterforms because I knew I would be undertaking a project where language is extremely important and therefore a custom typeface might be a suitable critical response.

Rather than creating a new typeface, I begun distorting and morphing existing fonts; specifically, those used most commonly in press releases. By slightly offsetting and then blending Arial, Tahoma and Verdana in a series of 11 stages, I created new letterforms that retains a corporate, bland appearance but with subtle elements that are inconsistent or ugly when viewed close up. By using existing fonts without acknowledgement, particularly those which are usually viewed with disdain by graphic designers, gives the typeface its subversive premise. The occasional stepped edges look aggressive and the irregular widths of the constituent parts give a sense of my critical position.

This new typeface, named after Bernays, has its ideological roots within theories of deconstruction that were explored within the sphere of graphic design in the 1990s. The pastiche of knowingly low-brow fonts, the focus on the methodology (rather than the outcome) and the questioning of accepted communications, all fit within the cannon of postmodern typography, popularised by *Émigré* magazine. Two outcomes, a thick book and a folded poster were designed to showcase this new typeface, using some of Bernays' quotes to demonstrate the qualities of the letterforms (Figure 8.3)

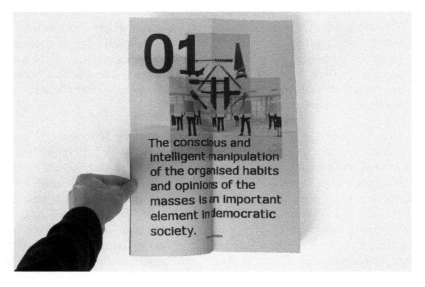

Figure 8.3 Bernays Typeface (i)

Reimagining propaganda as a manifesto

This lead to consideration of how graphic design could be used to persuade a new audience to read Bernays' *Propaganda*. Originally published in 1928, and still protected under copyright law, the entire text is easily available on the internet but receives surprisingly little public attention, given its historical significance. Given my self-imposed rules for these outputs, stock photography was the only kind of imagery allowed to create visual interest and potential new readings of the text.

Users of stock photos sites rely on keywords to find the pictures they require and I quickly became interested in how picture editors (or indeed designers) search and select their pictures. Using Getty Images, the process of entering a keyword, browsing and refining results, filtering tags and creating 'lightboxes' to organise potential purchases was documented. This lead to the idea of using stock imagery to act as a companion to Bernays's text, whilst also attempting to make the process behind the selection of the images visible.

Firstly, I read the text, making notes of keywords that I thought summarised each section. These would act as a critical counterpoint to Bernays' almost evangelical prose. Then, I searched Getty Images's UK website using these keywords, before selecting the images that I thought were most interesting and/or relevant. Placed on a double page spread with the keywords arranged over the top, these would act as a visual introduction to the forthcoming chapter. I could then juxtapose these images to illustrate important sections of the text, creating playful illustrations which either act as anchorage or as a relay (Barthes & Heath, 1977: 38).

There are strong contextual links between this project and Jan van Toorn's work and his ideas on the 'mechanics of manipulation'. Stock imagery is such an integral part of much of modern advertising and marketing (of which public relations is arguably a part) and yet the process of how images are selected is rarely considered. By intervening and exposing this practice, I hoped to draw attention to and encourage the audience to be critical of the ubiquitous, arbitrary and false nature of stock imagery. Poynor (2008: 96) writes "It is the designer's role and responsibility as a mediator, Van Toorn argues, to find ways to break open and demystify the message, to make its provenance and manipulatory character visible in its form, so that the receiver can engage fully in the communication's argument."

The imagery was intended to make the text more visually appealing, helping to break up the text and illustrate particular points whilst also forming a themed narrative within each chapter. Whilst these narratives might not be easily understood, I intended each individual illustration to be clearly critical of Bernays' position, creating an openly rhetorical response to Bernays' text. The lo-fi look and feel of cheap paper and black and white printing were chosen to echo the loose historical aesthetics of manifestos, of which this arguably one (Figures 8.4, 8.5 and 8.6)

Figure 8.4 Bernays Typeface (ii)

Figure 8.5 Bernays Typeface (iii)

Figure 8.6 Bernays Typeface (iv)

Crisis communication: a visual history of BP's response to the Deepwater Horizon incident

Searching for a single public relations event or campaign that I could an in-depth piece of visual research into, I moved away from a focus on media relations into areas of PR which have been the subject of greater controversy. For example, a visual investigation into the use of Western PR firms employed by the Kingdom of Bahrain to improve the image of the country – an attempt to restrict negative coverage and also lobby influential political figures during the 'Arab Spring' of 2010. These case studies all resulted in visual outcomes which chronicled an event using the narrative structure that is inherent in the format of printed books.

In 2010, the Deepwater Horizon oil platform, drilling in the Gulf of Mexico exploded, causing in the deaths of 11 workers, as well as the release of over 18 million gallons of oil into the sea. Working on behalf of BP, contractors made a series of mistakes which resulted in a 'blowout' and a high intensity fire which burned uncontrolled for two days. Although investigations found a catalogue of errors made by a number of firms, BP's business culture was questioned. Safina (2011: 9) writes 'In March and April 2010, audits by maritime risk managers Lloyd's Register Group identified more than two dozen components and systems on the rig in "bad" or "poor" condition, and found some workers dismayed about safety practices and fearing reprisals if they reported mistakes.' In the following weeks and months, the spill caused widespread damage to the surrounding ecosystem, as well as to the livelihoods of inhabitants along the Gulf Coast who rely on the tourism and fishing industries.

BP immediately received negative public and media criticism for its role in the disaster and quickly initiated its now infamous crisis communication response, or 'image restoration' strategy. After BP's then Chief Executive was photographed on a yacht off the Isle of Wight, a White House spokesman referred to the move as "one of a long line of PR gaffes and mistakes" (BBC News, 2010).

Their response strategy made extensive use of online methods of distribution, allowing members of the public, journalists and other stakeholders access to a huge archive of material which could then be reproduced or shared. A dedicated 'Gulf of Mexico response' section on BP's website featured press releases, information, diagrams, photos and videos; whilst their social media accounts regularly featured content aimed at restoring, or defending, the firm's reputation. All this easily accessible material is a veritable goldmine for researchers of all kinds. Therefore, a systematic methodology involving a set of design rules was required – encouraging analysis and critique of the company's multi-million-dollar campaign strategy.

Rather than only featuring content distributed by BP, a method of comparing their messages with those of other stakeholders was devised, potentially resulting in more insightful observations. This resulted in a visual timeline structure, with each page (divided into seven vertical sections) representing one week of time, starting just before the explosion on 20th April 2010. Imagery, press releases, quotations, and BP's share price are mapped against the dates, resulting in a book which covers a period of two years. Using a combination of publication dates,

EXIF data (embedded in most digital images) and time-specific Google image searches – each element can be accurately placed on the date it was created or publicly released. Although an editing process of the content occurred (because of a book's limited physical size) none of the images have been cropped, just simply left-aligned to their respective date marker. Other than controlling the size and horizontal position of each element, the only 'designerly' decision was to make the non-BP content black and white, so that the viewer can make easier visual comparisons. This draws on the widespread public understanding that black and white photography is somehow more truthful, which the author accepts is a deliberate decision to influence the way the viewer decodes the information. 'French folds' (a printing term which allows each page to overlap onto the next, on the non-spine edge) are used to emphasise the ongoing flow of time between pages. (Figures 8.7, 8.8, 8.9, 8.10, 8.11)

The narrative arc of BP's response to the accident is clear. At the start, the pages are almost bare; these quickly evolve into sections which are an overwhelming, confusing, dense field of imagery and text, before slowly quieting down during 2011. In conclusion, the book features BP's involvement with the 2012 Olympic Games in London, with its sponsorship of the US team featured prominently. These changes of flow and contrast hopefully make the book more engaging and communicate a message even if the viewer doesn't read the text. BP's PR 'gaffes' which begun very soon after the explosion on the rig are represented by using a contrasting colour (orange) and image distortion techniques. These deconstructed sections act as a visual metaphor for the disruptions in the continuity of the campaign.

Figure 8.7 BP Crisis Communications (i)

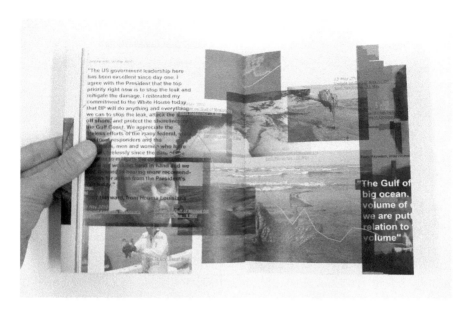

Figure 8.8 BP Crisis Communications (ii)

Figure 8.9 BP Crisis Communications (iii)

Figure 8.10 BP Crisis Communications (iv)

The most dominant elements in the book are high quality colour photographic images, centred on environmental measures and community engagement. These images were downloaded from BP's account on social media photography website Flickr which, at the time, hosted hundreds of commissioned professional photos of the clean-up operation and CSR activities in the Gulf states. The photographs were notable because, with a few rare exceptions, did they show any oil, instead they presented a sanitised, almost surreal, version of the clean-up operation as well as all the 'community events' that the company organised or sponsored after the spill. These contrast strongly with images taken by photojournalists or amateurs of the disaster itself and its negative impact on the environment.

Taken out of the context within which they were intended to appear, these juxtapositions use irony to challenge BP's version of events. Muralidharan et al. (2011: 226) suggest that BP's usage of social media during the crisis indicates that Flickr (and Twitter) were used for quick information dissemination; and whilst Facebook and YouTube are used for initiating dialogue with the general public, Flickr does not necessarily foster or even allow two-way communication. These still images, many of which were featured in BP's external communications are powerful in their own right but were always intended to appear alongside text. Presenting the photos in this format allows for readings that the company never intended. For example, the colours used in the imagery often closely match BP's corporate colour scheme, introduced in 2000 as part of a rebranding exercise to move the firm away from its original name 'British Petroleum'. The regular reoccurrence of bright green in the photos is perhaps surprising, given that this is a maritime disaster but is clearly part of a clear communication strategy.

Future developments

Whilst these projects help to push graphic design in to new fields of enquiry and hopefully add to the body of knowledge around public relations, they explore the grey area between the perceived neutrality and rigour of traditional research methods and the rhetorical messages inherent in artistic practice. The questioning of ideas surrounding authorship was a necessary and relevant part of the process, however I believe there is a requirement for this work to form the basis of something more clearly public-facing. In a 2005 essay in *Creative Review* magazine Nico Macdonald is scathing of much of this type of work and calls for graphic designers exploring these kinds of political, social or environmental subjects to engage with the public. He writes 'today's graphic activism is characterised by ill-informed, sanctimonious, grand-standing – verging on righteous anger. It is less about understanding the world and engaging in real debate, more about having one's views endorsed by like-minded colleagues. Less about effecting change, more about showing one's moral virtue through action or abstinence.'

Although rigorous in many ways, these initial explorations are hopefully just the start of many more projects which have some kind of measurable impact. The visual research techniques employed offer potential new directions for research and analysis within PR academia as well as commercial practice. The same 'visual timeline' technique could be used to record any PR event or campaign, with digital tools allowing the possibility of automating the documentation of an event as it unfolds. Also, the visual language ties all of the completed outcomes together into one body of work – and now established – could be used as the visual voice of critical PR.

References

Adbusters *et al.* (1999). *First Things First Manifesto 2000*. [online]. eyemagazine.com. Available at: www.eyemagazine.com/feature/article/first-things-first-manifesto-2000 [Accessed 29 Apr. 2017].

Barthes, Roland. and Heath, Stephen. (1977). *Image, Music, Text*. 1st ed. London: Fontana Press.

BBC News. (2010). *BP Boss Criticised for Boat Trip*. [online]. Available at: www.bbc.co.uk/news/10359120 [Accessed 28 April 2017].

Bernays, Edward. (1928). *Propaganda*. London: Routledge.

Davies, Nick. (2008). *Flat Earth News*. 1st ed. London: Vintage.

Dunne, Anthony. and Raby, Fiona. (2014). *Speculative Everything*. 1st ed. [S.l.]: MIT Press.

Garfield, Simon. (2010). *Just My Type*. 1st ed. London: Profile Books.

Kinross, Robin. (1985). The Rhetoric of Neutrality. *Design Issues*, 2(2), p. 18. [online]. Available at: www.jstor.org/stable/1511415&gt [Accessed 6 Apr. 2017].

L'Etang, Jacquie. (2005). Critical Public Relations: Some Reflections. *Public Relations Review*, 41(4).

Lewis, Justin., Williams, Andrew., Franklin, Bob., Thomas, James., & Mosdell, Nick. (2007). The Quality and Independence of British Journalism. *Cardiff School of Journalism, Media and Cultural Studies*. Available at: https://orca.cf.ac.uk/18439/1/Quality%20 %26%20Independence%20of%20British%20Journalism.pdf [Accessed 7 Apr. 2017].

Lupton, Ellen. And Miller, J. Abbott (1999). *Design Writing Research*. 2nd ed. London: Phaidon.

Macdonald, Nico. (2005). Practice, Don't Preach. *Creative Review*, (9).

Margolis, Eric. and Pauwels, Luc. (2011). *The Sage Handbook of Visual Research Methods*. 1st ed. Los Angeles, CA: Sage Publications.

McCoy, Katherine. (1994). Countering the Tradition of the Apolitical Designer. *Design Renaissance: Selected Papers from the International Design Congress, Glasgow, Scotland 1993*.

Meggs, Philip, B. and Purvis, Alston, W. (2011). *Meggs' History of Graphic Design*. 5th ed. New York: John Wiley & Sons, Incorporated.

Muralidharan, Sidharth., Dillistone, Kristie. and Shin, Jae-Hwa. (2011). The Gulf Coast Oil Spill: Extending the Theory of Image Restoration Discourse to the Realm of Social Media and beyond Petroleum. *Public Relations Review*, 37(3).

Noble, Ian. and Bestley, Russell. (2016). *Visual Research*. 1st ed. London: Bloomsbury.

Poynor, Rick. (2004). *Jan van Toorn: Arguing with Visual Means*. [online]. Design Observer. Available at: http://designobserver.com/feature/jan-van-toorn-arguing-with-visual-means/2027 [Accessed 28 Apr. 2017].

Poynor, Rick. (2007). *Obey the Giant*. 1st ed. Basel: Birkhäuser.

Poynor, Rick. (2008). *Jan Van Toorn: Critical Practice*. 1st ed. Rotterdam: 010 Publishers.

Poynor, Rick. (2014). *Observer: In a Critical Condition*. [online]. Print Magazine. Available at: www.printmag.com/imprint/observer-in-a-critical-graphic-design-condition/ [Accessed 29 Apr. 2017].

Rock, Michael. (1996). *2 × 4: Essay: Designer as Author*. [online]. 2x4.org. Available at: http://2x4.org/ideas/22/designer-as-author/ [Accessed 29 Apr. 2017].

Rock, Michael. (2009). *2 × 4: Essay: Fuck Content*. [online]. 2x4.org. Available at: http://2x4.org/ideas/2/fuck-content/ [Accessed 29 Apr. 2017].

Rose, Gillian. (2014). On the Relation between 'Visual Research Methods' and Contemporary Visual Culture. *The Sociological Review*, 62(1).

Safina, Carl. (2011). *A Sea in Flames*. New York: Broadway.

van der Velden, Daniel. (2011). Research and Destroy: Graphic Design as Investigation. In: A. Blauvelt and E. Lupton, eds., *Graphic Design: Now in Production*, 1st ed. Minneapolis: Walker Art Center.

White, Candace. and Park, Joosuk. (2010). Public Perceptions of Public Relations. *Public Relations Review*, 36(4).

9 Environmental multi-modal communication

Semiotic observations on recent campaigns

Andrea Catellani

Introduction

This chapter proposes an analysis of on-line visual communication in recent environmentalist campaigns by Greenpeace. Greenpeace is probably the most 'visible' and well-known environmentalist NGO in the world, and it is extremely able to attire media and public attention through images. The basic question of this study is: how does Greenpeace use visual images in its on-line discourse, in connection with verbal texts? The answer to this question can contribute to the understanding of a larger question: which is the role of images (moving and still) in environmentalist discourse? This study is a contribution to a developing research field, the study of NGOs' communication and PR practices, and focuses on the visual dimension of these practices as a part of multi-modal communication.

The other objective of this chapter is to see if some of the 'post-humanitarian' tendencies identified by J. Chouliaraki (2010) in communication aimed at collecting founds for humanitarian causes can be identified also in environmentalist communication. In her researches, Chouliaraki identified some traits typical of many recent humanitarian campaigns (in contrast with previous periods). I will focus on the following: an accent on 'textual games' (119), soliciting reflexivity (the inferential activity of the reader-receiver) and rhetoric (irony, juxtaposition of images and of images and text, etc.), and low levels of moral and emotional direct appeal ('low-intensity emotional regimes'). In the conclusion, I will clarify if these traits are present also in the case of some Greenpeace's campaigns, and if we can talk about something like a 'visual post-environmentalism'.

Semiotics is the scientific discipline that inspires this research. The version of semiotics applied here studies how specific systems of signs (like verbal languages, or visual codes), used by people to produce 'texts', influence meaning production and communication by social actors (see Floch 2001; Henault and Beyaert 2004; Catellani, 2011a, 2011b, 2012; Fontanille 2006, 2008). Semiotics focuses on the forms of the connection between specific sign configurations and *probable* meanings and effects. Visual images, their meanings and their agency, are one of the objects of semiotic analysis, as an important rhetoric tool. Semiotics cannot discover the real effects of texts on real social actors. It can only propose hypothesis on the most probable interpretations and results, basing on the analysis of the internal configuration of texts. Semiotic analysis of multi-modal texts can help in answering questions about the contribution of specific texts to a specific communication activity, like Greenpeace's campaigns.

The kind of semiotics developed here is, indeed, a form of qualitative approach. It can be a contribution to the improvement of the rhetorical approaches to communication and public relations (Catellani 2015; for a presentation of this area of research, see Oyvind Ihlen 2011, 2015, 2016). Semiotics is articulated into many different and evolving branches. Algirdas Julien Greimas and his disciples proposed a very important version of this discipline, which has evolved in recent years toward an effort to analyze sense-making and how specific significant forms create limits and opportunities to the sense-making production of social actors. I agree with T. Van Leeuwen (2005: 4) when he affirms that the social semiotics he practices is aimed at analyzing the 'semiotic potential' of "semiotic resources": this is indeed the same goal of the semiotic approach developed in this study.

The post-structural semiotics applied in this study is deeply influenced by thinkers like P. Ricoeur, who helps semiotics in getting out of the excesses of structuralism, and by phenomenology, which helps in focusing on the apparition and development of subjective experience. This approach is clearly aware that semiotic objects or 'texts' are significant only inside their interaction with specific actors; in this way, there is a possible reconciliation between post-structuralism, based on the notions of enunciation and subjective experience, and the semiotics inspired by Charles S. Peirce, based on notions like the 'interpretant', semiosis and abduction.

The semiotic approach of this study is a form of 'epokè', a selective attention to texts that temporarily does not take into consideration the context and the social situation in which texts appear, are produced and interpreted. This temporary 'epokè' helps in focusing on the internal configuration of texts, in order to understand this configuration and its possible agency. Text is defined here as a portion of reality that is supposed to be meaningful for someone (an 'interpreter'), and that can be isolated and observed. This definition can include material objects, 'texts' in the traditional sense, but also social situations and even cultures and forms of life (Catellani 2011a, 2011b, 2012, 2015; Fontanille 2008). Texts in this large sense are seen as 'traces' of interaction and social exchange, and of cultural phenomena. This 'epokè' focused on text can be integrated into more complex research strategies that include other forms of analysis, like the observation of behaviors or quantitative research; it is a candidate to a multi-disciplinary analysis of social and cultural facts and objects.[1]

As already said, the post-structural semiotics used in this study is closed to the social semiotics of Van Leeuwen (2005, 2010), even if the basic semiotic references are partially different.[2] Van Leeuwen defines multimodal analysis as the analysis of 'the combination of different semiotic modes – for example, language and music – in a communicative artifact or event' (Van Leeuwen 2005: 281). The approach proposed here can also be seen as a contribution to multimodal analysis of verbal and visual texts.

The author has also been influenced by another research tradition, critical discourse analysis (CDA), and in particular by Norman Fairclough, who proposes the analysis of the 'semiosic' aspects of social facts (2005). Like CDA, semiotics is a contribution to the understanding of sense making by social actors, and can be useful to uncover specific forms of oversimplification and ideology. This critical aspect of semiotic analysis is another link to the tradition of critical rhetorical analysis of public relations and communication by authors like Oyvind Ihlen (2016).

In the following pages, I will present some categories on which I based my research, and a part of the images that are presents on the international website (English version) of Greenpeace. I will focus in particular on some campaigns, going on in spring-summer 2014 and still retrievable in 2016, in particular 'save the bees', 'save the arctic' and the campaign for the protection of Indonesia forests. I explored also the photo gallery, as it was visible at the end of May 2014. The first result of this semiotic, qualitative observation will be a typology of different types of visual images – or, more precisely, of verbal and visual devices in which visual images are predominant – used by Greenpeace to complete and make more effective these campaigns. The second result will take the form of some observations on the links with Chouliaraki' research on post-humanitarian communication.

Basic tools: some opposition from semiotics and rhetoric

In this study, I will use some oppositions in order to build a classification of visual images used in Greenpeace's campaigns.

- The first is the opposition between high definition and low definition images, corresponding in part to the distinction between the pole of 'realism' and the one of 'abstraction': images can represent reality in different ways and with different degrees of fidelity.
- The second is the opposition between two different relations to the verbal text. On one hand, images and verbal text can be semantically complementary, like in the case of the 'relay' function described by Roland Barthes (1964): verbal text and images alternates in order to create a narrative sequence. The opposite situation would be redundancy (a same meaning is signified by both visual and verbal signs). The problem is that a perfect redundancy is not possible when the semiotic system of sign changes: a visual iconic image of a house will never be perfectly redundant of a description of that house. I propose the notion of 'inter-semiotic redundancy' to identify texts in which images and verbal texts point towards the same notions or objects, with a high degree of semantic redundancy.
- I refer also to the classical rhetorical distinction of ethos, logos and pathos, coming from classical Greece (see Ihlen 2011). We will see in the following section how to apply this old distinction of rhetorical strategies to environmentalist images.
- In order to identify different types of images, I will refer also to two other more recent authors. One is the French philosopher Michel Foucault. While studying texts aimed at supporting spiritual exercises and meditation (2001), he distinguished what he called 'pedagogy' (to teach and transmit data and

instructions for treating these data: reading instructions is a rational preparation for an experience) and 'psychagogy' (to 'drain' and to pull the soul by
proposing an intense experience: reading is an experience in itself). In previous researches on early modern texts, I applied this distinction to spiritual
and religious manuals (see for example Catellani 2010c). This opposition
can be useful also for the analysis of environmentalist campaigns, in order
to distinguish different forms of agency.[3]

•   Finally, the French semiotician Jean-Marie Floch proposed a distinction
    between four styles or strategies of advertising: referential, substantial,
    mythical, and oblique (2001). The first, the referential one, is based on
    the narrative representation of the product and of its practical character-
    istics. The second, the mythical one, is based on the construction of links
    between the product and symbols, values, stories. It is an attempt to create
    a 'different' and magical atmosphere around the product, and to link it to
    basic existential values. The substantial strategy puts in evidence the 'real'
    and sensorial aspects of the product as an object, in opposition to the
    mythical strategy. Finally, the 'oblique' strategy tries to imply the receiver,
    the consumer, via stratagems like irony, and opposes to the practical valo-
    rization of products by exalting the amusing and ludic aspects of them.
    These four strategies, identified in a different type of texts (commercial
    advertising), can be a useful source of inspiration for the analysis of envi-
    ronmentalist visual images. These last ones share indeed, at least in some
    cases, some characteristics with commercial advertising, like the necessity
    of 'hitting' and catching the attention in a short time, and the basic per-
    suasive nature.

I will try to apply these different oppositions in the conclusion after showing
some concrete examples of the different types of images founded in the Greenpeace's campaigns.

Save the Arctic and 'psychagogy'

The campaign 'Save the Arctic'[4] is an example of the fact that different types of
visual forms are used by Greenpeace to create a visual device. While opening the
main page of the campaign's website, the reader is asked to sign a petition, while
being immediately 'immerged' in a visual narrative world linked to the subject
(changing images that show the Arctic, the menace by oil drilling, and the fight to
preserve it). Dimensions and the absence of clear limits to the image (that coincides with the limits of the browser's window) create a (possible) effect of intensity
and immersion. The rest of the page is divided into different parts: each one proposes to sign a petition and offer a verbal text with some explanations. Visual still
images (a polar bear, a picture of the North Pole, a photo of activists on a bridge)
illustrate each one of these parts. It is indeed a more static, analytical and pedagogical part of the page, which proposes argumentations and information about
the campaign. In this way, the two basic strategies (pedagogy and psychagogy) are

present together on the same page, and create the premises for a multiple reading experience, leading the reader from an intense 'overture' (in a musical sense) to a less emotional and more informational development.

Scrolling down the page, in 2014 the reader met a video ('vicious circle', no more visible on the website of the campaign but still accessible on YouTube[5]) that sums up, once again in an intensive way, the contents of the campaign. The video combines beautiful images from the film *Home* by Yann Arthus-Bertrand, which shows different aspects of the Arctic. The editing of images (that reduces progressively their dimensions) creates a visual rhetorical effect: reduction is a representation of the progressive destruction of this environment (visual metaphor), and at the end the apparition of planet Earth creates a visual link to global menace. The 'voice off' (of the actor John Hurt) 'anchors'the meaning of the visual device, and music by the composer Johann Johannsson contributes to the atmosphere of melancholy and beauty. The video is indeed an example of 'psychagogy', in the sense of Foucault. The reader is captured by the semiotic device that is able to 'drain' him/her through space and time, to absorb and lead him towards the final revelation of planet Earth. The result of this intense experience should be engagement, through the invitation to 'sign up' on the website.

Specific time devices are aimed at improving this effect of 'pulling the soul': in particular, the slow pace of music and of the alternation of images, which focuses the attention of the reader and let him/her 'digest' and being affected by the video. To use an old expression coming from the book of "Spiritual exercises" by St. Ignace of Loyola (16th century, see Catellani 2010c), the video proposes the 'composition of place' of a narrative world. The viewer has to take position inside this world, in front of the situation, after having felt all the emotions that are connected to it. The image operates here as a tool for attiring attention and activating emotions, in connection with music and oral speech. The video is a strong combination of visual and sound rhetoric with a high-definition iconic text.

All about bees: notes on a galaxy of visual solutions

An even richer example of the multiplicity of the visual language developed by Greenpeace is the campaign on bees.[6] Greenpeace developed in 2014 a big international campaign to save bees, attacked by different menaces included (in a prominent position) human industrial farming activities and artificial substances like pesticides. The main page of the campaign opens with very large images (short films) of flowers, trees and bees in their environment. The point of view on bees is very close, and the image does not have borders: the probable effect is, here again, that the observer is 'immerged' in the natural (beautiful) reality of bees, fields and flowers. The same visual poetics of big, immersive images is present in the internal parts of the site ('situation', 'causes', 'solutions'; in these cases, sometimes images are not moving). These images could be considered, as in the case of 'Save the Arctic', as a sort of 'ouverture' that introduces in an intense way the world of the campaign, made of different parts and aspects. Images are not expressing specific emotions, but simply representing bees and flowers from a very short distance (alternating with immense views of fields: the very near and the very far).

The campaign about bees is rich of different visual solutions. The page on 'solutions' is full of different videos that present the testimonies of scientists, activists and peasants who apply and develop methods of agriculture that make no harm to bees. In these videos, the 'ethical' aspect (in the sense of rhetorical 'ethos', the character of the speaker used as a persuasive tool) is central. They are 'edifying' and instructive videos that present also 'logos', knowledge and information, but without precise quantitative data. These last ones are reserved for the 'reports', like the one entitled 'Plan bee – living without pesticides' that can be downloaded on the same website. Videos underline the figure of the protagonist, the hero (and the opinion leader in the sense of the 'two-step flow' theory of communication), like prof. Hans Herren,[7] or Yvonne and Steve Page who practice permaculture in France. These videos represent the speaker, but also his/her living and working environment. The video on prof. Herren (a specialist of eco-agriculture in Switzerland) alternates (in a very classical way for documentaries) images of him in his office and images of agro-business (industrial agriculture, fishing and rearing): the 'ethos' images alternate with emblematic (anonymous) illustrations of its speech. The 'pathos' dimension is less important, but present in particular through music. This last one creates a sort of 'secondary semiotic flux', capable of producing a dynamic (but discrete and unobtrusive) atmosphere and of creating a positive feeling about the speech and the images. In this way, pedagogy (the dominant strategy here) doesn't eliminate a component of 'psychagogy', the attempt to 'drain' and 'pulling' the soul in a non-rational way.[8]

Other videos of this page propose different combinations of the same 'ingredients'. For example, the interview of Claudia Daniel (researcher in Switzerland) is based on the same system of 'alternating' ethos and illustration images, which in this case are images of her while working with a colleague in the natural environment. The interview to prof. Dufumier (French expert of agro-ecology) offers only 'ethical' images of the speaker, without any illustration of his speech: his discourse (intense, quick, inspired), his beautiful and expressive face, and music are enough to enrich with a 'psychagogical' note the verbal content of the interview. In each case, ideas and information come to the viewer through the verbal text (mainly), and music creates an accompanying dynamic (with a psychagogical effect). Images have three functions: they show the enunciator, which is the producer of the discourse and the 'proof' of its importance through his/her personal testimony; they illustrate the discourse (showing for ex. anonymous examples of industrial agriculture); they show the enunciator in action, creating the space-time that confirms the identity of the speaker.

Showing the heroes creates a sense of positive collective involvement, it transfers credibility to the initiative (many of the "pioneers" are renowned scientists) and it creates also a sense of richness and abundance of people operating in favor of bees.

Another type of video is the presentation of events, like the 'Global Day of Action – Save the Bees' video.[9] In this case, music leaves its unobtrusive and

Figure 9.1 Save the Bees

'marginal' position and catches a very important place, accompanying images that show different moments of the event in different parts of Europe. The rhythm of music and of the cutting of scenes is rapid; music creates a climax with its internal structure (verses and chorus). The accumulation of places, actions, and faces produces a sense of feast and euphoria. The aim clearly is to show the success of the initiative, and indirectly the success and power of the association, with a quite strong psychagogical component – the reader is invited to involve him/herself in this positive movement).

Another radically different type of images is exemplified by the video on dying bees in Hungary,[10] posted by Greenpeace Hungary on YouTube. In this case, the music is absent; the voice off of the activist explains (or 'anchors', in the terms of the semiotician Roland Barthes) the images of the sunflower field with bees (seen from a short distance) dying after collecting nectar in the flowers. In this case, all psychagogy is absent. The video is a sort of visual 'proof' of a phenomenon: the simple fact of seeing becomes the argument, the proof; image is a semiotic tool for getting in touch with a real fact that is happening now. In this case, the image is not 'anonymous' (*a* field, *a* place) but specific (*that specific* field in a specific country).

This presentation of the visual dimension of the campaign continues by talking about another 'genre' of images, that is perhaps the most famous in the case of Greenpeace: the spectacular, rhetorical one. In this case, the visual world of ordinary experience is modified in a rhetorical way, creating surprises through mechanisms like metaphors, parody and other rhetorical figures. An example is the video on 'Greenbees'.[11] The video presents bees in action to defend their survival (and the one of humans) against pesticides and industrial agriculture.

Figure 9.2 Greenbees

Bees operate many iconic and typical actions of real Greenpeace (like exposing posters and following ships with speedboats). The video is a self-parody of
Greenpeace, which creates a different point of view and surprise. The visual
world connected to the organization is modified in order to create attention,
interest and involvement.

Parody is a 'coherent distortion' of texts aimed at the creation of meaning effects,
in particular the attack of specific social actors (Catellani 2012). Greenpeace is
very well known for its parodies of the symbolic universe of brands. Examples are
the campaign against Mattel with the parody of Barbie and Ken,[12] or the parody
of an advertisement by Volkswagen inspired by the world of Star Wars.[13] Parody
is an inter-textual work, because it modifies a pre-existing textual universe; and
it is also a form of attack and criticism.[14] In this case, 'Greenbees' presents the
first characteristic (inter-textual work): a quite well known visual world is evoked
in a modified and 'strange' (but coherent) form. Instead, the second aspect is not
present, because Greenpeace is not criticized. More precisely, the text is aimed
at showing an apparently ridiculous dynamic that is, at the end, a criticism of the
humans, of the viewer (the written text towards the end of the video says 'give
bees a chance – because without us, you don't have one'). In this way, an action
of criticism and blame is present, but deviated towards 'you', the public, and not
towards the symbolic capital of the organization (that is on the contrary valorized).
In this case Greenpeace creates the typical 'buzz video', made to be spread largely
on the Web, in order to attire people on the website.

Another example of spectacular, rhetoric video is RoboBees.[15] Built as a fake
promotional video for 'new bees', robots introduced to replace bees extinguished

because of pesticides, the video exalts the qualities of the 'product'. The video presents an idyllic environment (flowers, grass, sunshine), and ends with children playing with the 'new bees'. Music introduces (in an ambiguous way) a negative trait; the written text at the end asks 'should we create a new world or save our own?'. Immediately before that, we see a fake thanks to the main agribusiness companies. Children looking the viewer in the eye create a clear effect of direct call to our responsibilities. The fictional world is created as a coherent one, but some 'signs', some aspects of the global semiotic device, are there to 'break' this coherence and to drive the viewer towards the 'morality' of the show. It is a clear example of 'post-environmentalism', in which the 'zero degree' of meaning is bypassed and the text develops a second degree, using the old rhetoric figure of irony (real meaning is the opposite of what is said or showed, in this case the fact that "new bees" are better than the old ones), without a direct appeal to emotions.

Images are present also in the report 'Plan bee – living without pesticides', downloadable on the website. It is aimed at presenting a complete vision about how to manage the problem through a radical change in agricultural practices. In short, it is a text completely dominated by logos. In order to legitimate the seriousness of the discourse, an important rhetorical device is the abundance of bibliographical references. Another one is the presence of lists made of bullet points, a visual representation of 'enumeration', that is a central part of the rational 'method' proposed by the philosopher Réné Descartes, a central part of the scientific approach and a rhetoric tool for creating a sense of serious and rationality (see Catellani 2011a). Finally, another device is the relatively limited presence of visual images. There are illustrations at the beginning and between each chapter, a sort of visual opening and break in the flux of data and argumentation. They are very big photos that occupy the whole page, without borders (with a possible effect of immersion and visual pleasure). Another type of image that is present in the report is the one of illustrations: for example, the image of a specific type of bee, with a legend that specifies and anchors the content. More generally, each image in the report has a legend that explains and anchors the content, even in the case of the very big, full-page images. 'Logocentrism' (centrality of the verbal language) is evident, and it perfectly balances the (moderate) 'iconocentrism' of the website: people interested in deepening the subject will read the very long report, which offers the cognitive basis of the whole semiotic device of the campaign. From the 'RoboBees' and the 'Greenbees' videos to the quite an-iconic report, Greenpeace is able to use very different semiotic configurations, in order to 'create (symbolic) added value' around its message and its call to action.

Tigers and knowledge images

In other campaigns, we meet a different type of visual strategy, the one that I called in other texts 'knowledge images'.[16] Images of this type appear in the supports of the campaign against the use of tropical forest wood to produce pulp for paper and packages of toys.[17] These pages are a part of the 'core' website of the association (not a specific website for a campaign). The video on the top of the page presents in a didactic way an inquiry made by the association to unveil the links between deforestation and toy industry. It is a narrative presentation, made with written texts and images that show simplified and artificial images of toy boxes, stylized representations of machines and bulldozers, animated maps, etc. Music has here, as in other videos already observed, the role of adding 'psychagogy', in connection with the rhythm of images: music is obsessive and repetitive, quite "mechanic", and the effect can be an intensification of the dramatic atmosphere (and, as usual, the capacity of attiring attention).

Images are simplified, including some sorts of 'pictograms' (the heating planet, the jungle, two shaking hands with banknotes representing corruption), and some animated maps. They are different examples of the reduction of iconic 'definition': the amount of details is reduced and the global effect is the focus of the attention on more abstract notions, links and connections. Image tends to become a 'diagram', in which connections and interactions are in evidence. The expression 'knowledge image' can identify this pedagogical visual genre: 'visual text is not a spectacular, high-definition device, but a didactic and schematic support for teaching' (Catellani 2012: 5).[18]

Other examples of knowledge images are present in the same website. For example, we see some interactive maps, in which the viewer can identify precisely the area in which deforestation is taking place. This kind of images (simplified iconic definition, increased transparency of more abstract meaning, narrative or other) constitute in some senses the opposite pole of the 'proof' images, in which high definition supports the impression of a direct sensorial contact with a reality.

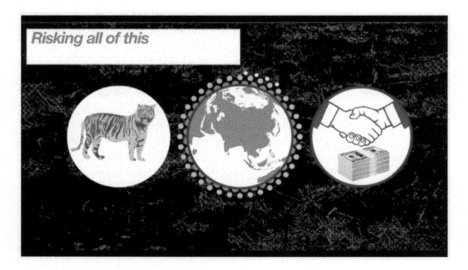

Figure 9.3 Save the Tigers

Some conclusions: towards a typology of post-environmentalist images

My observation of the use of visual images (both static and moving) by Greenpeace on the Web is aimed at creating a typology that can be used to understand other similar cases, like the visual universe of other big international environmentalist associations (Friends of the Earth, WWF, etc.). As a consequence, the conclusions take the form of a list of 'visual genres' with a short description of their characteristics. Each type can be described in particular from the point of view of the categories presented at the beginning of this article:

- the degree of visual 'definition' or fidelity, the 'iconisation' of images;
- the type of the relation with the verbal text (complementarity or inter-semiotic redundancy);
- the place of emotion (pathos), knowledge (logos) and the presence of the actor/hero who is portrayed (ethos);
- the specific combination of 'pedagogy' and 'psychagogy';
- the similarity with one of the four styles or strategies of advertising according to Floch 2001: referential, mythical, substantial and oblique.

Each type can include either moving and still images together, or only one of these two types. Of course, the types I identify here come from an empirical research on a limited 'corpus', and perhaps other combinations are possible and exist on the Web (or will exist in the future). Concrete verbal and visual (multi-modal) texts can include different types of images, and sometimes it can be difficult to categorize specific images. Nonetheless, this typology can contribute to the understanding of visual rhetoric.

1. Pictograms

I put in this category all small and simplified abstract images, in particular small pictograms, which can accompany verbal text. This category is not present in the website in an autonomous form; we find some pictograms incorporated into the video on deforestation. In this case, pictograms are the support of a pedagogical action.

2. Anonymous and specific illustrations; proof images

This very large category includes fixed images, but also videos (like in the case of the interview to prof. Herren). Generally speaking, an illustration proposes the visual equivalent of the accompanying verbal text. Images are used to create a 'composition of place', to propose to the reader the space and time that correspond to what is said verbally. I identified two different types of illustrations: the anonymous ones – the visual correspondent of indefinite articles (e.g. 'an' example of industrial agriculture, without specification of time and place) – and the 'specific' ones – e.g. images with legends that identify precisely the place and the time. Iconic definition is normally high (photos and realistic videos). The quantity of psychagogy is normally low; illustrative images are instead a possible ingredient of pedagogical texts.

Finally, illustrations are examples of a referential or substantial strategy (creation of an impression of contact with a reality). Specific illustrations include *proof images* as a sub-type. In this case, a high level of iconic definition is used to show the visual proof of a phenomenon, like in the case of photos (with legend) of deforestation in Indonesia, or of videos of dying bees in a sunflower field in Hungary. Proof images can be moving or still; they are linked to a specific space and time. Proof images are normally linked to a low level of ethos and pathos, while they are a support for logos. They are normally more pedagogical than psychagogical. Like other illustrations, they are examples of referential and substantial strategies.

3.   *Referential narrative images*

Mostly videos, these images (visual components of verbal-visual texts) present a situation, a phenomenon or an event (like the video on the Global Day of Action). They are normally narrative or with a narrative component (they contribute to the narration of the story of one or more characters, and are built around some modification or change to reality). Their iconic definition is high: they are built to appear as a 'window on the world', in order to put the viewer in direct contact with it. Psychagogy can be present in this kind of visual texts: the combination of verbal text, music and (edited) images can create a complete experience for the viewer, often with evident emotional aspects (pathos). The visual strategy is referential, even if some videos of this type can become mythical (because of the dramatic, intense evocation of basic values and principles). This type of images is not far from illustrations. The distinction between the two types has to be made case by case, observing if the visual images are simply a double of the text (inter-semiotic redundancy), or if they participate in creating the narrative meaning of the text (complementarity).

4.   *'Ethical' images (in the sense of Aristotelian 'ethos')*

These images are the place for exposing a character, normally a 'hero' of environmentalism (or an 'endorser' like a scientist), talking about a subject. They present the enunciator that is proposed as a source of persuasion and knowledge for the viewer. These images can alternate with others (in particular the narrative ones), in order to build specific persuasive videos. Ethos images can be part of pedagogical videos, but do not exclude a psychagogical component. An example of ethos images outside environmentalism is the one of photos of CEOs and managers in financial and CSR (corporate social responsibility) reports of business corporations (see Catellani 2015). Ethos images are often linked to a mythical style.

5. *Knowledge images*

This type of images is quite diverse, including maps, diagrams, images with abstract elements aimed at identifying relations and aspects (like arrows and lines, or artificial colors), schemes, etc. The basic characteristic is that iconic definition is 'broken' and reduced in order to put emphasis on a more abstract content, or in order to create a selective attention on some aspects. Image becomes (more directly) a cognitive tool. Logos and pedagogy are in this case clearly dominant. The basic visual style is referential: the basic connotation of this kind of images is the direct contact with a reality, in this case not by showing this reality in its sensorial appearance, but by expressing something of its invisible 'essence', identity or abstract configuration (quantity of deforestation, economic links between companies, etc.).

6. *Spectacular images*

It is the case of visual parodies and self-parodies (like 'Greenbees'). What defines more this type is the rhetorical modification of the visual world. In the case of the Ken's video, the basic visual technique (realistic, high-definition cartoon) is already a modification of the normal visual experience, but the real 'break' is made in relation to the fictional world of Barbie and Ken, on a narrative level. In the case of Greenbees, the break is the transfer of real scenes of activism to bees, keeping a high level of iconicity. These images are good examples of the 'oblique' strategy identified by Floch. Psychagogy can be present and important: the visual experience created by the video is aimed at attiring, amusing and mobilizing the viewer, even if these videos are clearly more based (at least in many cases) on amusement, spectacle and surprise than on moral emotions.

This last observation on spectacular (rhetoric) images leads to the conclusion of this text about a possible form of 'post-environmentalism', similar to the post-humanitarian communication studied by Chouliaraki. The presence of irony, parody and other rhetorical forms is a proof of the importance of the 'oblique' style, which creates a link with the 'post-humanitarian' tendencies studied by this author. Another aspect of the post-humanitarian communication in Chouliaraki'is analysis is that the viewer's look is often 'de-emotionalised' ('de-emotionalisation of the cause', 2010: 118).

Basing on the corpus under analysis, I affirm that this tendency is present, even if psychagogy identified in the corpus is a testimony of the importance of emotional aspects. The evocation of emotions is present, but it is not based on an intense, immediate and elementary evocation of passions; instead, it is the result of the immersion in a multi-semiotic experience in which images (rhetorically modified or not) have an important part, together with music. Emotions are not absent, but they are previewed as the result of a sophisticated visual and textual construction that stimulates the reflexivity and inferential activity of the viewer ('affective regimes . . . do not appear as immediate emotions that may inspire action but rather as objects of contemplation to be reflected upon', 2010: 118).

Another 'post-environmentalist' aspect present in the images I observed is the importance of the brand. As Chouliaraki wrote (2010: 118), 'it is not the verbalization of argument but the 'aura' of the brand that sustains the relationship between product and consumer'. In the case of Greenpeace, this observation has to be toned down: the aura is real, and self-parodies plays on the symbolic capital of the brand; but Greenpeace doesn't hesitate to verbalize in many different forms its arguments, and to mobilize different visual genres too.

In conclusion, some aspects of the visual rhetoric of Greenpeace are near to the post-humanitarian communication, and the expression 'post-environmentalism' can be used. It refers in particular to the richness of the visual languages of Greenpeace communication, to its mobilization of different rhetoric and multimodal forms, to the appeal to the inferential and reflective activity of the reader, to the indirectness of the appeal to emotions.

As we have seen, the visual world of Greenpeace is diverse, and it does not include only 'rhetorically modified' videos and parodies. Greenpeace plays on a rich visual 'blend' made of emotion, testimony and knowledge, in order to attire, interest and convince (and in order to 'emerge' in the hard competition for 'buzz' on the Internet). The 'post-environmentalist' visual language of Greenpeace is also made of knowledge and proof images, in which emotions and psychagogy are not very evident. The visual language of this association appears today as very mature, rich and developed, and this article was an attempt at exploring it. Other researches would be necessary to extend the application of the typology of persuasive images to other organisations.

Notes

1 Different kinds of "socio-semiotics" or "social semiotics" have developed, in order to improve the connection between text analysis and the study of social and cultural contexts (see Catellani 2011b, 2011a, 2012, 2015).
2 Van Leeuwen makes reference in particular, but not only, to the works of M. A. K. Halliday.
3 Examples in the following sections will clarify the meaning of "pedagogy" and "psychagogy" in Foucault's perspective (2001). See also Catellani (2012).
4 See Greenpeace campaign. 'Save the Arctic': http://savethearctic.org/en/ (accessed 29th February 2016). The website of the campaign has changed significantly between 2014 and the final observation in 2016.
5 See Greenpeace campaign, 'Save the Bees': www.youtube.com/watch?v=bL3luiNGshM (accessed on 29th February 2016).
6 See the 'Save the Bees' campaign homepage: http://sos-bees.org/ (accessed on 29 February 2016).
7 See Greenpeace campaign, 'Save the Bees': https://youtu.be/ICHOqrR8Dng (accessed on 29th February 2016).
8 "Non-rational" does not mean "anti-rational": it is simply another "way" of persuasion, that does not pass through data and reasoning (a distanced examination of elements), but through a more immediate involvement in a dynamic, like a narrative. This distinction, coming from the research of Michel Foucault, is not identical to the distinction between the two "routes" of persuasion studied by psychology (peripheral and central route proposed by Petty and Cacioppo in 1986), even if some connections can be identified between the two theories. In some senses, "psychagogy" is a third route, based on emotional vibration or "immersion" in an experience that creates the proof that something has to be believed or done.

9 See Greenpeace campaign, 'Save the Bees': www.youtube.com/watch?v=2tKs UyRZLpE#t=26 (accessed on 29th February 2016).
10 See Greenpeace campaign, 'Save the Bees': www.youtube.com/watch?v=PJ4os0WuFdE (accessed on 29th February 2016).
11 See Greenpeace campaign, 'Save the Bees': http://sos-bees.org/greenbees.
12 See Greenpeace campaign, 'Barbie, It's Over'. www.Greenpeace.org/international/en/ campaigns/forests/asia-pacific/barbie/ (accessed on 29th February 2016).
13 See Greenpeace: www.youtube.com/watch?v=nXndQuvOacU (accessed on 29th February 2016).
14 In the case of the campaign against Volkswagen, we can talk about a "double re-writing": the first one is made in the original advertisement by Volkswagen, that evokes one of the characters of the film series; the second one by Greenpeace, which creates the parody of the advertisement by Volkswagen by using other elements, characters and narrative aspects of the film series in order to change the meaning of the advertisement itself (see Catellani, 2012).
15 See Greenpeace, 'Robobees': http://robobees.info/ (accessed on 29th February 2016).
16 See Catellani (2012), in which a section is dedicated to this case.
17 See Greenpeace: www.greenpeace.org/international/en/campaigns/forests/asia-pacific/ app/toys/ (accessed on 29th February 2016).
18 Of course, the fact of using comic strip-like images to talk about packaging of toys creates a sort of internal coherence.

References

Barthes, Roland. (1964). Rhétorique de l'image. *Communications* 4 (1): 40–51.

Catellani, Andrea. 2010. *Lo sguardo et la parola. Saggio di analisi della letteratura spirituale illustrata*. Florence: Cesati.

Catellani, Andrea. (2011a). La justification et la présentation des démarches de responsabilité sociétale dans la communication corporate: notes d'analyse textuelle d'une nouvelle rhétorique épidictique. *Etudes de communication* 37: 159–176.

Catellani, Andrea. (2011b). Environmentalists NGOs and the Construction of the Culprit: Semiotic Analysis. *Journal of Communication Management* 15 (4): 280–297.

Catellani, Andrea. (2012). Critiques visuelles: observations socio-sémiotiques sur quelques campagnes parodiques environnementalistes. *Communiquer dans un monde de normes. L'information et la communication dans les enjeux contemporains de la "mondialisation"*. Proceedings of the congress "Communiquer dans un monde de normes. L'information et la communication dans les enjeux contemporains de la 'mondialisation'". Available at: http://hal.univ-lille3.fr/hal-00823885

Catellani, Andrea. (2015). Visual Aspects of CSR Reports: A Semiotic and Chronological Case Analysis. Melo, Ana Duarte, Somerville, Ian and Gonçalves, Gisela, eds., *Organisational and Strategic Communication Research: European Perspectives II*, 129–149. Braga: CECS – Centro de Estudos de Comunicação e Sociedade Universidade do Minho.

Chouliaraki, Lilie. (2010). Post-Humanitarianism: Humanitarian Communication Beyond a Politics of Pity. *International Journal of Cultural Studies* 13 (2): 107–126.

Fairclough, Norman. (2005). Peripheral Vision: Discourse Analysis in Organization Studies: The Case for critical realism. *Organization Studies* 26 (6): 915–939.

Floch, Jean-Marie. (2001). *Semiotics, Marketing and Communication: Beneath the Signs, the Strategies*. Hampshire: Palgrave (original version: 1990. *Sémiotique, marketing et communication*. Paris: PUF).

Fontanille, Jacques. (2006). *The Semiotics of Discourse*. Brussels: Peter Lang.

Fontanille, Jacques. (2008). *Pratiques sémiotiques*. Paris: PUF.

Foucault, Michel. (2001). *L'herméneutique du sujet. Cours au Collège de France 1981–1982*. Paris: Seuil/Gallimard.

Henault, Anne and Beyaert, Anne ed. (2004). *Ateliers de sémiotique visuelle*. Paris: PUF.

Ihlen, Øyvind. (2011). On *barnyard scrambles*: Towards a Rhetoric of Public Relations'. *Management Communication Quarterly* 25 (3): 423–441.

Ihlen, Øyvind. (2015). "It Is Five Minutes to Midnight and All Is Quiet": Corporate Rhetoric and Sustainability'. *Management Communication Quarterly* 29 (1): 145–152.

Ihlen, Øyvind. (2016). Critical Rhetoric and Public Relations. L'Etang, Jacquie, McKie, David, Snow, Nancy, Xifra, Jordi ed., *The Routledge Handbook of Critical Public Relations*, 90–100. London: Routledge.

Petty, Richard, E. and Cacioppo, John, T. (1986). The Elaboration Likelihood Model of Persuasion. *Communication and Persuasion*. Springer Series in Social Psychology. Springer, New York, NY.

Van Leeuwen, Theo. (2005). *Introducing Social Semiotics*. London: Routledge.

Van Leeuwen, Theo. (2010). 4. Materiality and Meaning: A Social Semiotic Approach. Jewitt, C. ed., *Routledge Handbook of Multimodal Analysis*. London: Routledge.

10 Exploring visual experiments

Measuring multi-modal messages in laboratory research

Anna-Sara Fagerholm and Karina Göransson

Introduction: measuring the unconscious

Our perceptual thinking is largely unconscious (Brumberger, 2003). When we decide which political party to vote for, what to eat for dinner, whom to sit next to, or where to spend our holiday, our unconscious thoughts play a big role, and previous research indicates how deeply the unconscious mind shapes our daily interactions (Bargh, 2014). According to scholars (Schreuder, 2014; Khushaba et al., 2013) it is important to know about the unconscious when we are interested in studying human behaviour and, in particular, human visual experiences.

Therefore, we have to better understand the role of the visual and consciously identify visual components and their relationships to one another (Brumberger, 2003). Almost a decade ago, scholars developed thoughts on the role of unconscious influences (Freud, 1915; Rorschach, 1921; Jung, 1934), and in recent years, the unconscious effects of environmental signals on human behavior have been deciphered by researchers of social cognition (Dijksterhuis, Smith, van Baaren and Wigboldus, 2005; Bargh and Chartrand, 1999; Aarts, Dijksterhuis, and Dik, 2008; Ferguson and Bargh, 2004b; Wegner and Bargh, 1998). In addition, when psychologists try to understand the way our mind works, they commonly come to the conclusion that we often make decisions without having given them much thought (Bargh, 2014).

The human senses can intensify the experiences of certain messages and environments and therefore have an impact on their reception (Leijon, 2010). Every day we meet visual communications and different design solutions arranged in specific ways and, according to Holsanova (2014), these visual messages are created with the purpose to either inform, instruct, explain, educate, entertain, persuade, sell or communicate. However, there is a need to develop our knowledge about how we interact with these messages and what catches our attention and what does not, as it would improve how different target groups in society deal with visualizations and integration of text and images. Furthermore, there is still a lack of empirical studies on recipients' interaction with visual and multimodal messages (Holsanova, 2012, 2013).

The possibility of measuring the unconscious opens up opportunities to study how to measure and strategically communicate to specific target groups. Previously, researchers have used methods like observations to describe for example a setting, a behaviour or an event. Also, interviews are often used to comprehend the perspective and goals of different target groups (Maxwell, 2013), although one of the main limitations is that interviews are probing conscious experience and do not provide objective measurements, moreover, people with cognitive limitations can have difficulties interpreting and expressing their feelings in interview situations (Jenkins, Brown and Rutterford, 2009; Abdipour, Lorentzen and Olin, 2016).

In comparison, problems with self-reported or projective techniques for examining effects of situational variables (Lachman, Lachman and Butterfield, 1979; De Camp Wilson and Nisbett, 1978), can be reduced by doing experiments in research laboratories. According to Jenkins et al. (2009), there are a variety of methods used to measure response to emotional stimuli in experimental research studies, such as skin conductance (Electrodermal response, EDR or Galvanic Skin Response, GSR), cardiac function (Electrocardiogram, ECG), heart rate (HR), respiration, blood pressure (BP), facial musculature (Electromyogram, EMG) and more recently, gastric myoelectric activity (Electrogastrogram, EGG). Thus, these methods have been used in other scientific fields, but are rarely used in strategic communication.

In accordance, van Leeuwen (2014) argues that there is a crucial challenge to develop tools for analyzing the visual. Furthermore, he claims that today's reading is not 'linear', instead we gradually create meaning of parts to understand the whole spatial structure in a multimodal context. According to Jenkins et al. (2009) it is essential for researchers within the field of strategic communication to move beyond the limitations of methods built upon subjective conscious interpretations and explore the use of new experimental tools and multimodal methods to reach objective measurement of human experience.

Moreover, methodological improvements and additional psychological research are needed in the interpretation of multimodal messages to facilitate the development of valid measures of content in research (Weare and Lin, 2000). We live in a multimodal era and the future is likely to be even more multimodal, therefore the analysis methods must be multimodal too (Björkvall, 2009).

Consequently, strategic communication is multimodal: it activates eyes, ears, hands, and heart, stimulates several senses (Rasmussen, 2014). Multimodal analysis is relevant to the study of strategic communication since it is common to integrate multiple forms of communication into a communication campaign (Kress and van Leeuwen, 2001, 2006). Also, multimodality is about different modes employed simultaneously in conveying complex, sometimes even contradictory messages (Kress and van Leeuwen, 2001). From a reception perspective multimodality primarily concerns sensory modalities – vision, hearing, touch, texture, smell and taste – and focuses on the integration of information across the senses, so called cross-modal interaction (Rasmussen 2014; Holsanova, 2014).

Today the term has developed to denote the integrated use of different communicative resources such as language, image and sound in contexts of communicative events or messages and public communication has become increasingly multimodal (van Leeuwen, 2014; Jewitt, 2014). Language alone is not always sufficient when communicating, instead cross-modality meaning builds upon the collaboration of verbal and visual that together form mental representations, each modality contributing to the creation of thoughts and meaning (Hagan, 2007). Therefore, there is a need of multimodal research tools when exploring the multimodal nature of for example the web, to make a better understanding of the many layers of implicit meaning and cultural indicators (Pauwels, 2012). Multimodality methodologies used in experimental laboratory research could be the solution to this, enabling studies of the unconscious mind.

In accordance, experimental visual communication research offers a possibility to measure both the conscious and the unconscious in a research lab, where traditional multimodal methods are combined with laboratory research equipment for measuring psychological signals probing emotional responses (Abdipour et al., 2016). Previous studies indicate that verbal stimuli affect the unconscious, for example, people walk more slowly after hearing words that are associated with elderly people, for instance words as 'Florida' and 'bingo' (Bargh, 2014). Also, research shows that visual stimulus matter even more for unconscious priming effects – an image of a pair of eyes increases contribution to a public good (Bateson, Nettle and Roberts, 2006). Visual stimuli has added to our understanding how different brain regions are activated when making judgments or undertaking certain behaviors (Bargh, 2014).

Moreover, confronting the challenges posed by the information age and the visual turn in society (Mitchell, 1995; Becker, 2004; Felten, 2008; Holsanova, 2012; Teruggi Page, 2014), developing new methods for studying communication and multimodal messages are significant. Abdipour et al. (2016: 1), claim that there is a need for an 'extended tool box addressing the part not accessible to human conscious knowledge'.

Literature review

Here, we present a brief overview of controlled experiments in a laboratory setting. In addition, a literature review on experimental research was conducted in the field of strategic communication, and like previous researchers (Barnhurst and Quinn, 2012; Barnhurst, 2004), we also inspected publications from the related discipline of public relations. The total selection of journals were made followed by searches in databases and the keywords visual, experiment, experimental method, experimental study and strategic communication were used. This is followed by a discussion of how to measure and customize visual communication strategies in terms of advertising campaigns, symbols and product designs, and targeting different groups in public spaces.

Controlled experiments are part of a scientific tradition. One of the semiotic protagonists, Charles Sanders Peirce (1839–1914), was among the first to make experimental studies in a laboratory. Peirce and his student Jastrow, assigned volunteers randomly to an experiment with the aim of evaluating the ability to discriminate weights (Peirce and Jastrow, 1884). This experiment inspired researchers in psychology and education to develop a research tradition with randomized experiments in laboratories, and were performed to get more knowledge of human perception and included a theory of representation and cognition which Peirce's studied under the name of semiotics (Liszka, 1996). Later, semiotic research developed into a multimodal approach, and the multimodal analysis is mainly based on theories developed by Peirce (Rasmussen, 2014).

A famous and attentive experimental study was carried out in 1963 by Milgram, a psychologist at Yale University. He conducted an experiment focusing on the conflict between obedience to authority and personal sense of right and wrong (Russell, 2011). In laboratory experiments, Milgram examined justifications for acts of mass murder offered by those accused at the World War II Nuremberg war-crimes trials: a defence often based on the claims that they were just following orders from their leaders. Milgram's aim was to see how far people would go when they were given an order and, as a result, these experiments showed that humans are capable of hurting others when obeying an authority. In his article 'Behavioral Study of Obedience' (1963), Milgram points out that the procedure created nervous tension, sweating and nervous laughter among the test persons. However, the design, interpretation and ethical aspect of this study has been criticised, and more than 50 years after the laboratory experiments, a team of cognitive scientists has carried out findings that may offer some explanation for Milgram's revelations. According to their research, people genuinely feel less responsibility for their actions when following commands (Caspar, Christensen, Cleeremans and Haggard, 2016).

Another early and famous experiment is the popcorn experiment by Vicary in 1957, where subliminal advertising were used at a movie theater with the aim to explore marketing techniques to increase the sales of popcorn and soda. The experiment was conducted by placing a tachistoscope in the theater's projection booth with the aim to exposure visual stimuli to the audience. All through the film *Picnic* different messages were flashed on the screen every five seconds, far below the viewer's conscious perceptibility. A tachistoscope is used in the study of perception and learning and the result showed that unwary buyers made purchases they would not otherwise have considered. Later, criticism of the experiment was that no explanation was presented of, for example, the differences in size of the percentages or other details, as to how or under what conditions the tests had been conducted (Rogers, 1992).

Even in 1987, Pavlik noted that virtually no experiments had been conducted in public relations research (Cameron, 1992) and our literature review shows that within the field of strategic communication it is still unusual to find experimental studies related to multimodality in a laboratory environment. The only example found is a study where Hallahan (2001), explores usability connected to products tested in a laboratory using an experimental method. The study examines the nature and value of usability research, and the elements of an effective web site analysed in laboratory environments. In strategic communication research, it is also unusual to study audience's unconscious experience of communication messages and environment. More commonly, the conscious behaviour is studied and some examples are presented below.

In several research articles focusing on the impact of social media, experimental methods are used (Wiencierz, Pöppel and Röttger, 2015; Kim, Kim and Sung, 2014; Haigh and Wigley, 2015; Haigh, Brubaker and Whiteside, 2013). In research of strategic communication and advertising there are experiments of visual framing, for example Chen and Kim (2011) examine message framing in political advertising by using a pre-test/post-test experiment. In the research field of public relations, several studies use experiments as the main method (Sallot, 1996; Hong and Len-Riós, 2015; Connolly-Ahern, Grantham and Cabrera-Baukus, 2010; Werder, 2006).

These tests explore how messages are perceived in an experimental setting. For example, Sallot (1996) conducted a design experiment in order to test effects of motives, communication style and licensing on the reputations of sponsors of public relations in USA. In the experiment four fictitious news articles was exposed randomly to 585 participants. The next example explores if the perceived credibility of a PR spokesperson is based on the spokesman's race. In the experiment, which was run in a media lab, participants viewed photos of 16 spokespersons accompanied by a crisis story in a short paragraph. In the test, participants were shown 10 adjectives that referred to each spokesperson and had to click *yes* or *no* as to whether they were a good description of the spokesperson associated with the story (Hong and Len-Riós, 2015). Another example is a study by Connolly-Ahern et al. (2010). In the experiment, the aim was to understand the effects of video news releases on news consumers and the assessments of credibility and risk. The material consisted of newscasts including four stories, one of which was manipulated. Two-hundred-thirteen students participated in the study and the conclusion shows that there is a complex mechanism through which decisions of credibility are made. The last example from the field of public relations is a controlled experiment by Werder (2006) using stimulus material based on a real case of activism where a well-known activist group made an attack campaign against McDonald's with the aim to make McDonald's change its suppliers' treatment of food animals. The study analyzed the influence of public relations strategies on attributes of publics towards an organization responding to activism and shows the need for further understanding of both message and receiver variables in public relations.

Even in crisis communication research, scholars practice experimental methodology in their studies (Schwarz, 2012; Dardis and Haigh, 2009; Jin, 2014; Wan and Schell, 2007). An example is an experimental study by Lachlan and Spence (2014) which explores the influence of print and video, and the findings indicate that the use of organisation-produced messages placed in print media may reduce the negative effects of the crisis communications.

As for the types of experiments that occur in strategic communication research, the most common are the various online experiments. These experiments aim to measure the effects of social media and web pages by testing research hypotheses and questions posited, with the most frequently used tool being the online survey. (Wiencierz et al., 2015; Schmeltz, 2017; Wang, 2012; Cameron, 1994 Bachmann and Ingenhoff, 2017; Burgoon, Bonito, Ramirez, Dunbar, Kam and Fischer, 2002). For example, Werder (2008) discusses the results from a controlled experiment using stimulus material based on Starbucks Coffee Company corporate social responsibility initiatives.

In summary, our literature review indicates that experimental research is uncommon in strategic communications and public relations. Also, experimental research of the unconscious experience of communication messages are very rare. By that means, in a laboratory environment we see that there is a possibility to measure the unconscious in order to work strategically with visual messages to customize and enhance visual messages communicated in public spaces. Further, we argue that this experience could give professionals valuable insights on the specific communication needs of different target groups in public spaces.

An example of laboratory research

To exemplify experimental visual communication research and how it can be relevant to strategic communication scholars and professionals, we present a design laboratory ('design lab') at Mid Sweden University. Here, a research group has developed a model of how to identify people's conscious and unconscious behaviour in a design process. In the lab, traditional methods are complemented with tools to measure physiological signals influenced by emotional and sympathetic responses of conscious and unconscious user reactions. According to Abdipour et al. (2016: 2), the research lab could offer a 'variety of user studies using a virtual reality environment combined with several measurement tools'.

When we first visited the lab, we entered an environment consisting of a user stage with video projectors and large displays that can show virtual visual content,

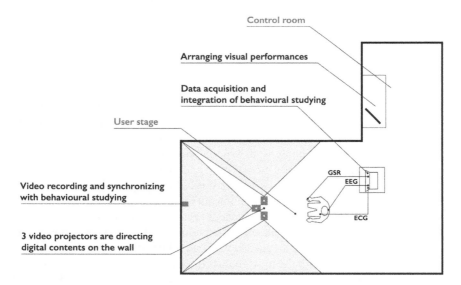

Figure 10.1 Overview of The Design Research Lab at Mid Sweden University. Used with permission of Morteza Abdipour.

and next to the user stege is a control room where the physiological measure-ment data is collected. Abdipour et al. (2016), describes this environment in their article, and adds that there are also various equipment to measure physiological reactions like brain activity, heart rate and hand sweat. Before a session starts in this laboratory, the participants receive an introduction to the lab with the aim of

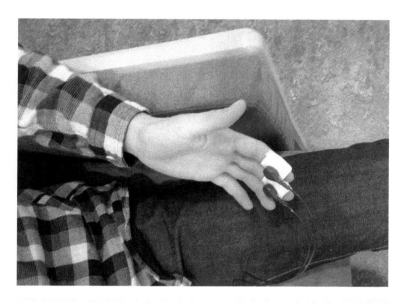

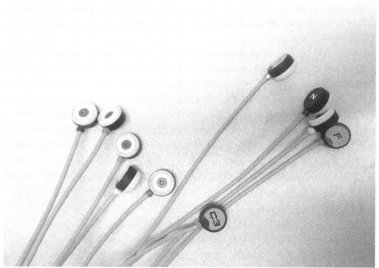

Figure 10.2 (i-iii) GSR connections (i), ECG (ii) and EEG Cap (iii): three solutions used to register emotional reactions. Used with permission of Morteza Abdipour.

Figure 10.2 (i-iii) (Continued)

bringing the test respondents to a calm starting point. The experiment goes on collecting data of brain- and heart activities and skin moisture. Observation and interviews can be used to complement when collecting behaviours, user experiences and concepts and sessions are recorded by video cameras and photographies (Abdipour et al., 2016).

According to Abdipour et al. (*ibid*), visual experiences can be evaluated by arranging a system in a lab registering participants brain activities from the scalp (Electroencephalography, EEG), the activity of the heart (Electrocardiogram, ECG) and by measurement of the electrical conductance of the skin influenced by moist of the skin (Galvanic skin conductance, GSR). One example of a study performed in the lab, is an experiment evaluating emotional reactions of users with and without Attention Deficit Hyperactivity Disorder (ADHD), and in their article the research group present results examining the impact of large displays used for advertisement in public (Abdipour et al., 2016). In the test experiment, participants were surrounded by three different commercial film clips projected onto three walls, and the physical measurements of GSR combined with interviews indicated that people without ADHD were able to focus on a single screen, while the participants with ADHD lacked this focus and tried to look at all screens simultaneous. According to the research group, this could help researchers to understand what target groups are looking at and why they show a typical behaviour, both from a conscious and unconscious perspective (Abdipour et al, 2016). Currently, there are ongoing experimental projects in the lab, and we are looking forward to more research to come.

Figure 10.3 Demonstration of a visual experiment where evaluation of environmental design and behavioural observations are integrated with psycho-physiological reactions.

Used with the permission of Morteza Abdipour

The double-edged sword

The pluralism of theoretical perspectives that exist within strategic communication is relevant to the use of different methods, which means that there are high demands on the ones to choose and apply as a method. The choice of perspective becomes crucial and important to how a method is applied and how the results are presented. (Thelander and Eksell, 2014). Nevertheless, there are some methodological challenges with laboratory research. In this section of the chapter, we focus on the use of the experimental method as well as a critical reflection.

Scholars have pointed out a range of arguments about the value of combining methods (Bryman, 2011; Fielding and Schreier, 2001; Kelle, 2001; Mason, 2006). According to Mason (2006) mixed-method research is relevant because reality is multi-dimensional and experienced at a macro and micro scale. But also, this mixed-method approach raise challenges in conciliating different epistemologies and ontologies, and in integrating different forms of data and knowledge.

In studies with experiments as method, researchers use standardized procedures and operationalisations. For example, in carefully designed controlled experiments it is possible to investigate, in a systematic way, people's experiences and the processes for the reception of multimodal messages. By that means, experimental studies offer more conclusive answers about what caused the effect observed in the behavior (Holsanova, 2012). Although, a limitation of laboratory research is the large amount of data created by the experiment. Sorting and filtering the data must be done with the aim to get the most valuable data in order to use analysing tables (Abdipour et al., 2016). After collection of raw data from experiments, the data must be processed. The complex reality can be summarized and simplified into a matrix which is a schematic view of reality. Data processing usually takes place through: coding, categorizing, systematic loss (for example, questions), unsystematic loss (eg mistake, time). Quality of the study and ethical aspects are linked to the management of the concepts of reliability and validity. That is, to what extent a measurement gives the same result if it is repeated on the same phenomenon, *reliability*, and to what extent a measurement measures it as it is based on measuring, *validity* (Esaisson, Gilljam, Oscarsson, Towns and Wängnerud, 2017).

Inherently in all experimental research, it is important to be cautious in generalizing from samples (Hong and Len-Riós, 2015), and a problem might be the sampling of large unknown amounts of data where researchers have to be more critical and explicit about choices (Pauwels, 2012). Hence, the analytical model is essential in experimental studies of multimodal resources. In studies of, for example, people's experiences of advertising campaigns, events or product design, the coding scheme and coding instructions, a visual grammar, underlies the analysis (Björkvall, 2009).

Another reason why multimodal methodologies are relevant to experimental studies of strategic communication is that there has been a trend towards using more forms of communication in one and the same product or service (Kress and van Leeuwen, 2001, 2006; Rasmussen, 2014). For example, on the web, interactive design, motion design, images, illustrations, text, typography, audio and video are used in one channel. A multimodal approach makes it possible to understand the common characteristics, differences and integration of several forms of communication (van Leeuwen, 2005). Beyond studying typography and layout (Rasmussen, 2014) and colors (van Leeuwen, 2011), multimodal analysis can also study sounds and music (van Leeuwen, 1999; Machin, 2010), monuments (Abousnnouga and Machin, 2013) and texture (van Leeuwen and Djonov, 2011). In the last decade, Pink (2009) argues that there are new approaches in understanding research such as the multisensory and the visual. Furthermore, Pink argues that we should add neurological perspectives to the multi-sensoriality paradigm of visual communication research and use visual methods in new ways. For example, the use of images as the dominant sensory modality should be complemented with video or sound and aural senses.

In an experimental setting, sometimes the researcher explores the participants sensory experiences of products and practices. Therefore, in the analysis the researcher has to have in mind that the material itself can awake the participants memories, rather than the experiences of the research content and context itself (Pink, 2015). According to Loftus and Palmer (1974), the original memory can be supplemented, modified or changed. Also, memory can easily be distorted by questioning techniques which can merge with original memory causing inaccurate recall or reconstructive memory, and this could affect the results of the experiment. Therefore, we argue that a possible weakness of the method is how validity could be guaranteed. Since small changes in information can cause distortion in memory (Loftus and Palmer, 1974) it is important that all participant receive the same information in the initial part of the experiment session, and this is one way of how this weakness could be prevented.

Furthermore, each research project needs to consider its own ethical practises, depending on the specifics of its situation. For researchers using experimental visual methods it is necessary to be careful of what the researcher does and why, and to be aware of the possible consequences when it comes to power relations. There is a need to develop other kinds of ethics, not what is right or wrong, but rather to explore the grounds of the relationship between the researcher and the researched (Rose, 2016).

Conclusion

In this chapter, we have attempted to summarize a wide range of arguments that critically reflects on the use of experiments as method in visual strategic communication research. It is becoming obvious that laboratory research employing multimodal analysis techniques can address essential issues of how to measure and customize strategic communication efforts. Furthermore, experiments as method have the potential to analyze multimodal resources and measure emotional reactions of communication activities and design in our daily life.

Consequently, in an experimental setting it is possible to evaluate communication strategies by measuring different target groups' conscious and unconscious experiences of advertising campaigns, symbols, product designs and environments. Nevertheless, combining multimodal methodologies with research in laboratories has rarely been employed in strategic communication research until recently, probably due to some of the challenges of this approach. Particularly, experiments as method in visual research do pose special technical difficulties, and sophisticated analysis software is often needed to process the large amount of data. In sum, by examining multimodal messages in laboratory research, knowledge of adequate and meaningful communication, strategically customized to different target groups, can develop and we look forward of more studies with visual experiments to come.

Acknowledgement

We would like to express our great appreciation to Morteza Abdipour for his valuable knowledge in the development of this book chapter.

References

Aarts, H., Dijksterhuis, A, & Dik, G. (2008). Goal Contagion: Inferring Goals from Others' Actions-and What It Leads to, in J. Shah and W. L. Gardner (eds.), *Handbook of Motivation Science,* 265–280. New York: Guilford Press.

Abdipour, M., Lorentzen, L., & Olin, H. (2016). A Design Research Lab: An Integrated Model to Identify Conscious and Unconscious Behavior in the Design Process, in

Advances in Intelligent Systems and Computing: Design for Inclusion (Vol. 500, pp. 553–563), Switzerland: Springer International Publishing.

Abousnnouga, G., & Machin, D. (2013). *The Language of War Monuments*, London: Bloomsbury.

Bachmann, P., & Ingenhoff, D. (2017). How Do Media Companies Gain Legitimacy? An Experimental Study on the (Ir)Relevance of CSR Communication, *International Journal of Strategic Communication, 11*(1), 79–94.

Bargh, J. A. (2014). Our Unconscious Mind: Unconscious Impulses and Desires Impel What We Think and Do in Ways Freud Never Dreamed of, *Scientific American*, January.

Bargh J. A., & Chartrand, T. L. (1999). The Unbearable Automaticity of Being, *American Psychologist, 54*(7), 462–479.

Bateson, M., Nettle, D., & Roberts, G. (2006). Cues of Being Watched Enhance Cooperation in a Real-World Setting, *Biology Letters, Sep 22, 2*(3), 412–414.

Becker, K. (2004). Where Is Visual Culture in Contemporary Theories of Media and Communication, *Nordicom Review, 25*(1–2), 149–158.

Björkvall, A. (2009). *Den visuella texten, multimodal analys i praktiken*, Stockholm: Ord och stil, Hallgren & Fallgren.

Barnhurst, K. G., & Quinn, K. (2012). Visual Studies in Political Communication, in H. A. Semetko and N. Scammell, (eds), *Sage Handbook of Political Communication*, 276–291, Los Angeles: SAGE Publications.

Barnhurst, K. G., Vari, M., Rodríguez, Í. (2004). Mapping Visual Studies in Communication, *Journal of Communication, 54*(4), 616–644.

Brumberger, E. R. (2003). The Rhetoric of Typography: The Persona of Typeface and Text, *Technical Communication, 50*(2).

Bryman, A. (2011). *Samhällsvetenskapliga metoder*. Liber, Stockholm.

Burgoon, J. K., Bonito, J. A., Ramirez, A., Dunbar, N. E., Kam, K., & Fischer, J. (2002). Testing the Interactivity Principle: Effects of Mediation, Propinquity, and Verbal and Nonverbal Modalities in Interpersonal Interaction, *Journal of Communication, 52*(3), 657–677.

Cameron, G. T. (1992). Memory for Investor Relations Messages: An Information-Processing Study of Grunig's Situational Theory, *Journal of Public Relations Research, 4*(1), 45–60.

Cameron, G. T. (1994). Does Publicity Outperform Advertising? An Experimental Test of the Third-Party Endorsement, *Journal of Public Relations Research, 6*(3).

Caspar, E. A., Christensen, J. F., Cleeremans, A., & Haggard, P. (2016). Coercion Changes the Sense of Agency in the Human Brain, *Current Biology, 26*, 585–592.

Chen, H-T., & Kim, Y. (2011). Attacking or Self-Promoting? The Influence of Tone of Advertising and Issue Relevance on Candidate Evaluations and the Likelihood of Voting for an Emerging Challenger in Korea, *International Journal of Strategic Communication, 5*, 261–280.

Connolly-Ahern, C., Grantham, S., & Cabrera-Baukus, M. (2010). The Effects of Attribution of VNRs and Risk on News Viewers' Assessments of Credibility, *Journal of Public Relations Research, 22*(1), 49–64.

Dardis, F., & Haigh, M. M. (2009). Prescribing versus Describing: Testing Image Restoration Strategies in a Crisis Situation, *Corporate Communications: An International Journal, 14*(1), 101–118.

De Camp Wilson, T., & Nisbett, R. E. (1978). The Accuracy of Verbal Reports about the Effects of Stimuli on Evaluations and Behavior, *Social Psychology, 41*(2), 118–131.

Dijksterhuis, A., Smith P. K., van Baaren, R. B., & Wigboldus, D. H. J. (2005). The Unconscious Consumer: Effects on Environment on Consumer Behavior, *Journal of Consumer Psychology*, *15*(3), 193–202.

Esaisson, P., Gilljam, M., Oscarsson, H., Towns, A., & Wängnerud, L. (2017). *Metodpraktikan: Konsten att studera samhälle, individ och marknad*, Stockholm: Lund. Wolters Kluwer.

Felten, P. (2008). Visual Literacy, *Change: The Magazine of Higher Learning*, *40*(6), 60–64.

Ferguson, M. J., & Bargh, J. A. (2004b). Liking is for Doing: The Effects of Goal Pursuit on Automatic Evaluation, *Journal of Personality and Social Psychology*, 87, 557–572.

Fielding, N & Schreier, M (2001). Introduction: On the Compatibility between Qualitative and Quantitative Research Methods [54 paragraphs]. *Forum Qualitative Sozialforschung / Forum: Qualitative Social Research*, *2*(1), Art. 4. Retrieved from http://nbn-resolving. de/urn:nbn:de:0114-fqs010146.

Freud, S. (1915). The Unconscious, in Freud, S. (1963), *General Psychological Theory: Papers on Metapsychology*, P. Rieff (ed.), New York: Collier Books, Macmillan Publishing Company.

Hagan, S. M. (2007). Visual/Verbal Collaboration in Print: Complementary Differences, Necessary Ties, and an Untapped Rhetorical Opportunity, *Written Communication*, *24*(1), 49–83.

Haigh, M. M., Brubaker, P., & Whiteside, E. (2013). Facebook: Examining the Information Presented and Its Impact on Stakeholders, *Corporate Communications: An International Journal*, *18*(1), 52–69.

Haigh, M. M., & Wigley, S. (2015). Examining the Impact of Negative, User-Generated Content on Stakeholders, *Corporate Communications: An International Journal*, *20*(1), 63–75.

Hallahan, K. (2001). Improving Public Relations Web Sites through Usability Research, *Public Relations Review*, 27, 223–239.

Holsanova, J. (2012). New Methods for Studying Visual Communication and Multimodal Integration, *Visual Communication*, *11*(3), 251–257.

Holsanova, J. (2013). In the Eye of the Beholder: Visual Communication from a Recipient Perspective, in D. Machin (ed.), *Visual Communication: Handbooks of Communication Science*, (Vol. 4), Boston: De Gruyter.

Holsanova, J. (2014). Reception of Multimodality: Applying Eye-Tracking Methodology in Multimodal Research, in C. Jewitt (ed.), *Routledge Handbook of Multimodal Analysis*, (2nd ed.), London: Routledge.

Hong, S. & Len-Riós, M. E. (2015). Does Race Matter? Implicit and Explicit Measures of the Effect of the PR Spokesman's Race on Evaluations of Spokesman Source Credibility and Perceptions of a PR Crisis' Severity, *Journal of Public Relations Research*, *27*(1), 63–80.

Jenkins, S. D., Brown, R. D. H., & Rutterford, N. (2009). Comparing Thermographic, EEG, and Subjective Measures of Affective Experience during Simulated Product Interactions, *International Journal of Design*, *3*(2), 53–65.

Jewitt, C. (2014). A Multimodal Lens on the School Classroom, in D. Machin (ed.), *Visual Communication, Handbooks of Communication Schénce*, Berlin and Boston: De Gruyter Mouton.

Jin, Y. (2014). Examining Publics' Crisis Responses According to Different Shades of Anger and Sympathy, *Journal of Public Relations Research*, 26, 79–101.

Jung, C. G. (1934–1954). *The Archetypes and the Collective Unconscious* (1981 2nd ed. Collected Works Vol. 9 Part 1), Princeton, NJ: Bollingen.

Kelle, U. (2001) Sociological Explanations Between Micro and Macro and the Integration of Qualitative and Quantitative Methods, *FQS (Forum: Qualitative Social Research)* *2*(1). Retrrieved from hwww.qualitative-research.net/fqs/fqs-eng.htm

Khushaba, R. N., Wise, C., Kodagoda, S., Louviere, J., Kahn, B. E., & Townsend, C. (2013). Consumer Neuroscience: Assessing the Brain Response to Marketing Stimuli Using Electroencephalogram (EEG) and Eye Tracking, *Expert Systems with Applications*, *40*(9), 3803–3812.

Kim, S., Kim, S., & Sung, K.H. (2014). Fortune 100 Companies' Facebook Strategies: Corporate Ability versus Social Responsibility, *Journal of Communication Management*, *18*(4), 343–362.

Kress, G., & van Leeuwen, T. (2001). *Multimodal Discourse: The Modes and Media of Contemporary Communication*, London: Arnold.

Kress, G., & van Leeuwen, T. (2006). *Reading Images: The Grammar of Visual Design*, London: Routledge.

Lachlan, K., & Spence, P. R. (2014). Does Message Placement Influence Risk Perception and Affect? *Journal of Communication Management*, *18*(2), 122–130.

Lachman, R., Lachman, J. L., & Butterfield, E. C. (1979). *Cognitive Psychology and Information Processing: An Introduction*, London & New York: Psychology Press, Taylor & Francis Group.

Leijon, M. (2010). *Att spåra tecken på lärande. Mediereception som pedagogisk form och multimodalt meningsskapande över tid* (Malmö Studies in Educational Sciences No. 52), Malmö: Malmö Högskola.

Liszka, J. J. (1996). *A General Introduction to the Semeiotic of C.S. Peirce*, Bloomington: Indiana University Press.

Loftus, E. F., & Palmer, J. C. (1974). Reconstruction of Auto-Mobile Destruction: An Example of the Interaction between Language and Memory, *Journal of Verbal Learning and Verbal Behavior*, *13*, 585–589.

Machin, D. (2010). *Analyzing Popular Music: Image, Sound and Text*, London: Sage.

Mason, J. (2006). Mixing Methods in a Qualitatively Driven Way, *Qualitative Research, London: Sage Publications*, *6*(1), 9–25.

Maxwell, J. A. (2013). *Qualitative Research Design: An Interactive Approach*, London: Sage.

Mitchell, W. J. T. (1995). *Picture Theory*, Chicago: University of Chicago Press.

Pauwels, L. (2012). A Multimodal Framework for Analyzing Websites as Cultural Expressions, *Journal of Computer-Mediated Communication*, *17*, 247–265.

Peirce, C. S., & Jastrow, J. (1884). On Small Differences in Sensation, *Memoirs of the National Academy of Sciences*, *3*, 73–83.

Pink, S. (2015). *Doing Sensory Ethnography*, London: Sage Publications.

Rasmussen, J. (2014). Multimodal analys – att förstå det visuella varumärket, in Eksell, J. & Thelander, Å. (eds.), *Kvalitativa metoder i Strategisk kommunikation*, Lund: Studentlitteratur.

Rogers, S. (1992). How a Publicity Blitz Created the Myth of Subliminal Advertising, *Public Relations Quarterly; Rhinebeck*, *37*(4) (Winter 1992–1993), 12.

Rorschach, H. (1921). *Psychodiagnostics: A Diagnostic Test Based on Perception*, Switzerland: Huber (Hans) Verlag.

Rose, G. (2016). *Visual Methodologies: An Introduction to Researching with Visual Materials*, London: Sage.

Russell, N. J. C. (2011). Milgram's Obedience to Authority Experiments: Origins and Early Evolution, *British Journal of Social Psychology*, *50*, 140–162.

Sallot, L. M. (1996). Considering the Source: What the Public Thinks of Sponsors of Public Relations, *Journal of Communication Management*, *1*(2), 145–165.

Schmeltz, L. (2017). Getting CSR Communication Fit: A Study of Strategically Fitting Cause, Consumers and Company in Corporate CSR Communication, *Public Relations Inquiry*, *6*(1), 47–72.

Schreuder, A. D. (2014). *Vision and Visual Perception: The Conscious Base of Seeing*, Bloomington: Archway Publishing.

Schwarz, A. (2012). Stakeholder Attributions in Crises: The Effects of Covariation Information and Attributional Inferences on Organizational Reputation, *International Journal of Strategic Communication*, *6*, 174–195.

Thelander, Å., & Eksell, J. (2014). Introduction, in Eksell, J. & Thelander, Å. (eds.), *Kvalitativa metoder i Strategisk kommunikation*, Lund: Studentlitteratur.

Teruggi Page, J. (2014). Images with Messages: A Semiotic Approach to Identifying and Decoding Strategic Visual Communication, in D. Holtzausen and A. Zerfass (eds), *The Routledge Handbook of Strategic Communication*, Abingdon: Routledge.

Van Leeuwen, T. (1999). *Speech, Music, Sound*, London: MacMillan.

Van Leeuwen, T. (2005). *Introduction to Social Semiotics*, London: Routledge.

Van Leeuwen, T. (2011). *The Language of Colour: An Introduction*, London: Routledge.

Van Leeuwen, T. (2014). Multimodality and Multimodal Research, in E. Margolis & L. Pauwels (eds.), *The Sage Handbook of Visual Research Methods*, London: Sage Publications.

Van Leeuwen, T., & Djonov, E. (2011). The Semiotics of Texture: From Tactile to Visual, *Visual Communication*, *10*(4), 541–564.

Wan, H., & Schell, R. (2007). Reassessing Corporate Image: An Examination of How Image Bridges Symbolic Relationships with Behavioral Relationships, *Journal of Public Relations Research*, *19*(1), 25–45.

Wang, A. (2012). Visual Priming of Pharmaceutical Advertising Disclosures: Effects of a Motivation Factor, *Corporate Communications: An International Journal*, *17*(1), 73–88.

Weare, C., & Lin, W. Y. (2000). Content Analysis of the World Wide Web: Opportunities and Challenges, *Social Science Computer Review*, *18*(3), 272–292.

Wegner, D. M., & Bargh, J. A. (1998). Control and Automaticity in Social Life, in D. Gilbert, S. T. Fiske, & G. Lindzey (eds.), *Handbook of Social Psychology* (4th ed., pp. 446–496), Boston: McGraw-Hill.

Werder, K. P. (2006). Analysis of Public Relations Strategy Influence on Attributes of Publics, *Journal of Public Relations Research*, *18*(4), 335–356.

Wiencierz, C., Pöppel, K, G., & Röttger, U. (2015). Where Does My Money Go? How Online Comments on a Donation Campaign Influence the Perceived Trustworthiness of a Nonprofit Organization, *International Journal of Strategic Communication*, *9*, 102–117.

11 Conclusions and future directions

Sarah Roberts-Bowman and Simon Collister

The importance of the non-textual aspects of PR and strategic communications has long been overlooked. It is hoped that this edited collection has gone some way to start to rectify this situation by drawing on a range of interdisciplinary scholarship that pulls together a number of related threads. We believe that the themes emerging from the contributors' chapter start to articulate a coherent picture of the ways in which the visual and spatial dimensions of communication play a much richer and increasingly important role in public relations and strategic communication. Whether it is a concern over the practicalities of the skills required for public relations practitioners to do their job; the transformation of research methods and conceptual approaches to what communication means in a scholarly environment through to broader concerns about public relations' role within a contemporary societal and cultural setting, we believe that it is increasingly clear that all of the threads explored in this text require further research and critique in order for the discipline to better understand and shape itself for the future.

PR comes home: past, present and future

On one hand, the visual and spatial dimensions of communication have always been part of human history and, at times, the chapters in this collection provide fresh and contemporary insights into centuries-old issues. Architecture and art were used in Ancient Egypt, to impress a particular message on the public of the greatness of the pharaohs. In England, the Bayeaux Tapestry was used to commit one account of the importance of the Norman Conquest into history; the network of Norman castles established after the Conquest become not just material, military sites but also symbolic icons of power. Maps and cartography too can be seen as symbolic abstractions of reality. In essence: all such phenomena have been strategically designed and deployed to tell a story.

Fast forward to the twentieth-century and, as L'Etang (2004) points out, in the UK the government was the driving force behind the early use of public relations. During World War I and World War II the need to unite people in a single cause stimulated creative persuasive approaches using a greater variety of printed means. This adoption of visual communication arguably begins with the growth of the poster with leading designers, such as Tom Eckersley, Abram Games, F.H.K

Henrion and Hans Schlege, being commissioned to produce highly impactful print work to educate mass populations on matters of public interest and safety.

All of these figures established their graphic design reputations during WW2 and subsequently revolutionised communication design post-war. From the 1930s too, film units were increasingly attached to public organisations' publicity or public relations departments, including the Post Office, Empire Marketing Board, and later during World War II the Ministry of Information.[1] Such techniques and approaches further stimulated the use of film by commercial organisations, including Dunlop, ICI and Shell.

The notion of spatiality, too, while conceived in this text as a distinctly contemporary concern has antecedents in history. One of the most quoted historically significant public relations moments, the 1929 'Torches of Freedom March' in New York, when women joined the Easter Parade in a collective public of public smoking, was not only a visual stunt but also demonstrated the importance of time and space. Orchestrated by Edward Bernays and A.A. Brill, the march intended to challenge the taboo of cigarette smoking among women (and thus aimed to increase sales for the American Tobacco Company). Although scholars such as Murphree (2015) suggest that Bernays subsequently over inflated the importance of the event in changing attitudes towards the social acceptability of smoking among women and the subsequent media coverage, it nevertheless points to the early significance of the performative and spatial dimensions of strategic communication.

While this book explores afresh the role of graphic design, visuality and spatiality in the context of contemporary public relations, it can be argued that such a distinction between the disciplines is not born out of historical precedent. Acknowledging, returning to and learning from such an historic inter-disciplinary perspective could enable strategic communications to become much more resilient to the field's future needs and challenges. Public relations practitioners and scholars should see themselves continuing the tradition of creating and studying powerful ideas that tell emotionally-compelling stories across time and space.

Sense-making

Another thread emerging from these chapters is how visual and spatial forms of communication help people to make sense of reality and the world around them. This links to the growing body of research around the concept of sense-making. Although there is no single agreed definition of sense-making (Brown *et al.*, 2015), broadly it is taken to mean the processes by which people seek plausibility to understand ambiguous, equivocal or confusing events (Colville *et al.*, 2012; Maitlis, 2005; Weick, 1995). This has relevance to how people construct the realities of their day-to day lives (Holt and Cornelissen, 2014).

Although much attention has been paid to sense-making in communications scholarship from a textual perspective, most notably by Taylor and van Every (2000), visual and spatial communications are also forms of narrative and discourse. Often illustrations, pictures and drawings can be used to give voice to emotions and contribute to understanding (Barner, 2008) with greater efficacy that simply text. In addition to purely functional sense-making uses of imagery, visual metaphors – defined as a way if enabling the understanding of one kind of concept in terms of another (Lakoff and Johnson, 1980) – and other types of visual cues can help people engage more deeply in important debates and topics. In doing so, meaning becomes co-created between the communicator and receiver, arguably fostering a deeper emotional connection and resonance.

The strategic significance of such phenomena is being explored within organisational and management studies and is a growing area of exploration (Davison *et al.*, 2012; Meyer *et al.*, 2013; Mitchell, 2011; Vince and Warren, 2012). These scholarly perspectives argue that visual materials, such as images, photos, drawings and, importantly, physical objects are being used to add depth and richness to organisational culture and communication. The role of such artefacts in constructing or directing meaning in organisational and, even, public (or 'quasi-public') spaces is also an area worthy of further examination by public relations and strategic communications scholars.

The recent 'cultural turn' in public relations theory has also challenged the functional and managerial focus arising from system theories. Here the work of scholars such as Edwards, Curtain and Gaither, Hodges, Holtzhausen and Ihlen have heeded the call made by L'Etang (2004) of the need to expand the analysis of public relations to become more interdisciplinary and critical. At the forefront of attempts to link public relations with concepts drawn from media and cultural studies is a concern with dicsourse, framing, semiotics and representation (Dan and Ihlen, 2011; Edwards and Hodges, 2011). Yet these fields are changing too.

Moving beyond the 'visual turn' in cultural studies, that has refocused critical attention on 'visuality' and 'visual technology' (Mirzoef, 2005) and the role such factors play in mediating the range of consumer, cultural and informational experiences, cultural and critical scholars have started to explore the physical and spatial elements of communication. Such approaches, termed the 'spatial turn' '[s]ituates communication and culture within a physical and corporeal landscape' where 'infrastructure, space, technology, and the body become the focus' (Packer and Wiley, 2012: 3).

As with the increasingly visual nature of contemporary society, so is the material interaction between individuals and the built environment becoming a central domain in which strategic communication occurs. Central to the creation and reception of these experiences is the role of the public relations practitioner. Thus, understanding in more detail the way the visual, material and, in totality, the experiential nature of strategic communication is deployed is vital – both in terms of evolving effective practice as well as being able to adequately analyse and critique such approaches.

Exploring pre-communicative contexts

Moving the focus of public relations and strategic communication beyond text and out to the full physical and bodily experience in which information is received opens up fertile – and potentially controversial – routes for practice and scholarship.

Taking such a perspective means recognising that the visual and material attributes of the communicative environment in which messages will be decoded play a dual role. Firstly, the environment operates at a functional or representational level in that it acts as a medium to carry persuasive messages. Thus, the communicative context has intrinsic communicative value. Secondly, however, this communications environment also functions at a *pre*-suasive level. That is, the affective context in which functional or representational communications are received and consumed can play a vital role in influencing and determining the ways in which such messages are decoded.

This, then, presents wider implications and challenges for practitioners and scholars alike in terms of extending key considerations for the efficacy of strategic communications and the factors influencing sense-making on an individual and social scale. The significance of this *pre-communicative context* is a largely unexplored area within public relations studies, although Cialdini (2016) recently has taken steps to articulate pre-suasion as key component of persuasion. In his work Cialdini argues that pre-suasion, which includes visual cues, operates as a way to prime and prepare audiences for any following functional, persuasive communication.

Validating the importance of public relations and strategic communications scholars paying attention to this pre-communicative context is evidence from wider marketing research demonstrating that visual priming, particularly in advertising, has strong links with information processing (Fahmy *et al.*, 2006). Moreover, recent work by Baxter *et al.* (2014) has shown how phonetic cues can in product messaging can influence consumer-decision-making and improve preference among consumers.[2] Crucially, such findings indicate how it isn't the intrinsic, representational or rational value of marketing communication that persuades here, rather it is the sounds in words which convey meaning. And, arguably, phonemes can be primed at a pre-suasive level to improve the efficacy of whole words operating at a more conventional, representational level.

Specifically, then, priming plays an important role in helping to encourage the understanding, retention and cognition of information in receivers.

While the contributors to this book have focused primarily on the visual and spatial dimensions of public relations, the pre-communicative context discussed here opens up much broader affective dimensions for strategic communication. For example, seeking to understand a multi-sensory world of communication is likely to become increasing relevant. Although, scholars from marketing disciplines have arguably had a longer tradition in exploring multi-sensory consumer experiences – the manufactured 'new car' smell is a classic example – this domain is not as well researched from a public relations perspective. Bartholme and Melewar (2009) have done much to reassess corporate communications by bringing reflecting on corporate identity from the perspective of sound, smell and taste, but the ways in which a multi-sensory world relates to the full plethora of organisational stakeholders is something that public relations scholars needs to grasp.

Ethical concerns

As with all forms of public communication, there are ethical concerns and dilemmas especially in relation to the concept of communicative power (Perloff, 2010). It could, however, be argued that such concerns are amplified in the context of presusasion, priming and the strategic creation of immersive environments to affectively enhance or degrade the efficacy of functional communication. For example, where Clark and Mangham (2004) talk of organisational theatre whereby corporate events are used to produce immersive experiences in which to communicate strategically planned and, usually, commercially-oriented outcomes. This raises issues of ensuring persuasive efficacy or corporate compliance through affective means, an area little researched in scholarly terms and thus even less likely to have been considered as part of ethical frameworks at the level of industry regulations and guidelines, let alone at a societal, legislative level.

Here the debate focuses on organisational power and its legitimacy – or otherwise. While public relations can be used for good through its role in community building, creating shared understanding and conflict resolution, it is arguable that the economic resources and large-scale planning required to establish such an immersive environment is likely to be affordable by large corporations and/ or governments and states, rather than NGOs and community groups. Thus, while Davis (2002) argues that public relations' cultural capital ensures that its social power is not directly related to economic capital, such a transformation of strategic communication into a fully immersive experience challenges this perspective.

Challenges and opportunities

Moving forward there are both challenges and opportunities for public relations and strategic communication practice and scholarship. For practice, there is a framework and emerging creative space within which strategies can be planned and implemented that embrace visual, spatial and – potentially – other multisensory forms of communication. This offers a landscape rich with opportunities for highly original and immersive experiences that will improve the efficacy of communications. However, making full use of such a domain extending beyond text will require a better understanding what this means for professional practice in terms of skills and behaviours necessary for this twenty-first century discipline.

Moreover, as noted above, how practitioners engaging in such types of multimodal public relations ensure they act professionally will inevitably raise ethical questions around the enhanced persuasiveness and communicative power that practitioners may have at their disposal. And the need to navigate – and potentially regulate – these forms of multi-sensory communications to ensure a level-playing field between corporate and civic organisations and actors will likely need to be addressed.

For researchers and scholars, the chapters in this collection assert an urgent need to grasp and apply interdisciplinary perspectives to public relations. This includes extending the range of theoretical approaches used to inform and underpin scholarship in the field as well as well as recognising that studying strategic communications beyond text will require the researcher to draw – and, crucially, build – on a wide variety of methodologies to evaluate, de-construct and understand public relations effectively from this new stand-point.

Moreover, collaboration with colleagues from different fields needs to be encouraged and welcomed. Fields as diverse as spatial and graphic design, urban planning, architecture, built environment, psychology, performing arts, fine art, museums and heritage, organisational studies. Not forgetting, of course, public relations' fellow-travellers in cultural and critical studies, as well as marketing and advertising. As Jawaharlal Nehru, the Prime Minister of India before and after Independence observed: 'We live in a wonderful world that is full of beauty, charm and adventure. There is no end to the adventures that we can have if only we seek them with our eyes open' (Merchey, 2005). We hope this book has helped to open public relations scholars and practitioners eyes and encouraged them to take some initial steps on a strategic communications adventure.

Notes

1 See: Scott Anthony's (2013) history of public relations in the UK for a comprehensive overview of these developments.
2 See: Baxter *et al.* (2016) for a good summary of recent discussions on phonetic priming.

References

Anthony, Scott. (2013). *Public Relations and the Making of Modern Britain: Stephen Tallents and the Birth of a Progressive Media Profession.* Manchester: University of Manchester Press.

Barner, R. (2008). The Dark Tower. *Journal of Organisational Change Management,* 21 (1), 120–137.

Bartholme, R. H. and Melewar, T. C. (2009). Adding New Dimensions to Corporate Identity Management and Corporate Communication: Exploring the Sensory Perspective. *The Marketing Review,* 9 (2), 155–169

Baxter, S., Ilicic, J., Kulcynski, A. and Lowrey, T. M. (2016). Vipiz Is Fast, Vopoz Is Slow: Phonetic Symbolism Is the Way to Go! In Moreau, P. and Puntoni, S. (Eds.). *Advances in Consumer Research, 44,* 32–36.

Baxter, S. M., Kulczynski, A. and Ilicic, J. (2014). Revisiting the Automaticity of Phonetic Symbolism Effects. *International Journal of Research in Marketing,* 33 (4), 448–451.

Brown, Andrew D., Colville, Ian. & Pye, Annie. (2015). Making Sense of Sense-Making. *Organization Studies,* 36(2), 265–277.

Cialdini, R. B. (2016). *Pre-Suasion: A Revolutionary Way to Influence and Persuade.* New York: Simon & Schuster.

Clark, T. and Mangham, I. (2004). Stripping to the Undercoat: A Review and Reflections on a piece of Organisation Theatre. *Organisation Studies,* 25 (5), 841–851.

Colville, I., Brown, A. D., and Pye, A. (2012). Simplexity: Sensemaking, Organising and Storytelling for Our Time. *Human Relations,* 65, 5–15.

Dan, V. and Ihlen, O. (2011). Framing Expertise and Media Framing: A Cross-Cultural Analysis of Success in Framing Contexts. *Journal of Communication Management,* 15 (4), 368–388.

Davis, A. (2002). *Public Relations Democracy: Politics, Public Relations and the Mass Media in Britain.* Manchester: University of Manchester Press.

Davison, J., McLean, C. and Warren, S. (2012). Exploring the Visual in Organisation and Management. *Qualitative Research in Organisations and Management: An International Journal*, 7 (1), 5–15.

Edwards, L. and Hodges, C. E. M. (Eds.). (2011). *Public Relations, Society and Culture: Theoretical and Empirical Explorations*. Abingdon: Routledge.

Fahmy, S., Cho, S., Wayne, W. and Song, Y. (2006). Visual Agenda Setting after 9/11: Individual Emotion, Recall and Concern about Terrorism. *Visual Communication Quarterly*, 15 (4), 4–15.

Holt, R. and Cornelissen, J. (2014). Sensemaking Revisited. *Management Learning*, 45, 525–539.

Jawaharlal Nehru, quoted in Merchey, J. A. (2005). *Building a Life of Value: Timeless Wisdom to Inspire and Empower Us*. Beverly Hills, CA.: Little Moose Press.

L'Etang, J. (2004). *Public Relations in Britain: A History of Professional Practice in the 20th Century*. Mahwah, NJ: Lawrence Erlbaum Associates.

Lakoff, G. and Johnson, M. (1980). *Metaphors We Live By*. Chicago, IL: University of Chicago Press.

Maitlis, S. (2005). The Social Processes of Organisational Sensemaking. *Academy of Management Journal*, 48, 21–49.

Meyer, R. E., Hollerer, M. A., Jancsary, D. and Van Leeuwen, T. (2013). The Visual Dimension in Organising, Organisation, and Organisation Research. *The Academy of Management Annals*, 7 (1), 487–553.

Mitchell, C. (2011). *Doing Visual Research*. London: Sage.

Mirzoef, N. (Ed.). (2005) *An Introduction to Visual Culture*. New York and London: Taylor and Francis.

Murphree, V. (2015). Edward Bernays's 1929 Torches of Freedom March: Myths and Historical Significance. *American Journalism*, 32 (2), 258–281.

Packer, S. and Wiley, S. B. C. (Eds.). (2012). *Communication Matters: Materialist Approaches to Media, Mobility and Networks*. London and New York: Routledge.

Perloff, R. (2010). *The Dynamics of Persuasion: Communications and Attitudes in the 21st Century* (4th Edition). Abingdon: Routledge.

Taylor, J. R. and van Every, E. J. (2000). *The Emergent Organisation*. London: Lawrence Erlbaum.

Vince, R. and Warren, S. (2012). Participatory Visual Methods. In Cassell, C. and Symon, G. (Eds.), *The Practice of Qualitative Organisational Research: Core Methods and Current Challenges*. London: Sage, pp. 275–295.

Weick, K. E. (1995). *Sensemaking in Organisations*. Thousand Oaks, CA: Sage.

Index

Note: Page numbers in italic indicate a figure on the corresponding page.

For Product Safety Concerns and Information please contact our EU
representative GPSR@taylorandfrancis.com
Taylor & Francis Verlag GmbH, Kaufingerstraße 24, 80331 München, Germany

www.ingramcontent.com/pod-product-compliance
Ingram Content Group UK Ltd.
Pitfield, Milton Keynes, MK11 3LW, UK
UKHW020955180425
457613UK00019B/693